# Female Embodiment and Subjectivity in the Modernist Novel

# Literary Criticism and Cultural Theory

WILLIAM E. CAIN, *General Editor*

**Machine and Metaphor**
The Ethics of Language in
American Realism
Jennifer Carol Cook

**"Keeping Up Her Geography"**
Women's Writing and Geocultural
Space in Twentieth-Century U.S.
Literature and Culture
Tanya Ann Kennedy

**Contested Masculinities**
Crises in Colonial Male Identity from
Joseph Conrad to Satyajit Ray
Nalin Jayasena

**Unsettled Narratives**
The Pacific Writings of Stevenson,
Ellis, Melville and London
David Farrier

**The Subject of Race in American
Science Fiction**
Sharon DeGraw

**Parsing the City**
Jonson, Middleton, Dekker, and City
Comedy's London as Language
Heather C. Easterling

**The Economy of the Short Story in
British Periodicals of the 1890s**
Winnie Chan

**Negotiating the Modern**
Orientalism and Indianness in the
Anglophone World
Amit Ray

**Novels, Maps, Modernity**
The Spatial Imagination, 1850–2000
Eric Bulson

**Novel Notions**
Medical Discourse and the
Mapping of the Imagination in
Eighteenth-Century English Fiction
Katherine E. Kickel

**Masculinity and the English
Working Class**
Studies in Victorian Autobiography
and Fiction
Ying S. Lee

**Aesthetic Hysteria**
The Great Neurosis in Victorian
Melodrama and Contemporary Fiction
Ankhi Mukherjee

**The Rise of Corporate Publishing
and Its Effects on Authorship in
Early Twentieth-Century America**
Kim Becnel

**Conspiracy, Revolution, and
Terrorism from Victorian Fiction
to the Modern Novel**
Adrian S. Wisnicki

**City/Stage/Globe**
Performance and Space in
Shakespeare's London
D.J. Hopkins

**Transatlantic Engagements with the
British Eighteenth Century**
Pamela J. Albert

**Race, Immigration, and American Identity in the Fiction of Salman Rushdie, Ralph Ellison, and William Faulkner**
Randy Boyagoda

**Cosmopolitan Culture and Consumerism in Chick Lit**
Caroline J. Smith

**Asian Diaspora Poetry in North America**
Benzi Zhang

**William Morris and the Society for the Protection of Ancient Buildings**
Andrea Elizabeth Donovan

**Zionism and Revolution in European-Jewish Literature**
Laurel Plapp

**Shakespeare and the Cultural Colonization of Ireland**
Robin E. Bates

**Spaces of the Sacred and Profane**
Dickens, Trollope, and the Victorian Cathedral Town
Elizabeth A. Bridgham

**The Contemporary Anglophone Travel Novel**
The Aesthetics of Self-Fashioning in the Era of Globalization
Stephen M. Levin

**Literature and Development in North Africa**
The Modernizing Mission
Perri Giovannucci

**The Tower of London in English Renaissance Drama**
Icon of Opposition
Kristen Deiter

**Victorian Narrative Technologies in the Middle East**
Cara Murray

**Ruined by Design**
Shaping Novels and Gardens in the Culture of Sensibility
Inger Sigrun Brodey

**Modernism and the Marketplace**
Literary Culture and Consumer Capitalism in Rhys, Woolf, Stein, and Nella Larsen
Alissa G. Karl

**The Genesis of the Chicago Renaissance**
Theodore Dreiser, Langston Hughes, Richard Wright, and James T. Farrell
Mary Hricko

**Haunting and Displacement in African American Literature and Culture**
Marisa Parham

**Misery's Mathematics**
Mourning, Compensation, and Reality in Antebellum American Literature
Peter Balaam

**The Politics of Identity in Irish Drama**
W.B. Yeats, Augusta Gregory and J.M. Synge
George Cusack

**Female Embodiment and Subjectivity in the Modernist Novel**
The Corporeum of Virginia Woolf and Olive Moore
Renée Dickinson

*For a full list of titles in this series, please visit www.routledge.com*

# Female Embodiment and Subjectivity in the Modernist Novel
The Corporeum of Virginia Woolf and Olive Moore

Renée Dickinson

Taylor & Francis Group

New York   London

First published 2009
by Routledge
711 Third Avenue, New York, NY 10017

Simultaneously published in the UK
by Routledge
2 Park Square, Milton Park, Abingdon, Oxfordshire OX14 4RN

First issued in paperback 2014

*Routledge is an imprint of the Taylor & Francis Group, an informa business*

© 2009 Taylor & Francis

Typeset in Sabon by IBT Global.

All rights reserved. No part of this book may be reprinted or reproduced or utilised in any form or by any electronic, mechanical, or other means, now known or hereafter invented, including photocopying and recording, or in any information storage or retrieval system, without permission in writing from the publishers.

**Trademark Notice:** Product or corporate names may be trademarks or registered trademarks, and are used only for identification and explanation without intent to infringe.

*Library of Congress Cataloging in Publication Data*
Dickinson, Renée, 1966-
 Female embodiment and subjectivity in the modernist novel : the corporeum of Virginia Woolf and Olive Moore / by Renée Dickinson.
  p. cm.—(Literary criticism and cultural theory)
 Includes bibliographical references and index.
 1. Woolf, Virginia, 1882–1941—Criticism and interpretation. 2. Moore, Olive—Criticism and interpretation. 3. Women in literature. 4. Body image in literature. 5. Subjectivity in literature. 6. Woolf, Virginia, 1882–1941. Mrs. Dalloway. 7. Woolf, Virginia, 1882–1941. Waves. 8. Moore, Olive. Spleen. 9. Moore, Olive. Fugue. 10. Modernism (Literature)—Great Britain. I. Title.
 PR6045.O72Z618 2009
 823'.912—dc22
                                        2008054735

ISBN13: 978-0-415-99383-8(hbk)
ISBN13: 978-1-138-82082-1(pbk)

# Contents

*Permissions* ix
*Acknowledgments* xi

Introduction: Articulating the Corporeum: Formulating the Feminine and Illuminating the Images of Physical, Geographical, National and Textual Embodiment    1

1  The Shape of Modernism: Female Embodiment and Textual Experimentation in *Mrs. Dalloway*    25

2  Exposure and Development: Re-Imagining Narrative and Nation in the Interludes of Virginia Woolf's *The Waves*    52

3  Modernist Con(Tra)Ceptions: Re-Conceiving Body and Text in Olive Moore's *Spleen*    74

4  Flight of the Feminine and Textual Orientation in Olive Moore's *Fugue*    110

Epilogue: Feminine Form and Textual Reform    135

*Appendix* 139
*Notes* 141
*Bibliography* 167
*Index* 175

# Permissions

I am grateful to the following for their generous permission to use these texts and images:

COLLECTED WRITINGS by Olive Moore and Steven Moore, ed. Copyright 1992 by Dalkey Archive Press. Reproduced with permission of Dalkey Archive Press in the format Other book via Copyright Clearance Center.

Excerpts from MRS. DALLOWAY by Virginia Woolf, copyright 1925 by Houghton Mifflin Harcourt Publishing Company and renewed 1953 by Leonard Woolf, reprinted by permission of the publisher.

Excerpts from THE WAVES by Virginia Woolf, copyright 1931 by Harcourt, Inc. and renewed 1959 by Leonard Woolf, reprinted by permission of the publisher.

The Society of Authors as the Literary Representative of the Estate of Virginia Woolf for the use of passages from *Mrs. Dalloway* and *The Waves* by Virginia Woolf.

# Acknowledgments

As with any great undertaking, this book would not be complete nor would its author be functional if it were not for the work of many parties. I would like to first thank my dissertation advisor at the University of Colorado, Jane Garrity, for her tremendously careful and detailed guidance, editing and care during each phase of the writing process, for her wisdom and grace, and for her laughter and friendship. In addition, Karen Jacobs, whose fine editing skills and lovely sense of humor and life perspective made this project more tolerable to read and my life within it more delightful. Eric White graciously opened his office and literary and film repertoire to me, often without notice, and our conversations greatly improved the direction and detail of this project as well as my film therapy. Both Susan Kent and Jeremy Green's editorial comments, questions and suggestions also propelled this project into deeper and more nuanced discoveries.

Two writing groups warmly welcomed me and generously entertained my often loosely connected ideas to help me formulate and revise them into sense. First, Robin Calland and Pam Albert intervened in this project at its beginning, proposing a direction I would eventually follow with passion. Their intellectual rigor and passion, and their personal integrity helped me to carve out an argumentative path that I could honestly pursue. Second, Patrick Hamilton, Matt Reiswig and Lorna Wheeler cultivated this project, the job market process and our academic friendships with fierce insight, humor and honesty, making all three worlds better places for their participation in them. I thank them especially for embracing Olive Moore and all that the research and writing on her requires and for keeping my fascination with her alive. In addition, I would like to thank the University of Colorado community of English graduate students whose willingness to take time off on Friday nights eventually led to a powerful group of academic friendships that has since set the bar for personal and work relationships at an extraordinary level. In addition, my work was furthered by comments from the Woolf community at conferences and online and by discussions with my students and colleagues at Radford University, all of which enhanced and deepened this project.

xii  *Acknowledgments*

In my research in particular I wish to thank the many teachers who have guided my academic career from its infancy—Rose Reynoldson, Luke Reinsma, Rob Snyder and Ken Macrorie—to its development with my discovery of Virginia Woolf, feminism and Literary Theory—Sara Blair, Elaine Jordan, Michael Wood and Francis Barker—to its maturity with professors at the University of Colorado at Boulder, namely, Jane Garrity, Karen Jacobs, Marty Bickman and Katherine Eggert. In addition, I would like to thank those on whose work I rely and build, especially Susan Stanford-Friedman, Leslie Heywood, Mariana Torgovnick and Julia Kristeva.

This project would not have progressed if it were not for the generous fellowships offered by the University of Colorado and Radford University communities. I am indebted to the benefactors of the Katherine Jacob Lamont Scholarship, the Emerson and Lowe Project Fellowship, the Bernice Udick Fellowship and the Thomas Edwin Devaney Project Fellowship at the University of Colorado and to the financial and scheduling wizardry of my department chair, Rosemary Guruswamy, at Radford University.

I also thank the people of my life who have held this project dear and held me together throughout its progress. My parents, Victor and Carol Gould, nurtured my love for literature and creativity, setting the stage for this very performance and setting the example of parenting that I daily strive to follow. My sister, Cynthia, taught me literally to write, setting this project in motion many years prior, and also nurtured my body and soul throughout the process of the book. Many, many friends have provided chocolate, coffee, conversation and their parallel emotional props, keeping me laughing and pulling my focus out to the real matter of living. Here I thank in particular Katie Bagby, Teresa Osborn, Jill Smith, Cindy Moran and Jessica Staheli. In addition, Cindy Moran, proving true friendship and academic curiosity, took the helm of research on Olive Moore at a crucial stage and provided new opportunities for information on Moore. Two students at Radford University have since continued in her footsteps, and I am deeply grateful for the diligence and patience of Shelley Gentry Jessee and Bethley Giles.

Ultimately, this project would mean little without those with whom I share it and my daily struggles and joys. To my husband, Rick, I offer thanks for his patience, endurance and deep love and belief in me and my ideas. Meeting him across the editing table, dinner table or the changing table, I find his pure commitment to living the kind of challenge that continues to make me a better writer, person and parent and also the person with whom I most want to take up that challenge. To my daughter, Hallie, I offer thanks for the new and unexpected joys and conversations, for the constraints of schedule that structured the completion of this project, and for providing a purpose to this making way for women's voices in literature. At five, already an avid reader and storyteller, I hope that she will, in some way, continue this story.

# Introduction
## Articulating the Corporeum: Formulating the Feminine and Illuminating the Images of Physical, Geographical, National, and Textual Embodiment

> It wasn't simply that something had been added to history; the *shape* of history had been radically altered.
>
> Samuel Hynes, *A War Imagined*[1]

When initially writing the first chapter of this project, on Virginia Woolf's *Mrs. Dalloway*, I saw the novel as a failed experiment. I found Woolf's traditional representations of women incongruous and irreconcilable with the experimental form of the text. I wondered what, if anything, Woolf exposes and criticizes about the anxieties surrounding the conflicts for women in their multiple and precarious identities in their bodies, the land and the nation. Indeed, a larger question loomed: Does Woolf's textual experimentation provide for alternatives to seeing women as embodiments of their physical, geographical, and national identities?

*Female Embodiment and Subjectivity in the Modernist Novel: The Corporeum of Virginia Woolf and Olive Moore* (*The Corporeum*) proceeds to investigate this question within the shape of British modernism by examining four crucial incarnations of female embodiment and subjectivity: female bodies, geographical imagery, national ideology, and textual experimentation. I propose that the ways *Mrs. Dalloway* (1925) and *The Waves* (1931) by Virginia Woolf and *Spleen* (1930) and *Fugue* (1932) by Olive Moore reflect, expose, and criticize physical, geographical, and national bodies in the narrative and form of their texts reveal the authors' attempts to try on new forms and experiment with new possibilities of female embodiment and subjectivity. These four material and theoretical bodies—physical, geographical, national, and textual—thus make up what I call the *Corporeum*, an interconnected and interdependent network of representations of physical and ideological embodiments that I argue play out on multiple levels in each text.

At first, I found that *Mrs. Dalloway* fails to provide viable alternatives for women. As women are continually implicated as willing and coerced participants in the systems of patriarchy and imperialism, even the textual experimentation seemed to fail to free them from these various identifications. The female characters remain trapped in their physical bodies despite their multiple incarnations, that is, in *Mrs. Dalloway*, the variously virginal, maternal, and aging body of Clarissa Dalloway, the "unlovable body" of Miss Kilman (129), the "handsome," "erect," "magnificence" of Lady Bruton (111), and the "light, glowing" body and "melodramatic" character of Sally Seton (35, 182).[2] Eventually, each female character is incorporated into or exiled from patriarchal systems, as opposed to granted a liberating existence apart from the laws of patriarchy and imperialism which inscribe and entrap them. Associations of these female characters with the land and landscape appeared to be attempts to release them from the trap of feminine physicality but instead recreated the same trap through the affiliation with what I and others argue is another already femininely marked body, the geographical body. These representations of the feminine within the physical and geographical bodies continue and in fact are required in the establishment and continuation of the ideologies of nation and empire: these female characters, despite their various positions on and within the British Empire, again become complicit with the national body of imperialism. My question was how could the experiments of the textual body, understood here as modernist experiments with form such as stream-of-consciousness, disruption of linearity, and the inability to conclude, possibly unwind such a multifarious knot without also penetrating, insinuating, and incorporating the feminine within its workings much like the feminine is implicated in the workings of the imperial apparatus?

Selected based on the thematic, imagistic, and narrative connections within them, the four novels I discuss were written between the two world wars, from 1925 to 1932, and similarly experiment with form and narrative. The texts range from the beginnings of modernist experimentation with the highly canonized Woolf to the vastly experimental and virtually unknown Moore. Woolf experiments with form in both *Mrs. Dalloway* and *The Waves*, but the narratives and the characters are not as experimental (and disturbing) as those found in Moore. The rootedness of Englishness in the English countryside and city in Woolf's texts is disrupted by the self-exile of the characters in Moore's texts. The suspended endings that provide for future possibilities in Woolf highlight even more the anxiety of ending in Moore's truncated texts. I conclude with Olive Moore, mostly ignored and excluded in criticism, whose texts are increasingly experimental in narrative, character, and form, and specifically in the obscurity of her own (lack of) conclusions, in order to reveal how pervasively these concerns for female British modernists extended across the generations of women writers. Both authors address and complicate the ideas in the Corporeum, connecting and challenging them in light of their own positions as British citizen (Woolf) and British exile (Moore).

I situate my argument at this site of tension between the content and form of the texts. In doing so, I argue that these four novels, despite their depictions of the feminine body and the feminized land, and their failure to provide a resolution to the questions they raise regarding female embodiment, ultimately resist these entrenched identities of the feminine body and land through their experiments in character, narrative, and form precisely because they refuse to operate within the confines of masculinist ideologies of patriarchy, imperialism, and male modernist form. In fact, in its creation of new shapes of narrative, the textual body provides for alternative ways of thinking about, accessing, and therefore, creating identity subjectivity for women. In *Mrs. Dalloway*, for example, Virginia Woolf deploys identical imagery to describe the body of Clarissa Dalloway, the pastoral landscape of England, and English nationalism, indirectly linking Clarissa to patriarchal and national structures of female identity and subjectivity. However, I argue that Woolf's textual experimentation with the form and sequence of the narrative levels monolithic structures of class and time, making way for the leveling of other monoliths such as patriarchy and imperialism. Ultimately, I propose that by investigating these four manifestations of the feminine in representations of body, land, nation, and text within British modernism that as modernist women writers experimented with the shape of texts, they also attempted to reshape female identities.

Just as Samuel Hynes suggests in the epigraph to this introduction that World War I altered the ways British history was imagined, it also altered the ways the shape of fiction and women's identities were imagined and how women's identities are shaped in fiction. Although I do not propose to discuss the specific consequences of World War I itself on literary production, I do pose a query into the awareness and development of women's subjectivity during the interwar period and its subsequent manifestations in the works of experimental British women modernists, specifically in the works of Virginia Woolf and Olive Moore.[3] By juxtaposing the highly discussed Woolf (1882–1941) and the unknown Moore (possible dates 1905–1970), I demarcate the concerns of women's subjectivity and textual experimentation across two generations of British women modernists. Through the analyses of four novels, I uncover the relationship between these authors' attempts to reconsider the ways women's identities have been shaped by their various identifications that I delineate later and, thus, the way Woolf and Moore re-imagine the shape of the modernist text which portrays them.

This book introduces Olive Moore's vastly experimental novels to literary criticism. After publishing four novels in the 1930s, she slipped into obscurity until the 1990s when her novels were republished posthumously by the Dalkey Archive Press. Her birth and death dates, most of her manuscripts and life are still largely subject to speculation and no literary criticism has yet been published on her work.[4] Situating Woolf's highly documented texts alongside Moore's obscure novels, and applying the multiple lenses of the Corporeum, I expose submerged anxieties about female subjectivity as pervasive concerns across generations of both mainstream and peripheral British women modernists.

Throughout this book, I examine each body within the Corporeum in relation to the others as layers in a stacking palimpsest of embodiments. Like a medical textbook, in which the outline of the physical body is layered with transparencies of the skeletal, muscular, and vascular systems, a new image of embodiment is created as each additional theoretical system (physical, geographical, national, and textual) is transposed upon the others. Typically, each theoretical "system" is considered and discussed by theorists as a whole in and of itself. As of yet, few literary critics have considered these bodies together as a new kind of whole, or read across (or through) them intertextually. Despite many theorists' emphases on permeable borders of the body and slippery subjects, these theories have as yet to be applied across the borders of all of these theoretical bodies. Although connections have been made between body and land, land and nation, nation and text, and text and body, no one has as yet laid the track of all of these connections at once. When done so within the spectrum of the Corporeum, the connections reveal the texts' awareness, criticism of, and resistance to the traps of embodiment inherent in female identity within patriarchy and imperialism such as marriage, maternity, and domesticity. In brief, I argue that these texts are not *just* about the physical bodies of the characters, but how, within each text, their bodies interact with the land; I then explore how that interaction depicts the national state, and how the text itself investigates and reveals the machinations and articulations of these bodies, lands, and nations. As further explanation next, I outline each body and the issues therein briefly and then highlight my analysis of each text within this theoretical collective.

## BODILY FORMS AND FEMININE CORPOREALITY

As I began to explore in the examples of the imagery of Clarissa's body, the landscape, and the nation in *Mrs. Dalloway*, within what I call the Corporeum, the physical body is the origination of the links between the body and the land. This connection then leads to the connections between the land and the nation in a type of theoretical skeleton of anklebones connected to shinbones, implying further connections to come. One *could* theoretically begin with the nation and lead *back* to the physical body, but it would be a digging back to the source of the metaphor in the physical body that then leads to the ideas of the land and nation, and, I will argue, to ideas of textual production and form. In the brief example from *Mrs. Dalloway* above, beginning with the descriptions of Clarissa's body foregrounds the connections between these descriptions and the ways in which they are used to conjure ideas of nationalism. Without initial analysis of these connections between body, land and nation, the subsequent analysis of the development of experimental form would not expose the ways in which the authors use experiments in form to attempt new possibilities for female subjectivity. The use of the physical body as an originary site of metaphor and language, as well as a springboard into the other bodies in the Corporeum, implies not only the body's place in origination of the metaphor, but also underscores the lack of agency in female corporeality; in an analysis of the physical body, the (here, female) body is filleted and demarcated, acted upon and analyzed, and essentialized. By tracing the trajectory of demarcations of female subjectivity from the body through images of land and ideology of nation and empire, the continuing essentializing of the feminine comes to the fore. It is up to the textual body, then, to reverse these entrapments of the feminine by setting free the form of the text. Because of the body's foundational place in metaphor and female subjectivity, the physical body, then, is the place to begin the theoretical mapping.

Each of the four bodies I discuss contains a realm of potential linguistic hazards. In my discussion of the physical body, the terms *female*, *feminine*, *the feminine*, and *woman/women* could easily slip from one to another. I use the terms *female, woman,* and *women* through strict dictionary definition to denote physical sex as compared to *male, man,* and *men.* I use *feminine* to denote gendered bodies be they human, land, nation, or text.[5] Finally, I use *the feminine*, often in contrast to *patriarchy*, to denote an ideological representation of that which is seen as female or feminized which, again, can occur in any of the bodies of the Corporeum. I use *patriarchy* then to signal the corresponding system of masculine ideology which has been adopted as a social system or "the Law of the Fathers" (Benstock, 124–128) in which the masculine is dominant and privileged. These ideological representations of "the feminine" and "patriarchy" also manifest beyond ideology into established institutions of political and social apparatuses, that is marriage, maternity, national identity, and imperialism.

The various theories, namely feminist, eco-critical, postcolonial, and poststructural theories, I use to analyze the Corporeum in these texts operate as the connective tissue which links each body of the Corporeum. In the medical textbook metaphor, the theory is not the focus, but serves as the light behind the body transparencies that illuminate the issues of female embodiment within the texts of the novels. For the sake of this introduction, I want to draw attention to the theories relevant to my study within each body of theory and then provide brief examples of how these theories prove productive in revealing the traps of female embodiment imposed by patriarchy and imperialism and possible escape routes created by the texts. Specifically, in my analysis of the physical bodies in these texts, I investigate the inscriptions of and on the female body, its subsequent identitifications and the opportunities and attempts to escape them.[6]

The issues of escape and containment encourage my use of Julia Kristeva's work on the abject. Her theories on the abject concern issues of physical and metaphorical borders and border crossings that then determine law and taboo and therefore the abject. Kristeva's theories therefore allow for an analysis of the ways in which patriarchal systems impose limits on the feminine body.[7] Kristeva also sees the corpse as the primary reminder of the body's materiality and its remainder, but it is also represented by anything which transgresses the boundary of self: blood, pus, semen, and so forth. The abject, then, is not abject when it is a part of the body, only when the body's excess is expelled from the body, or when it "strays" outside of the borders of the body. There is, therefore, a profound connection between ideas of the abject and the feminine, especially the maternal, as through childbirth a part of the self transgresses the boundary of the self to become the other. Through maternity, then, woman is both abject and abjecting.[8] The rejection of the feminine asserts the abject status of the feminine as physical excess, societal contamination, threat of death, and a straying from the body and society. In sum, the feminine is inherently abject in its excess bodily presence and, as abject, is necessarily rejected.[9] For example, Ruth, in Olive Moore's *Spleen*, gives birth to (she abjects) a deformed child (the abject) which she then takes with her into exile on a remote Italian island (she abjects them from England). Her actions are improper, taboo, and specifically related to her status as feminine through her maternity as well as contrarily to her lack of motherliness with her son, Richard. Ruth's abject status also manifests through her disturbance of the patriarchal family system and of her English identity through her self-imposed exile.

In order to explore how the demarcations of the body further affect the subject's understanding of her body and its place in her physical and political environments, I extend my analysis of female embodiment from the body itself to consider the slippery borders between psyche and body, or body image, specifically to the theories developed by Elizabeth Grosz. Grosz notes, echoing Kristeva: "the limits or borders of the body image are not fixed by nature or confined to the anatomical 'container,' the skin. . . . Its borders, edges, and contours are 'osmotic' . . . incorporating and expelling outside and inside in an ongoing interchange" (Volatile 79). The body image, then, is a kind of projection of the body that can change and "reorient" (Volatile 84) itself according to its experiences, surroundings, and governing psyche. Grosz's theories show the body image as something that the body performs with the mind, not something that the mind performs upon or through the body. Even so, the body is always the tool of or acted upon by another, even if the other is the psyche or identity of the subject. In *Spleen*, with the character of Ruth, we see that her body image changes with the changes of her corporeal as well as her national and geographic landscapes. When she can no longer deny that she is pregnant due to the swelling of her belly through the bath water, she then decides that this is her opportunity to make something new. When that experiment "fails" with Richard's deformity, her body image is reduced to her body in exile: the stuffy propriety of an Englishwoman who has unaccountably dismissed her child now established in the hot, dry, and "savage" landscape of a remote Italian island.

If we take Kristeva and Grosz's theories of the physical body together, the body becomes a text that the individual herself and society at large read, use, manipulate, metaphorize, and objectify. The body moves, reacts, interacts, performs, and leaks but does not have complete agency on its own. When the body is marked as female, this acting upon typically indicates an action of containment, even when conducted by the female subject herself. In looking at the works of Woolf and Moore, these theories trigger queries into the types of body images performed by these texts' characters, how they change with or against their changing environments, and what specifically these texts challenge about the female embodiments in the texts. To use Clarissa Dalloway as an example again, the work of these two theorists evokes questions about the possibility for Clarissa to escape the physical markings of her female embodiment and her identifications as wife and mother. I argue that Clarissa's abject status is reified in her affiliations with the land and nation and contributes to her understanding of her body as "nothing at all" (11). If, as Joseph Allen Boone suggests, "in Woolf's vision of subjectivity the boundaries of identity are at once shifting and porous, for although consciousness may arise from within, it is not ultimately contained by the corporeal body" (174), then what is evidenced about the physical body through the leaky consciousnesses in the textual body is the feminine body's inherent abject, leaky status. In addition, if, as Makiko Minow-Pinkney suggests, Woolf's "modernism was . . . a feminist subversion of conventions. . . . Of the very definitions of narrative, writing, the subject—of a patriarchal social order" (x), Woolf then succeeds in subverting conventional narrative and, I argue, ideology through her deployment of modernist forms such as stream-of-consciousness. Thus, I consider first how Clarissa is compared to the English pastoral landscape and then incorporated into national and imperial ideology, and, eventually, by considering how, as Boone and Pinkney suggest, the experiments of the text respond and subvert these identifications.

## BODILY NATURE: MAPPING THE FEMININE ONTO THE LANDSCAPE

For many of the female characters in the texts I discuss, their affiliation with the land initially appears to grant them an escape from the patriarchal demarcations on their physical bodies. But, as the land is often gendered female, this proves to be another site of feminine embodiment in service to patriarchy. I argue that, in these texts, the feminized land becomes the site of a feminized geographical and, eventually, national identity. As these bodies of land are feminized, female embodiment is implicated in them and in the violence involved in controlling them. The process of identity formation, located on the geographic and social borderlands, demarcates people and place, inclusion and abject. I argue that during the interwar period, as England struggled to re-form its national identity, the homeland becomes another feminized frontier.[10] This then implies the possibility of conquering, invading, and controlling the feminine through the metaphors of land and landscape if not or as well as through the physical body by patriarchy.

Within the analysis of the geographical body, the terms *land* and *landscape* depict two different manifestations, one physical and one ideological. In my analyses of the novels, I focus specifically on the depictions of the physical "land" of England, looking closely at the differences between the ways that rural and pastoral England are compared to urban spaces of England, specifically of London as well as to European spaces such as Italy and the Alsace. These depictions participate in the creation of an imagery of the English "landscape" that figures as an image or reflection of the land which reveals the cultural valuations placed on the various "lands" of England.

My analysis of the geographical body in the novels also centers on issues of borders and identity. In this, the issues of excess and the stray of the feminine of Kristeva's theories extends to the feminizing of the land and to the ways the imperial project and its exploration and subsequent cartography took advantage of and required the feminizing of the land. The ways in which the borderlands were "ritualistically feminized" (24) as part of the imperial project, as Anne McClintock suggests, contributed to the ways that "women served as mediating and threshold figures by means of which men oriented themselves in space, as agents of power and agents of knowledge" (24). The land is further feminized through the "myth of the virgin land" which "is also the myth of the empty land" (McClintock 30), making the land (and, by association, women's bodies) an empty, abject lack, that must need filling, conquering, and containing. In addition, the consequence of "disavowing male loss of boundary by reinscribing a ritual excess of boundary," is the accompaniment of "an excess of military violence" on the feminine (McClintock 24). Thus, the contradictory excess and empty feminine land becomes necessary in the orientation of masculine power and identity and also becomes the site of patriarchy's dominance and violence.

I deploy the theories of the geographical body to illuminate the connections between feminine and geographical embodiments in the texts, revealing the association of the feminine with the land as well as the subsequent power struggles that occur with, on, and for that feminine land and landscape. In *Mrs. Dalloway*, for example, both Clarissa's abject feminine body and the feminine land with which she is compared are cultivated, contained and controlled through allegiance and complicity with patriarchy. In contrast, Sally's abject status continues in the descriptions of her as wild and as living in the wilds and borderlands of Manchester. Yet, Sally, too, becomes tamed by domesticity, gardening, and maternity. Therefore, I argue that in *Mrs. Dalloway* women's affiliation with the land heralds only another demarcation of the feminine by patriarchal inscription, an inscription that reifies women's variously abject and stray statuses and situates them as potential territories on and for which patriarchy battles to control in an attempt to control feminine, masculine, and national identity.

## BODILY STATES: NATION, EMPIRE, AND THE FEMALE FIGURE

I continue to extend this argument to suggest that both physical and geographical bodies are revealed as being in service to the national body of patriarchy and imperialism. The theories on national bodies (demarcated by ideas of nation and government rather than strictly by ideas of land and geography) are also concerned with issues of the (re)filling of empty land and with the necessary exclusion involved in the creation or maintenance of national identity. As national identity is inherently concerned with borders, with lines drawn between us and them, and how or how not to cross them, I therefore foreground the issues of boundary, identity, and imperialism in my analysis of the national body.

In articulating the national body, the terms *nation, empire, colonialism,* and *imperialism* arrive loaded with various complications and controversies. I use "nation" to denote the supposed originary site of the British homeland, specifically as England itself and "empire" to denote the extension of that nation into the colonies and subsequent protectorates and commonwealth. I refer to imperialism and colonialism according to the following definitions:

> "*Imperialism*" is the concept that comprises all forces and activities contributing to the construction and the maintenance of *transcolonial empires*. Imperialism presupposes the will and the ability of an imperial center to *define* as imperial its own national interests and enforce them worldwide in the anarchy of the international system. (Osterhammel 16–17)

"'*Colonialism*' is a relationship of domination between an indigenous (or forcibly imported) majority and a minority of foreign invaders. The fundamental decisions affecting the lives of the colonized people are made and implemented by the colonial rulers in pursuit of interests that are often defined in a distant metropolis" (Osterhammel 16–17). Thus, colonialism implicitly requires the physical force and domination of one group over another, whereas the ideologies and materialities of imperialism, which may result in colonialism, do not. Imperialism does, however, involve:

> an incursion, or an attempted incursion, into the sovereignty of another state . . . one power has the will, and, if it is to succeed, the capacity to shape the affairs of another by imposing upon it. The

> relations established by imperialism are therefore based upon inequality and not upon mutual compromises of the kind which characterize states of independence. (Cain & Hopkins 54)

Thus, imperialism does involve the forcing or "imposing" of the "sovereignty" of one state onto another, which necessarily results in an unequal relationship.

Defining the spaces of the British Empire also requires the clarification of terms. The geographical spaces of empire, England and Britain contribute to the determination of national and imperial identity of English and British subjects. In articulating the difference between English and British space, Ian Baucom explains that "'British' space was thus read as homogeneous, interchangeable, everywhere alike, while 'English' space remained unique, local, differentiated" (10). In addition, he claims that:

> Englishness has been identified *with* Britishness, which in its turn has been identified as coterminous with and proceeding from the sovereign territory of the empire, and that Englishness has also defined itself *against* the British Empire, first by retaining a spatial theory of collective identity but privileging the *English* soil of the 'sceptered isle' or, more regularly, certain quintessentially English locales, as authentic identity-determining locations. (12)

Thus, the geographical space of "the *English* soil" centrally determines English identity, which contradictorily both includes and excludes the space of the British Empire.

For English and British female subjects, national identity becomes increasingly complicated. Mariana Torgovnick suggests that European female subjects were designated a similar status to colonized subjects, thereby excluding them from the national subjectivity and space that Baucom describes earlier. Specifically, Torgovnick argues that "[b]oth European women and colonized peoples were, relative to European men, associated with the childlike, the irrational, and the dependent—and so linked" (37). She also argues that this association has been extended by the work of modernist writers as:

> immediate precedents for gendering the land female and symbolizing Africa in female terms were available in popular writers like Rider Haggard and Joseph Conrad. In addition, the popularity and renown of historical figures like La Malinche in Mexico and Pocahontas in Virginia tended to make females into symbols of access to indigenous peoples and their land. (37)

The feminine then extends from women's bodies to the "gendering [of] the land female" (Torgovnick 37) and specifically to colonized land. Eventually, this creates an association between the feminine and the primitive as "the primitive was coded metaphorically as feminine, collective, and ecstatic, and civilization was coded as masculine, individualistic, and devoted to the quotidian business of the family, city, or state" (Torgovnick 14), linking the ideas of the abject and the feminine to the primitive as well. This association then also extends the primitive from feminine embodiment to the workings of the feminine in the imperial project:

> [t]he primitive continued to be associated with heathenism, sexuality, and excess in a way that supported the idea that primitives needed Western guidance and control—in short, the goals of imperialism and empire. But alternatively . . . primitivism became a medium of soul-searching and self-transformation in which the idea of merging has been key, especially for people who feel ill at ease or constrained in the West. (Torgovnick 13)

Both of these alternatives—the idea that "primitives needed Western guidance" and the idea of primitivism as a "medium of soul-searching"—emerge in the novels I discuss. In each alternative, the feminine plays a significant role in guiding the masculine empire or explorer through the feminine, primitive territories, situating the feminine paradoxically as that which provides enlightenment to patriarchal and imperial subjects.

Additional consequences of the association of the feminine with the primitive in national and imperial ideologies, specifically the consequences, criticism, and incorporation of violence and hybridity emerge in the four novels I analyze in this project. For one, the association of the feminine with national and imperial identity becomes complicated by the presence of violence inherent in imperial activity. Kathy Phillips suggests that "[w]hen a society converts sexuality into militarism, or a need to be included into the desire for an all-embracing Empire, one effect may be a pervasive cultural image linking women and land" (239–40). Phillips locates not only the connection between imperial activity and violence but also the subsequent link between "women and land."

A second consequence of imperial activity which these four novels explore concerns the development of cultural hybridity. Homi Bhabha describes the effects of hybridity in detail as:

> the sign of the productivity of colonial power, its shifting forces and fixities; it is the name for the strategic reversal of the process of domination through disavowal. . . . The revaluation of the assumption of colonial identity through the repetition of discriminatory identity effects. It displays the necessary deformation and displacement of all sites of discrimination and domination. It unsettles the mimetic or narcissistic demands of colonial power but reimplicates its identifications in strategies of subversion that turn the gaze of the discriminated back upon the eye of power. (*Reader* 34–35)

As the authors of and characters in the four novels I discuss conduct experiments with physical, national, and textual hybridity, the role of the hybrid to unsettle or unseat dominate forces of power also emerges in these novels through contact with the feminine Other. The contact with the Other affects both the colonizer and the colonized, what Bhabha calls the "strategic reversal of the process of domination through disavowal." This "disavowal" is impossible, though, as both home and abroad are "unsettle[d]" and, specifically, the colonial power undermined through "strategies of subversion" such as the return of the colonized gaze, and body, into the homeland. Ultimately, Bhabha argues, "[t]he paranoid threat from the hybrid is finally uncontainable because it breaks down the symmetry and the duality of self/other, inside/outside. In the productivity of power, the boundaries of authority—its reality effects—are always besieged by 'the other scene' of fixations and phantoms (*Culture* 116). Like the feminine, the hybrid crosses borders and is "uncontainable" and always present even if as "phantoms." In the extension of the feminine into association with the primitive as argued by Torgovnick, the feminine here also becomes implicated in the workings and effects of empire. The manifestations of hybridity, too, then are also present in the novels I discuss.

The theories on the national body extend the theories on the feminizing of the land into the roles of the feminine in national and imperial ideologies, thereby further interweaving the concerns of the feminine in the first three bodies of the Corporeum: body, land, and nation. When placed in a national and imperial context, the feminine conjures images of the primitive, violence, and hybridity, placing women in a similar position as colonized subjects. In the texts of Woolf and Moore, issues of identity and containment of feminine bodies and land betray their concerns about national identity. In their work, the homeland embodies national identity in its notion of the pastoral and productive countryside as well as in the idea of the city, London, as the patriarchal hub of the empire. Despite the attempts of the texts to remove them from patriarchy's control through their geographical and ideological displacements, women's bodies, especially, become a site of creating nation through maternity as they become (re)producers of the national body. Clarissa Dalloway, for instance, becomes contained and controlled and put to (some) use as facilitator of empire both in her maternity which, when completed, leaves her empty and useless, and in her hostessing which succeeds her role as the physical "host" to instead entertain the Prime Minister. In the national body, therefore, the feminine is continually re-inscribed, replicating women's status in promoting empire. In these novels, women's identities, multiply marked in their physical bodies, geographical affiliations, and national cooperation, find no recourse for identity apart from that established by patriarchy. It is left, then, to the textual body to provide an alternative to these deeply entrenched notions of feminine embodiment and subjectivity in the body, land, and nation.

## TEXTUAL ANATOMY

I consider the four novels of this project as "texts" which function like bodies as their own organic entities. Just as a physical body is marked by its own borders and functions, the texts I discuss exist in physical containers the borders of which, I argue, they continually attempt to cross. The "body" of *The Waves*, for example, overloads the page with dense, blocky paragraphs in its episodes and disrupts even this push toward the margins through the interspersal of the interludes, undermining the attempt of the main "body" of the text to fill all the empty spaces on the page in a mock replication of colonialism's attempt to fill the empty spaces on the map. I suggest that how these bodies function, specifically in their experimentalism, what they look like on the page, and how they participate in or subvert the machinations of patriarchy and imperialism, reveal the authors' attempts to create new kinds of textual spaces that exist outside of these restrictions.

Woolf and Moore's experimentation with literary form inherently links to alternative ways of imagining identity as it acknowledges and creates space for alternative imaginings of language and culture and, I argue, alternate ideas of female subjectivity. In essence, alternate ways of writing suggest alternate ways of thinking, and alternate ways of thinking suggest alternate ways of constructing identity. The textual body, then, is that which contains, or attempts to contain, the physical, geographical, and national bodies of the characters and places within it. The concerns of the text—what to do with female embodiment and the feminine (or feminized)—and the literal textual embodiment of the novels—what they look like on the page, how they perform structurally—and how it continues or complicates the ideological embodiments of the feminine depict the accumulation of the Corporeum's layering, its web of intertextuality. In this, body, land, and nation, too, are all texts that are written and read.

I argue that the operations of the texts then pose a reversal to the ways in which the feminine is inscribed in and on women's bodies, the English landscape, and British nationalism and imperialism within the texts. I propose that the textual strategies work against or undo the modes of female bodily understanding and representation at work elsewhere in the texts. For example, although Clarissa Dalloway's body is conflated with depictions of the cultivated and pastoral countryside and these depictions are then conflated with ideals of national identity, the text's deployment of the stream-of-consciousness form imbues the character of Clarissa with a psychic interiority that complicates her function as imperial figurehead. Therefore, these authors' textual practices of stream-of-consciousness, linear disruption and inconclusion mitigate or subvert conventional scripts of female embodiment, modern female subjectivity, and literary modernism. This convergence of narrative experimentation and identity formation signals a radical political proposal within textual experimentation as well as a radical shift in narrative style. To be clear, I do not advocate for the discovery or creation of a specifically or essentialized feminine text or a kind of "l'écriture féminine."[11] Instead, I argue that texts, theoretically those written by men or women although only those written by women are discussed here, can self-consciously figure the feminine differently within the text and can deploy textual strategies such that space is created for new feminine subjectivities to be represented in the form of the text, such as stream-of-consciousness, if not in the characterization within the text. Specifically, I argue that Woolf and Moore attempt to create these spaces and that their textual strategies are often posed in direct contrast to their characterizations of the women they narrate. For example, Olive Moore's portrayal of Lavinia in *Fugue* positions Lavinia as both an independent and dynamic woman and as dependent on men. Moore's lack of conclusion, or doubled conclusion, to the novel disrupts the male modernist's attempts to contain the feminine and proposes the disruption of male-dependent narratives such as Lavinia's. This project, therefore, is aligned with Woolf's arguments on androgyny in *A Room of One's Own* which advocates a writing beyond or outside of gender by considering the ways in which the feminine as well as the masculine emerge and operate in these novels.[12]

In addition, I situate this project specifically during the interwar period, drawing attention to the extensive development and practice of textual experimentation by British women modernists during a moment of tremendous cultural change, singling out Woolf and Moore as two examples among many and furthering the implications for women at stake in textual production. The pervasive experimentalism by such writers as Dorothy Richardson, Rebecca West, Gertrude Stein, and Djuna Barnes, as well as Woolf and Moore, signals the need, desire, and opportunity for new representations of the modernist text and, I argue, of the feminine. Rather than see this as mere coincidence or a continuation of textual experimentations already developing with male modernists such as Ezra Pound, James Joyce, and Marcel Proust, I propose that these women authors' experimentations reveal the latent anxieties about the feminine in the practices of literary modernism. These women modernists' experimentations, most often represented in the excess of narrative and form as witnessed in the length and density of many of their novels such as *Pilgrimage, The Making of Americans, The Judge,* and *The Waves,* reveal an attempt to explore the absent territory of the feminine and to give voice to an alternate form of modernist literary experimentation. Rather than trying to create a form of writing that is purely or only feminine, I argue that these experimental women writers instead attempted to create a form of writing that included the feminine that was not purely or only masculine in production or in narrative strategy. I suggest, then, that these experimental women authors attempt to force a confrontation with the feminine and reveal the collusion of male modernist literary production to excise it.

To this end, I use narrative theory to investigate how these women writers conflate physical, geographical, and national bodies in their own textual bodies. Specifically, I incorporate theory detailing the relationship between cultural ideas about the body and the ways those ideas resisted, reflected, and developed in various deployments of words on the page. For instance, as I discuss in detail later, Leslie Heywood argues that male modernists such as T. S. Eliot and Ezra Pound proffered an anorexic aesthetic, a highly edited and impersonal textual body, tightly controlled, and with the fleshy bits erased. For Woolf and Moore, who instead utilize an aesthetic that extends the sentence and the paragraph on the page as well as the page(s) itself, their texts further explore the interiority of their female characters through stream-of-consciousness and excessive textual form.

I argue that British women's experimental modernism sought out textual strategies to replace the fleshy feminine once missing in modernist texts. Male modernist form, as Leslie Heywood continues, can be seen as "anorexic" in its "insistence on purification, dissection, [and] cutting to arrive at the work of art" as seen specifically in the "'hard body' of the imagist poem" and the "'extinction of personality'" (69). This anorexic style attempts to not only excise the body of the text, but also the body of the woman which "as both 'too much' and a sign of nothingness, contributes to the anorexic structure" (60–61). The excising of the feminine, though, extends beyond the removal of its fleshy form in a text; it also extends from a response to the cultural feminizing of literature in general:

> [r]ather than problematizing traditional notions of gender, the negation of the body in literary modernism seems, quite explicitly, a negation of the feminine, a reinscription and privileging of masculine prerogative in a realm of human activity that in the nineteenth century had become progressively "feminized," that of literary production. (Heywood 63)

British women modernists such as Woolf and Moore, then, in seeking to reincorporate the feminine back into their texts, situate themselves in conflict with male modernist form in particular as well as the move to masculinize modernist literature in general as demonstrated by "the male creative principle [as] defined in opposition to feminine flesh, a creativity made possible by an expurgation of the flesh as female" (Heywood 63).[13] If male modernism practices the erasure of the feminine in its anorexic form, then for a woman writer to deploy this male modernist form is to subject herself to another form of patriarchy and to deny her female subjectivity and embodiment.[14] A female modernist form must then reincorporate what "the male creative principle" has sought to remove—the female body—and seek to reflect it in her textual strategies. This project, then, proceeds to explicate those strategies and explore the ways in which they return the feminine to the modernist text.

The practices of British women modernists, in contrast to male modernist strategies, can be further understood by examining the associations between the gendered body and writing. For example, in her discussion of hysteria and language, Vicki Kirby describes the use of imitation by the hysteric as

> so entirely persuasive that the difference between reality and theater, disease and its imitation, is difficult to determine.... It is as if the hysteric is a mirror of her surroundings, incorporating the signs from an other's body as the reflection of her own. (57)

Kirby's theories on hysteria elucidate the position of the hysteric as mimic and the way that this hysteria is specifically situated in the body of the hysteric. I argue that, within the scope of this project, Kirby's suggestions, laid alongside Heywood's, reiterate the problems for the modernist woman writer who, in taking on male modernist form, may subsequently take on the position of the hysteric.[15] Olive Moore exemplifies the danger of hysteria for the modern woman in *Fugue* as Lavinia and the landscape with which she is affiliated in the novel are both described in terms of the fleshy feminine and hysteria. Thus, not only are the writers themselves threatened into the position of the hysterical subject, so, too, are the female characters who must constantly navigate the inscriptions of the hysterical feminine on their bodies and in their associations with the feminine land.

The fleshy feminine is also inherently connected to the abject, making the women in the novels and the women who wrote them situated outside of what Julia Kristeva calls the "symbolic system" (*Powers* 65), which here can be read as created by patriarchy in general and male modernism in particular. Thus, in addition to Heywood and Kirby, I continue with Julia Kristeva's theories on the abject and language which provide further underpinnings to the outside and abject position of female modernists. Kristeva states that "[i]t is the Word that discloses the abject" (*Powers* 23), linking the activities of writing to the inclusion and exclusion of the feminine in determining the abject. Specifically, Kristeva argues that "[i]f language, like culture, sets up a separation and, starting with discrete elements, concatenates an order, it does so precisely by repressing maternal authority and the corporeal mapping that abuts against them" (*Powers* 72). Language, therefore, enacts and contains the abject, and if that containment is conducted by patriarchy, women are inherently excluded from language which does not o/abjectify them.[16] The experiments with style and form by British women modernists respond to this exclusion by demonstrating their attempt to rewrite not only the body of the text but also their attempt to rewrite the abject body of the female character and the female writer. As such, the struggle to conclude these stories demonstrates their struggle to imagine the possibilities of their experimentations and resistance.

Creating a new narrative form, then, can be seen as a way to create a new female subjectivity. To begin to understand the relationship between narrative and identity, I refer to Susan Stanford Friedman's explanation of the effect of narrative on identity:

> . . . identity is literally unthinkable without narrative. People know who they are through the stories they tell about themselves and others. As ever-changing phenomena, identities are themselves narratives of formation, sequences moving through space and time as they undergo development, evolution, and revolution. . . . Narrative texts—whether verbal or visual, oral or written, fictional or referential, imaginary or historical—constitute primary documents of cultural expressivity. Narrative is a window into, mirror, constructor, and symptom of culture. Cultural narratives encode and encrypt in story form the norms, values, and ideologies of the social order . . . around which institutions of gender, race, class, and sexuality are organized. (8–9)

I argue that narrative and identity work reflexively: if narrative contributes to, if not constructs, identity, then the construction of not only new narratives but new forms of narrative can be seen as creating new forms of identities, specifically of women's identities. As examples of "cultural expressivity," these narratives reflect the changes of the culture as well as the identity politics of the author and thus reveal their positions on the gendered implications of narrative construction.

British women modernists' experiments in narrative, though, do more than just mirror the social order and chart its potential trajectories; they attempt to shatter that mirror and alter the sequence of traditional narrative. As Rachel Blau DuPlessis argues, "Any literary convention—plots, narrative, sequences, characters in bit parts—as an instrument that claims to depict experience, also interprets it. No convention is neutral, purely mimetic, or purely aesthetic" (2), for

> narrative structures and subjects are like working apparatuses of ideology, factories for the "natural" and "fantastic" meanings by which we live. Here are produced and disseminated the assumptions, the conflicts, the patterns that create fictional boundaries for experience. (3)

Narrative in its basic function, then, as well as in its experimental forms, is not "purely mimetic" of culture but also an interpreter and producer of culture (DuPlessis 2). I argue that British women modernists' textual experimentation attempts to not only interpret their culture in order to expose its troping of the female figure in male-dominated literary production, but also attempts to produce new forms of narrative that may in turn produce new cultures for women.

The development of narrative, then, connects not only to the construction of new identities but specifically to the development of new gender identities. As Rita Felski states, "If our sense of the past is inevitably shaped by the explanatory logic of narrative, then the stories that we create in turn reveal the inescapable presence and power of gender symbolism" (1). Specifically, experimentation with these new narratives emerged during this interwar period. As Maroula Joannou explains: "Much writing between the wars is concerned with the expression of cultured and gendered identities in ways appropriate to the new social conditions in which women found themselves" (191). Joannou asserts here an interdependent relationship between "new social conditions" and the new textual strategies developed between the wars. I argue that British women modernists' textual experimentation is not only a reflection of these new social conditions but a contributor to them. In fact, I suggest that they developed their experiments with narrative and form in order to wedge wider the openings of new opportunity for women and for women's subjectivities.

The textual experimentations of *Mrs. Dalloway*, for instance, reveal that despite Clarissa's apparent complicity with patriarchy and imperialism, she remains the center of the novel and the characters' consciousnesses in the final line of the novel: "for there she was" (194). Despite these seemingly inescapable embodiments, the text reasserts the continuing presence of Clarissa. She is ever present in the characters' consciousnesses and in the text, proffering the feminine as an inescapable identity with which patriarchy and imperialism must contend. Woolf then shows an alternative to the containment of the feminine through the escape of the psyche. Her experimental form, with its extended use of stream-of-consciousness, here allows for a new kind of border-crossing identity for women outside of the realm of patriarchal control. Through the portrayal of women's psyches, which are not contained within their femininely-marked bodies, Woolf signals the creation of a specific kind of identity for women, one which transcends the boundaries of women's physical, geographical, and national demarcations. Woolf does not just create a room of their own, she creates a new narrative imaginary in which these characters think, feel, and live out their lives, each part of which is everyday, extraordinary, and expressed. The alternative shape of the text allows for an alternate shape of women's identities which operate outside of patriarchal and imperial ideologies. Through the stream-of-consciousness form, then, Woolf asserts the interiority of not only Clarissa but also of Lady Bruton, Peter Walsh, Miss Kilman, Septimus Smith, Sarah Bletchley, Mr. Bowley, and Emily Coates, including upper class, working class, psychotic, and colonial subjects. Thus, Woolf's deployment of stream-of-consciousness situates women (as in the example of Clarissa earlier) as being more than body and its markings by demonstrating their psychic interiority and levels structures of gender and class as well through the equal access to the psychic interiority it provides.

From the voyage into stream-of-consciousness in *Mrs. Dalloway* to the juxtaposition of the two conclusions in Olive Moore's *Fugue*, the analysis of form highlights these authors' attempts to reshape not only the body of the text and of female subjectivity but also to re-imagine women's inscription within each of the bodies of the Corporeum. Accompanied by the analysis of their experiments with narrative, I reveal these authors' attempts to re-imagine the modern female subject beyond their sutured or highly sculpted corporeal and literary incarnations. Although I begin by delineating each theoretical body and how it is at work in a text, I continue by considering how these bodies work with and against each other. In each chapter, different pieces of the Corporeum come to the fore and, thus, are not necessarily divided into four sections, one for each body. Although in the first chapter on *Mrs. Dalloway*, I do progress through each body, I do so to lay out a template of my argument about the connectivity of the bodies in the Corporeum and how they lead up to the textual experimentation in the textual body. To explicate the workings of the textual body, in this chapter I linger longer on theory of textual experimentation and how it developed during the interwar period and for women writers. In later chapters, for example in Chapter 2 on *The Waves*, the national body dominates my analysis in order to further determine the extent to which the feminine is implicated in the workings of empire and how a text might imagine and propose alternatives for women, nation and narrative. I return to a detailed analysis of narrative strategy in Chapters 3 and 4 on Olive Moore's novels in order to discern the different deployments of textual experimentation, specifically in the lack of conclusions to her novels. I delineate each chapter and its concerns in detail later.

As a model for my theories of the Corporeum, I begin with Virginia Woolf's *Mrs. Dalloway* (1925) and with its depiction of Clarissa's body, the ways in which her body is compared to and placed within the pastoral and urban landscapes, what these landscapes represent for the nation, and the ways in which her character performs within the textual body itself as well as how the textual body itself performs. In its clear articulations of the characters as well as its explicit connections between each of the bodies in the Corporeum, Chapter 1, "The Shape of Modernism: Female Embodiment and Textual Experimentation in *Mrs. Dalloway*," lays bare how the physical, geographical, and national representations of women in the novel implicate them as willing and coerced participants in the systems of patriarchy and imperialism. However, the textual body, in its exploration of the stream-of-consciousness form, heralds a new representation of the female subject. Through its acknowledgement of and access to women's psychic interiority and through its leveling of monolithic structures such as class and gender identity, Woolf's use of stream-of-consciousness creates a new narrative imaginary in which woman can be, what Rachel Blau du Plessis calls, a consciously "speaking subject" (56).

Clarissa's body, described in its middle age as physically and sexually cold, hard, and lacking, revives only when contemplating or remembering encounters with women, specifically with Sally, or in anticipation of her party (*Mrs. Dalloway* 32). It is at these moments of physical and sexual awareness that the text becomes most effusive in its language, the stream-of-consciousness form exploding the language of Clarissa's sexual and social reveries and granting psychic rather than sexual interiority. In contrast, her younger body is idealized as fertile and productive land. This pastoral landscape with which the young Clarissa is associated is also, in other places in the novel, a symbol of the national body. The connection of her body and the land reflect the ways in which the geography of England is gendered and represents the various aspects of national identity, specifically in its production and sustenance. This is, in fact, the same national body for which Septimus went to war, an ideal of Shakespeare and schoolteachers. Through these initial three embodiments; Clarissa's character fully embodies ideals of patriarchy and empire, operating as both canvas and conduit for ideas of body, land, and nation.

The text poses a reversal to these depictions of female embodiment through its exposure and criticism of the ways in which women's bodies are made complicit within the machinations of patriarchy and imperialism by creating an alternate space in which new identities for women can be created. It is as if Woolf creates the space or the shape of women's identities yet to emerge through her challenges of traditional narrative structures and her criticism of the patriarchal structures that they embody. Simultaneously, Woolf undermines these societal and narrative structures through the use of stream-of-consciousness form, the unavoidable presence of the feminine as embodied by Clarissa, and her development of a fleshy, fluid text. It is the outline of their possibility that had as yet to be filled in with the details of this new woman's experience. I explore the nuanced shading of these new identities in the subsequent chapters' concern with the additional textual experimentation of Woolf and Moore. Their construction during the 1930s grants a further look at the possibilities for new shapes of the modernist text and modern identities for women.

Chapter 2, "Exposure and Development: Re-Imagining Narrative and Nation in the Interludes of Virginia Woolf's *The Waves*," again exposes the overtly femininely gendered bodies, lands, and nations that reveal the implicit participation of women in the patriarchal imperial project. I argue that this imperial project ultimately turns on the homeland and both directly employs and condemns women within its machinations. Specifically, I consider the imagery of the sun in the interludes in order to show how women's bodies and bodies of land are incorporated into the work of the national body. The textual body of *The Waves* (1931) experiments with its shape in its full-throttle, dense form that pushes the text to the margins in long, blocky paragraphs and avoids dialogue, situating itself in stark contrast to other Woolf texts. The texture of the novel provokes my queries into the novel's position on empire and women's role within it. I suggest that rather than a text that, as Jane Marcus proposes, depicts the decline of empire, the interludes of *The Waves* reveal the continuance of the imperial impulse by depicting a new site of imperial activity within the homeland through the movement of the sun from the east to the west.

I argue that, through the textual experimentation of the interludes, Woolf proposes a new shape of female subjectivity through the shape of a new textual form which re-imagines narrative construction and, with it, national identity and the feminine inscriptions upon which they rely. I argue further that through the use of the interludes, Woolf creates an alternative space that is variously feminine and masculine that operates outside the reaches of the narrative. Despite ending with an episodic chapter solely in Bernard's voice, the novel proposes that there is yet a more powerful and persistent voice that is beyond the containment of the narrative and that, through its cyclical and perpetual nature in the elements of solar and oceanic repetition, is one that will survive even Bernard's attempts to conquer death. In addition, the effects of light and shadow throughout the interludes create an alternate textual space for female identity and subjectivity. These alternate spaces in the novel ultimately promise alternate spaces of feminine personal and national identity where nonpatriarchal and nonimperial stories may be created and, eventually, enacted.

Olive Moore's novel *Spleen* (1930) portrays one woman's attempt to achieve new possibilities of physical embodment. Chapter 3, "Modernist Con(Tra)Ceptions: Re-Conceiving Body and Text in Olive Moore's *Spleen*," considers how Moore explores the tensions between the realities of female identity and embodment essentialized in maternity and the possibilities of new identities and embodiments through physical and textual (re)production. Moore moves beyond Woolf's refiguring of the feminine and the text to attempt, as my title suggests, to *re-conceive* of the ways in which the feminine body and text are both imagined, or conceived, and created, or (re)produced. In each re-conception, Moore presents a complex, conflicted, and critical position on the feminine as located in women's bodies, feminized land and nations, as well as proposing new identities of body, land, and text.

The narrative of *Spleen* unravels in disordered flashes between the England of Ruth's childhood, father's death, marriage, and childbearing and the Italian island where she exiled herself after her discovery of her child, Richard's, mutancy. Ruth's attempt to make something new with her body and her destruction of her husband's archetypal family manor home disrupts established notions of female subjectivity in its undermining of stereotypical female embodiment and patriarchy. Ruth's physical body is disrupted when she becomes pregnant and plunges herself into denial until, many months pregnant, she cannot ignore the bulging of her stomach in the bath. Deciding that this is her chance to create something new, she accepts her pregnancy. When her son, Richard, is born mute and with waxen feet, she accepts it as punishment for her denial and deviance surrounding the pregnancy. Ruth's body is deeply affiliated with nature, but this geographical affiliation, too, is undermined, as her walking barefoot in the grass is at times blamed for Richard's deformity. It is as if this geographical affiliation not only continues her entrapment in female subjectivity rather than an alternate release as promised by her father, it proves toxic to her attempts to develop alternate embodiments and identities. Despite her early connection with the British soil, after Richard's birth, Ruth chooses not the grayness of England, but the "blue expanse of sky" (230) of Italy.

*Spleen* further disrupts the connections within the Corporeum by utilizing women's bodies as interactive and interchangeable canvases of landscape and as part of empire production. Although Moore does much to undermine these paradigmatic positions, they are still inscribed within the discourse of empire and patriarchy that Ruth attempts to resist. Still, the feminine, land, and landscape are pivotal to female and national identity and narrative construction. I suggest, therefore, that Ruth's desire to create something new with her body correlates directly to the modernist impulse to make it new.[17]

Despite the failed attempts at physical hybridity in the novel through maternity and the creation of Richard, Moore's textual experimentation of excess and fragmentation and hybridity of fusing a fleshy, female form of textual experimentation to the traditions of male modernist ideals, continues to assert the possibility for change in the social realm as signaled by her changes in the discursive landscape in the body and of the text. The textual body of *Spleen* removes Ruth's body from the empire to Italy rather than imprisoning it within the trope of Britishness. Ruth does not appear to be reincorporated into the stream of empire and is set free from the trap of patriarchy, but even this move is frighteningly figured within the imagery of a similar patriarchy of Roman Catholicism in the novel's final paragraph. Although the experimental form of this novel's excessive language and fragmented narrative structure, hybridized with male modernist ideals of myth and tradition, and the uncertainty of its conclusion, allow for possibilities of resistance to patriarchy, colonialism, and containment, the direction of this resistance remains unclear, leaving the possibility of a new identity for women unfulfilled.

The final chapter, "Flight of the Feminine and Textual Orientation in Olive Moore's *Fugue*"[18] (1932), examines how Moore discards her attempt in *Spleen* to re-conceive the feminine, and instead abandons any hope of changing feminine corporeal inscriptions of body, land, and nation, and with them, any hope of creating a new embodiment of female subjectivity. Like *Spleen*, *Fugue* is also told through a series of flashbacks and flashforwards. These follow the progression of Lavinia Reade's relationships with men, primarily her disturbing relationship with Harrion whom she tracks to the Alsace when she discovers she is pregnant. Olive Moore creates even greater dissonance within the Corporeum, moving the narrative to the Alsace (only the flashbacks are in England) and annihilating the body (first of Harrion's daughter and then of strangers) in the crematorium. Lavinia Reade's body is also pregnant (and highly sexualized), and she spends most of the novel in search of a partner (initially the father, Harrion and then, Sebastian, with whom she walks through the countryside at the end of the novel) and a future for her child. But, unlike Ruth, she is not portrayed as a sympathetic figure. The future of the physical body is linked directly to the land, as it is the "bacchic frieze of grapes, the tumbling children and burdened fields" of the Alsace (not England) that causes her to see that "there is an eternity" (333) for these people and for herself. *Fugue* locates the future not in a land or image of England or Englishness, but in a classical, European image of pagan ritual and agrarian production, one that in its seasonality foreshadows another dead end for the possibility of escaping the traps of female embodiment.

Even as physical, geographical, and national bodies merge in what appears to be a return to an ideal of land, nation, and maternity, and a criticism of these ideals within Englishness, the narrative of *Fugue* also incorporates the destruction of each by the character of Harrion. The conclusion, with the above scene of Lavinia and Sebastian in juxtaposition with Harrion's vision of the smoke from the crematorium, complicates the ideal future initially proposed about body, land, and country through Lavinia and Sebastian. For Harrion, he "could only love humanity when it suffered as it suffered here" (329). As he watches the smoke "with its stench and putrescence," he "smiled and held up his face" (333). If Harrion's smoke and ashes can be seen as an offering to the gods (and perhaps these are the same pagan gods that Lavinia and Sebastian seem to worship), this shows him as an active part of the pagan ritual that Sebastian and Lavinia only observe. There is a future, but it is a future still embedded with idealism about gender, land, and nation, and, potentially, a future still under the control of patriarchy and its ability to contain and destroy. The textual body, again highly experimental in form, resists ending through the dual proposals of Lavinia–Sebastian and Harrion, neither of which are conclusive.

Only through her textual experimentations, specifically of the twinned (in)conclusions, does Moore seek to navigate a way out of the abject status of female subjectivity which she so carefully depicts in each of the bodies of the Corporeum, and offers instead of a closed, predictable textual form, an open-ended, inconclusive one. These experiments in form and narrative which disrupt narrative linearity and modernist techniques such as the circadian novel, that is, *Mrs. Dalloway* and *Ulysses*, spawn my queries into Moore's proposals for viable alternatives to the traditions of patriarchy, maternity, and nationality. I argue that *Fugue* poses the split subjectivity of the modern subject through its characterizations of bodies, lands, and nations and through its textual form of doubled (and multiple) narratives, offering possibility in its opening of a fissure through which the feminine may stray and ultimately become its own story.

Throughout this project, the four embodiments within the Corporeum as a whole so that in reading them intertextually they enlighten new aspects of body, land, nation, and text. Through looking at the individual embodiments and the ways in which they work together, I seek to demonstrate their interconnectedness and interdependence. In doing so, I question the ability to utilize one without signaling the others, and I question the various performances of these texts to examine the role of female embodiment in establishing ideals and identities of land, nation, and narrative. I argue that if these individual embodiments are inextricably connected, so too are the identities of each. The Corporeum then reveals the complicated web of ligature that connects these bodies, revealing a complex body of thought concerned with issues of borders and identity, containment and exclusion inherent in confronting feminine embodiment and subjectivity within British Modernism.

Ultimately, I argue that these authors and texts attempt to resist the demarcations of the feminine body and land and their use in sustaining and propelling national identity and free the feminine from patriarchy and empire. Through experiments in character, narrative, and form, these texts resist the use of the feminine body and land. Their inability to conclude and firmly establish the possibilities of resistance they suggest indicates the anxiety and difficulty in imagining new possibilities of female identity and textual form. Though Clarissa, Ruth, and Lavinia provide resistance through their attitudes and actions, this resistance is still as yet only made manifest in the authors' textual experimentations as they attempt to create a new space for female identity.

# 1 The Shape of Modernism
## Female Embodiment and Textual Experimentation in *Mrs. Dalloway*

At the beginning of Virginia Woolf's *Mrs. Dalloway*, Clarissa Dalloway takes a well-known walk through London, encountering—along with many other Londoners—the grey car of (possibly) royalty that proceeds through Westminster to Buckingham Palace. Throughout the novel, the symbolism attached to the grey car demarcates it as a signifying landmark in the identity and identification of Clarissa, connecting her to both images of the landscape and ideologies of the nation. As the grey car passes a men's club, the club is described as a still life that summons images of nation: "The white busts and the little tables in the background covered with copies of the *Tatler* and syphons of soda water seemed to approve; seemed to indicate the flowing corn and the manor houses of England" (18). It is as if the siphons and *Tatler*s not only approve of the royal car but approve of it and access it specifically, I argue, via English pastoral images.[1] Later in the novel, Peter tells us that Clarissa for him was always "recalling some field or English harvest" (153). Here, Clarissa is associated, at least for Peter, with the English pastoral countryside. In fact, he says that "he saw her most often in the country, not in London" (153). This passage is surprising in its correlation of Clarissa—such a well-known Londoner—with the English countryside, but in conjunction with the earlier passage on the grey car, it also serves to connect and extend Clarissa's identity to the images of pastoral land and then to the nation as these same images of pastoral England are conjured by the royal grey car.[2] Clarissa's identity then becomes collapsed not only with a kind of pastoral geographical identity but with an idealized national identity as well. There is a familiar trajectory here in the tracing of how women and women's bodies become figureheads for nationalism, this time via geographical imagery. I argue that the novel's depictions of the physical, geographical, and national bodies as well fail to provide alternative identifications for women outside of patriarchy and imperialism.

Yet, the textual body reverses the trajectory of these demarcations of the feminine in its exploration of the stream-of-consciousness form, heralding a new representation of the subject, including the female subject, through its acknowledgement of and access to women's psychic (not just physical) interiority and leveling monolithic structures such as class and gender identity. After examining the text and its experiments with form, I argue that despite the exposure of the failure of women to escape the pre-established feminine embodiments of their physical form, their affiliation with land and landscape, and the ways they are depicted as necessary representations of, for, and within nation, Woolf exposes and criticizes these various demarcations of female embodiment in physical, geographical, and national bodies. Through her textual experimentation, specifically with her use of the stream-of-consciousness form, Woolf provides for alternative ways of thinking about, accessing, and, therefore, creating identity subjectivity for women and for the modern female subject.[3]

Within this chapter, I begin by looking closely at the portrayals of women's physical bodies in *Mrs. Dalloway* and then at how these portrayals are both continued and contradicted in the text's images of landscape, rhetoric of nationalism, and experiments in form.[4] If I were only to consider the first three incarnations of female identity and subjectivity—physical, geographical, and national—as in previous paragraphs, this analysis would conclude by noting Clarissa's affiliation via geography with nationalism and the complicit relationship between women's bodies and national identity. But, with the additional analysis of the textual body, I argue that Woolf's textual strategies provide an interiority and consciousness to the female body so often portrayed as only superficially inscribed with physical, geographical, and national identity markers. In essence, I argue that the text, through its use of stream-of-consciousness, provides alternate corporeal and psychic identities to those identities imposed upon and interpreted to be contained within women's bodies, the English landscape, and British nationalism. The body of the text, in granting interiority and consciousness to women like Clarissa Dalloway, also grants a separate, specific identity and presence to women, and this consciousness constructs different possibilities for and perspectives on, as well as criticism of, the physical, geographical, and national bodies within the text.[5] In extending the development of a new literary form into the psyches of women and the working class, Woolf makes it possible to imagine the form of women's identity outside of their traditional physical inscriptions.

## FEMALE EMBODIMENT: CLARISSA'S COMPLICIT CORPOREALITY

As Clarissa Dalloway traverses London in the opening of the novel, she describes her body as follows:

> But often now this body she wore (she stopped to look at a Dutch picture), this body, with all its capacities, seemed nothing—nothing at all. She had the oddest sense of being herself invisible, unseen; unknown; there being no more marrying, no more having of children, but only this astonishing and rather solemn progress with the rest of them, up

Bond Street, this being Mrs. Dalloway; not even Clarissa any more; this being Mrs. Richard Dalloway. (11)

In this passage, several representations of and conflicts about female embodiment are immediately apparent from her adjacent statements that her body has "all its capacities" and yet "seemed nothing . . . at all" (11). First, Clarissa sees her body as something she wears, "this body she wore" (11), indicating that this is an external part of her identity, something such as a coat that she puts on over something else: her body acts as a cover to another, internal identity. In acknowledging that the body is something that she puts on, she recognizes that it is in a sense something that she performs or has a choice about wearing or enacting; it implies that her body is also something she can take off like a costume.[6] This idea of conscious body performance is underscored by her reflection on the "Dutch picture" (11). Her body, like a painting, is a representation, a portrayal of an idea. Specifically, I argue, her body is the corporeal manifestation of patriarchal ideas of femininity, specifically those of marriage and maternity. Initially, this idea of her body performance denotes a type of freedom from the body and its inscriptions by implying that she has a choice of whether to and how to wear it. Unfortunately, she does not have the option of taking off her physical embodiment and its inscriptions.

In considering Clarissa's relationship to her body in this passage, I refer to Elizabeth Grosz's work on the slippery borders between psyche and body, or body image, in *Volatile Bodies*, where she states that:

> the limits or borders of the body image are not fixed by nature or confined to the anatomical "container," the skin. The body image is extremely fluid and dynamic; its borders, edges, and contours are "osmotic"—they have the remarkable power of incorporating and expelling outside and inside in an ongoing interchange. (79)

In other words, the body image is inherently involved in determining borders, specifically the borders that determine what is included and excluded in the body image. We see in the Bond Street passage earlier that Clarissa's body image has become "nothing—nothing at all" (11). It is as if all meaning attached to her body has evaporated or been "expell[ed] outside" of her body so that she sees herself as "invisible, unseen, unknown" (11). Because of the inherent connection, or "ongoing interchange," between the body and psyche that Grosz discusses, Clarissa reveals her sense of her interior identity as well as her physical identity so that she is "not even Clarissa anymore." The correlation between body and psyche grants that Clarissa sees herself as absent in both her public or physical corporeality and her private or psychic identity.

Second, Clarissa's description of being "invisible, unseen, unknown" relates directly to her body's use and status in the institutions of marriage and maternity: "there being no more marrying, no more having of children" (11). Her body has fulfilled its use as wife and mother and is now used up; without an individual identity, she is instead incorporated into the social body with "the rest of them" (11). In a sense, she sees herself as without specific bodily form or identity unless it is a body defined as wife and mother. In particular, the sexual body becomes, through marriage, regulated and incorporated into a social rather than an individual ideal as Kathy Phillips argues, "marriage seems to have tamed sexuality itself into a tourist landscape of uniformity for all" (103).[7] Marriage leaves Clarissa with no specific external physical or internal psychic identity. As Patricia Moran argues in *Word of Mouth: Body Language in Katherine Mansfield and Virginia Woolf*, this condition of detachment represents "women's orphaned state within the symbolic, an orphaned state Woolf connects to the cultural appropriation of the female body for the uses of patriarchy" such as marriage (149). The problem for Clarissa, of course, is that outside or after the body has been used, the body and the identity attached to it become unnecessary, discarded, or at the very least, unimportant, leaving her body and, therefore, her internal identity not only "orphaned" but also discarded.

As Clarissa asserts, through her joining of "marrying" and "having children" (11), the association between female embodiment and its use for patriarchy extends metaphorically and physically from the use of women's bodies for marriage to include their use in maternity. In fact, as Makiko Minow-Pinkney argues in *Virginia Woolf and the Problem of the Subject*: "maternity is the only female identity which is valorized by patriarchy. Only as a mother is a woman allowed to have her sexuality as difference, to own her body and social place" (71). Thus, women are orphaned from their identity within the symbolic system except in their accommodation to/valorization by patriarchy through maternity. Women must then both embody the signs of femininity that accommodate patriarchy or face possible expulsion from the patriarchal system. For Clarissa, the description of her physical body as apart from the maternal or postmaternal leads to her conclusion about her identity as "Mrs. Richard Dalloway" (11) absent of any specific Clarissaness. Here we see her reluctant acknowledgment of her status in maternity, abandoning her sense of creating an individual identity because of her place in marriage, maternity, and their operations which require her complicity.

Clarissa must remain in this position of "Mrs. Richard Dalloway" (11) in order to avoid the status of what Julia Kristeva describes as the abject who, among other things, "disturbs identity, system, order" (*Powers* 4) or who becomes a "stray" (*Powers* 8) by wandering outside of the symbolic system (here of marriage, maternity, and patriarchy). In addition to Kristeva's definition of the abject, Patricia Moran connects the abject to patriarchy when sees that "the abjection associated with female embodiment necessitates accommodation to the fathers' law and the Father's Word" (155), so that women must comply with or be exiled from the symbolic system. In order to remain within the symbolic system, Clarissa absents herself from any separate identity markers that would push her across the border of "the fathers' law" (Moran 155) into abjection or expulsion from patriarchy.

The effects of this complicity emerge in Clarissa's description of her body throughout the novel as absent or discarded. As Clarissa ascends the stairs to her attic room, she describes herself as: "a nun who has left the world . . . blessed and purified" (29), as "suddenly shriveled, aged, breastless . . . out of her body and brain which now failed" (31), and that "[s]he could not dispel a virginity preserved through childbirth which clung to her like a sheet" (31). All of these descriptions of herself show Clarissa to be physically or at least sexually absent as she is invisible, nun-like, breastless, with a body that has failed, and yet virginal. She is both pre- and postsexuality, but mostly she is outside of sexuality, outside of anything that would make her body sexually or physically present, namely maternity. In denying access to a present body, she denies any relation between her body and its potentially abject feminine status, but she also denies access to her own corporeal identity as well. As the abject is the undeniable presence of not only the body but the body's filth, Clarissa is able to remove herself from her body's transgression. Because she sees that both "her body and brain . . . now failed" (31), she also demonstrates that her body image replicates itself in the image of her psyche as Grosz's argument about body image previously suggests. Thus, Clarissa attempts to remove herself from the "fail[ure]" of her body and mind and from the abject feminine inherent in each. Although this can be seen as a potentially subversive act, a resistance to the external meanings placed on her body, Clarissa does not take advantage of this subversion but rather accommodates her abject status through her acceptance of her marriage and the loss of her marriage bed.

At the same time that she exposes Clarissa's reluctant complicity with her physical, and therefore, psychical, markers, Woolf also exposes the conflicted position for women who, like Clarissa, operate as both sexually reproductive and asexually pure. Clarissa describes her body as having "failed" (31) in its sexual relations with Richard, but it has succeeded in reproducing her daughter Elizabeth. Apart from this physical expulsion or abjection, her sexuality and physical presence must be denied in order for her to maintain the feminine ideal of purity. Hence, she also sees herself as "virginal" despite having had a child.

As a hallmark of Clarissa's physical presence and sexuality, the following passage, while revealing the possibility of her own identity in her corporeality, ultimately also denies it. Upon describing how she has repeatedly failed Richard sexually, she then also describes how:

> she could not resist sometimes yielding to the charm of a woman, not a girl, of a woman confessing, as to her they often did, some scrape, some folly. And whether it was pity, or their beauty, or that she was older, or some accident—like a faint scent, or a violin next door . . . she

did undoubtedly then feel what men felt. Only for a moment; but it was enough. It was a sudden revelation, a tinge like a blush which one tried to check and then, as it spread, one yielded to its expansion, and rushed to the farthest verge and there quivered and felt the world come closer, swollen with some astonishing significance, some pressure of rapture, which split its thin skin and gushed and poured with an extraordinary alleviation over the cracks and sores! Then, for that moment, she had seen an illumination; a match burning in a crocus; an inner meaning almost expressed. But the close withdrew; the hard softened. (32)

Sexual arousal, despite granting her some access to patriarchal power as she "then did undoubtedly feel what men felt" (32), does not offer a position of sexuality or physical presence that she can maintain. It is instead "only for a moment" (32). Clarissa's description associates sexual arousal to the abject through the oozing of her own interiority and sexuality as the blush spreads, expands, splits, and pours. Sexual contact with an/other body makes her body abject in the leaking of her body as it strays across her body's borders. Although the homoerotic implications of this passage promises subversion to patriarchy and marriage as Clarrisa's moments of bodily presence are alone or with women, away from the outside world of men/patriarchy she again does not pursue this course (either here or in her youth with Sally). Instead of following her body into a sexual but abject (or doubly abject) state, she recoils and contains her sexuality and potentially her physicality as "the close withdrew; the hard softened" (32).[9] As the "inner meaning" is "almost expressed" (32), it indicates both the removal of her sexuality and physical presence, and of her possibility as a phallic, patriarchal power.[10] As she withdraws any presence of sexuality, she also removes the possibility of a separate physical and internal identity apart from the symbolic system. And, as she chooses to remain within the system, she remains without agency for sexual or self-expression. She is both trapped within and complicit with the system's requirements of her physical embodiment as chaste and, therefore, abjectless.

The text, though, does not just represent the conflicts of the external identity of her physical embodiment, but also reveals its conflicts with the internal identity of her psychic self by showing Clarissa's physical/sexual presence and by showing Clarissa's psychic interiority. Through Woolf's use of the stream-of-consciousness form, the text reveals and represents the inner workings of Clarissa's female embodiment in ways that show how Clarissa is not just physically, but psychically and textually present. The stream-of-consciousness form acts as a leveling agent that portrays both men's and women's psyches, that accesses the thoughts of upper and lower class citizens, and that transcends the physical barriers imposed by the rules and regulations of patriarchy on female embodiment: the text is not contained by the physical bodies of the characters and, unlike its portrayal of Clarissa's sexuality, disregards concerns for abject leakage

*The Shape of Modernism* 31

by freely moving across the borders of the characters' minds and bodies. Specifically, except for two deviations—Peter's walk through the park and Richard's meeting with Lady Bruton—the Clarissa storyline (as opposed to the Septimus storyline) asserts the presence of the feminine by situating Clarissa at its center.

In the previous passages, the text grants interiority to Clarissa's physical embodiment by accessing her thoughts about her physicality, her marriage, the uselessness of her body, her sexual arousal, and the choices she makes around them. These thoughts are interrupted when she sees a Dutch painting, walks in a crowd, sees her narrow bed and bed sheets, and shuts down sexual expression. Part of the leveling effect of stream-of-consciousness not only grants access to these thoughts alongside the representations of the body, but also grants access to all levels of thought—to ideas about marriage as well as to their interruptions by the sight of a Dutch painting. Mostly, the form of the novel, in revealing the psychic interiority of Clarissa, undermines or at least counters the notion of Clarissa as only female embodiment: this is a body with a mind, a mind of its own, even if it does not fully have a physical identity of its own.

In addition, the use of the flashbacks to Bourton, to the summer when Clarissa lived unattached to Peter or Richard, and the summer when Sally kissed her, provide an escape to and reassert a time and place in which Clarissa could still identify her own specific identity, one in which she still held power over the choices of her body and future life, albeit a life that was rapidly changing. The emergences of and insistence on the Bourton moments and characters into the text are another way in which the text reminds Clarissa and the reader of a time before her marital and maternal complicity. It is another way in which the text exposes and criticizes the ways marriage and maternity compromise female identity through its demonstration of the contrast between the two Clarissas and another way in which the text disrupts the sequence of patriarchal narrative.[11]

## GEOGRAPHICAL GENDERING: ATTEMPTING AN ALTERNATIVE FEMININE EMBODIMENT

The geographical body continues the pervasive feminine presence as seen in the character of Clarissa in three ways: the natural or wild land, the pastoral or cultivated countryside, and the urban city.[12] The bodies of women, and specifically of Clarissa, are associated with all three of these landscapes in varying ways. Through the associations with the various lands and landscapes, the text explores a possibility for escape from female physical embodiment, extending the tropes of feminine embodiment onto the land.

The text does provide alternative feminine presences through the use of geographical imagery. It is as if the text reproduces the anxiety of the repressed abject feminine presence as already examined in the previous section on the physical body by continually asserting the feminine through imagery of the land. In casual references (Peter's fiancée is named "Daisy" 43), and metaphors, ("[t]he word 'time' split its husk" 69), the text relies upon imagery from nature. These smaller instances are extended in longer descriptions so that Peter says of Daisy to Clarissa: "'I am in love,' he said, not to [Clarissa] however, but to some one raised up in the dark so that you could not touch her but must lay your garland down on the grass in the dark" (45). Clarissa responds by having "leant forward, taken his hand, drawn him to her, kissed him,—actually had felt his face on hers before she could down the brandishing of silver flashing—plumes like pampas grass in a tropic gale in her breast" (46–47). Here, the nature imagery asserts not the typical English pastoral imagery I later discuss, but imagery from India which Peter helps colonize, as if Peter's experience and imagery also invades Clarissa's. In almost all these extended passages, nature imagery heralds the pastoral as a chivalric ideal especially in this moment between former lovers in which the one who wooed (Peter) is again "lay[ing his] garland down on the grass," and the imagery responds in Clarissa's action with that of Peter's colonial environment, with "pampas grass" and "a tropic gale." Summoned forth are specific instances of these characters' pasts and these memories are laden, if not haunted, with the presence of the feminine land.

Most often, nature imagery describes female characters such as Rezia or Elizabeth. Septimus sees that "[Rezia's] sigh was tender and enchanting, like the wind outside a wood in the evening" (141), that "[Rezia] held her hands to her head, . . . waiting, looking down, he could feel her mind, like a bird falling from branch to branch, and always alighting, quite rightly" (147), and that "sitting beside him, he thought, as if all her petals were about her. She was a flowering tree; and through her branches looked out the face of a lawgiver, who had reached a sanctuary where she feared no one" (148). The character of Rezia continually conjures up the use of pastoral nature imagery, of wind in the trees, birds, and flowering trees (23, 24, 50, 65, 89, 93, 141, 147) connecting her to the pastoral ideal and the ideal feminine. The association of nature imagery with female characters is not surprising in its reliance on pastoral tropes, but it does come laden with its inherent feminine associations, reasserting the presence of the feminine throughout the text.

The character of Elizabeth Dalloway, who also conjures nature imagery, complicates the association of nature and the feminine. She is "like a poplar . . . like a river . . . like hyacinth" (188)—even Clarissa describes her as "like a hyacinth, sheathed in glossy green, with buds just tinted, a hyacinth which has had no sun" (123). That Elizabeth is aware of the correlation suggests a fissure in the nature–feminine connection. Elizabeth states that "[p]eople were beginning to compare her to poplar trees, early dawn, hyacinths, fawns, running water, and garden lilies, and it made her life a burden to her" (134). For Elizabeth, these metaphors are not useful; instead, the feminine here is "a burden." Her awareness of them and her rejection of them grants the possibility of a new kind of association for women, one that is not trapped in feminine-inscribed embodiments.[13] Instead, Elizabeth desires to "[be] left alone to do what she liked in the country . . . and London was so dreary compared with being alone in the country with her father and the dogs" (134–35), a desire which places her again in what the text has shown via Clarissa to be the feminine-inscribed countryside.[14]

These geographical affiliations, further complicated by their inherent feminine demarcations, place the feminine in its geographical incarnation again in the power of patriarchy. Just as Woolf describes the English countryside at the beginning of *Between the Acts*: "From an aeroplane, [Mr. Oliver] said, you could still see, plainly marked, the scars made by the Britons; by the Romans; by the Elizabethan manor house; and by the plough, when they ploughed the hill to grow wheat in the Napoleonic wars" (4), we see the land, like women's bodies, as another site that is variously marked and scarred by man's encounters with it and attempts to possess it, and on in which these processes are made legible. In *Mrs. Dalloway*, the embodiment, feminizing, and inscription of the land is more subtle and insistent than in the above passage in the text's reliance on pastoral metaphors and the use of the pastoral in describing female characters.[15] At the same time, the feminized, pastoral land is pervasive throughout the text, infiltrating both memories of youth and the moments of the present day as well as descriptions of characters and urban locales.

The use of the women–land association by patriarchy is further suggested by Clarissa's affiliation with the land and its mitigation through the character of Peter Walsh. Peter associates Clarissa with the pastoral landscape, as for him she was "always in this way coming before him without his wishing it, cool, lady-like, critical; or ravishing, romantic, recalling some field or English harvest. He saw her most often in the country, not in London" (153). In fact, "he saw her most often at Bourton, in the late summer" (154). He also sees her as his guide and aid in that land, as this is a country in which Peter is disoriented, and it is Clarissa who would "break off to get her bearings, pilot him back across country" (154). For Peter, as Clarissa is the country and the homeland, she is the beacon which guides the (colonial) traveler through it. As she becomes the representative of the homeland for him, she also becomes the hostess of his travels in the homeland and the ideal of Englishness that he takes with him to the colonies. For example, during his walk through London, he exclaims,

> A splendid achievement in its own way, after all, London; the season; civilization. . . . There were moments when civilization, even of this sort, seemed dear to him as a personal possession; moments of pride in England; in butlers; chow dogs; girls in their security. (55)

Peter links ideas of national purity and its "civilization" to female "purity" and "security," ideas which I argue implicate women generally and Clarissa specifically. For Peter, then, Clarissa must remain fixed in her identity, must remain secure and bounded in order for his binary ideas of home and colony to remain secure and fixed as well. For Peter, at least, Clarissa is the countryside, and this association continues to layer her character with another feminine embodiment: the feminine, pastoral land. As this connection is witnessed through the male projection of Peter, it again asserts the use of this connection by men/patriarchy.

The feminizing of the land in *Mrs. Dalloway* gains credence through work of geographical theorists such as Nancy Duncan, Margaret R. Higonnet, Kathleen Kirby, and Linda McDowell, who document the feminizing of the geographical body. For example, patriarchy's role in gendering the land, as seen in Peter's projections of the pastoral ideal onto Clarissa's body, can be understood through Linda McDowell's contention that "places are made through power relations which construct the rules that define boundaries" (4). In addition, place is often gendered female as

> women are seen as closer to nature, as irrational, as polluters, as sacred but as inferior because they menstruate and because of their ability to bear children. Men, on the other hand, are seen as civilized, rational and superior, mind to women's body, even, indeed, unbodied or disembodied. (44)

For McDowell, then, the feminizing of the land begins with women being affiliated with nature in general and that to escape this affiliation is to deny the body, to be instead like the civilized men who are seen as "unbodied or disembodied." The "disembodi[ment]" of Clarissa, then, can also be understood as an escape from not only the feminine inscription on her physical body but also on the geographical body with which she is so affiliated.

The feminizing of the land advanced in England, specifically during the interwar period when Woolf was writing *Mrs. Dalloway*, as the relationship between women and the land developed in response to World Ware I. Anne McClintock's assertion that "as European men crossed the dangerous thresholds of their known worlds, they ritualistically feminized borders and boundaries" (24), places the activity of feminizing the land within the activity of war. In the process, as McClintock also claims, "women served as mediating and threshold figures by means of which men oriented themselves in space, as agents of power and agents of knowledge" (24), so that the feminine, like Clarissa in *Mrs. Dalloway,* becomes that which demarcates borders and, therefore, grants understanding of men's "orient[ation] in space" (24). The feminizing of the land results in the "disavowing male loss of boundary by reinscribing a ritual excess of boundary, accompanied, all too often, by an excess of military violence" (24). McClintock points out that the "myth of the virgin land is also the myth of the empty land" (30) implying not only the gendering of the land, but violence connected to the (re)filling of it. During the war and after, the land of England, affiliated with purity, became feminized and, in the trajectory of this theory, therefore needed to be protected. Historian Samuel Hynes states that after the war, writers such as Edmund Gosse "looked back, and saw a lost rural England that had been simpler and more decent and, somehow, more English" (13). The feminized land, then, is also a rural and pastoral land and, eventually in *Mrs. Dalloway*, I argue, a symbol for the nation and Englishness itself. Affiliation with this feminized land is then another way in which women are femininely inscribed.

Within *Mrs. Dalloway*, as rural England emerges through descriptions of the female characters, it and the ideals of England it represents are complicated through the novel's primary urban setting of London which situates the characters in the same position as Gosse: looking back in time at an ideal rural England as represented through the flashbacks at Bourton. Clarissa describes herself in relationship to both the rural and urban landscapes, often within the same passage. In contrast to Peter's strict affiliation of Clarissa with the pastoral landscape, Clarissa tells Hugh Whitbread, "'I love walking in London. . . . Really it's better than walking in the country'" (6), perhaps asserting her resistance to Peter/patriarchy's use of her as a pastoral/English ideal. Mostly, Clarissa describes herself in direct association with the land and its people, whichever land she currently inhabits:

> somehow in the streets of London, on the ebb and flow of things, here, there, she survived, Peter survived, lived in each other, she being part, she was positive, of the trees at home; of the house there, ugly, rambling all to bits and pieces as it was; part of people she had never met; being laid out like a mist between the people she knew best, who lifted her on their branches as she had seen trees lift the mist, but it spread ever so far, her life, herself. (9)

She reveals that the landscape, the "streets of London," the "trees at home," "the house there," all of these places are points of connection for her, are essential to her identity. The people, of whom she is also a part, also operate like part of the landscape, lifting "her on their branches" (9). In this association with the landscape, she is mostly bodiless, a mist that spreads, fixed only and briefly in multiple materialities of people and objects. In this passage, her bodilessness allows for a kind of leaky abjection that allows for an escape from the identifications demarcated on her physical body that contain her within maternity and patriarchy.

This same kind of multiple identification with the land and its people develops later in the novel as Clarissa describes herself as:

> everywhere; not "here, here, here"; and she tapped the back of the seat; but everywhere. She waved her hand, going up Shaftesbury Avenue. She was all that. So that to know her, or any one, one must seek out the people who completed them; even the places. Odd affinities she had

with people she had never spoken to, some woman in the street, some man behind a counter—even trees, or barns. It ended in a transcendental theory which, with her horror of death, allowed her to believe, or say that she believed (for all her skepticism), that since our apparitions, the part of us which appears, are so momentary compared with the other, the unseen part of us, which spreads wide, the unseen might survive, be recovered somehow attached to this person or that, or even haunting certain places after death. (152–53)

Here, Clarissa identifies herself as a spreading presence which is "everywhere" with "odd affinities" with people as well as "trees, or barns."[16] Again, she identifies a part of herself which is "unseen" or an "apparition" that "spreads wide." This is distinct from Clarissa's understanding of her physical body in association with the land: Clarissa does find herself to be a presence, but only dimly so, that still operates within the symbolic system by locating itself in the materialities of the land and its people. Yet, through Clarissa's affiliation with the land, the text indicates a subversive quality which elides the boundaries of the physical body and escapes its confinement, her transcendence offering momentary liberation. Like her brief moment of sexual arousal (32), this "apparition" of herself is "momentary compared with the other, the unseen part of us, which spreads wide." But, unlike her understanding of her sexuality and physicality, she acknowledges and allows for another kind of presence through her association with the land, one that remains somewhat present in embodying herself as pastoral landscape.

Although her affiliation with the pastoral and urban landscapes could be seen as a way for Clarissa to escape the trap of her physical embodiment because the pastoral land is inherently feminized, colonized, and used for the imperial project, it reproduces the same trap of embodiment in a femininely marked space. Affiliation with the pastoral geographical body does not enable her to get outside of the symbolic systems which confine her to a feminine identity that is seen as inherently secondary and subordinate to masculine identity. Although Woolf does question the association of women to the land through Elizabeth's awareness and criticism of it, none of the women of the novel completely escape these pervasive associations or their accompanying ideology.

Even in her affiliation with urban landscapes, linked through masculinity to the disembodied self, Clarissa is still held within the patriarchal system by becoming part of it rather than escaping it. She and the other female characters in the novel may move about the city, and, like Lady Bruton, may appear to be able to move men of the city to action, but they are still and always incapable of taking the action themselves. Even Lady Bruton is reliant on Hugh Whitbread, the faithful but, according to Peter, "mere barber's block" (6) of an imperial servant, to make sense of the tangles of her letter to the editor (110). Affiliation with the city may again offer an alternative to female embodiment, but it is not one that allows for a separate feminine identity outside of the system of patriarchy.

The use of nature imagery, however, is not limited to describing trivial moments or female characters. In other passages, it is used to describe the postwar society: "and the passing generation—the pavement was crowded with bustling middle-class people—vanished, like leaves, to be trodden under, to be soaked and steeped and made mould of by that eternal spring" (82). Yet, this association again works to feminize the land, as postwar society was seen as more feminine in its state of peace: "Since war, whatever its horrors, is manly, there is something both lower-class and effeminate about peacetime" (Light 7). Nature imagery also explains and expands crucial moments such as Peter reflecting on his friendship with Clarissa: "You were given a sharp, acute, uncomfortable grain—the actual meeting . . . would flower out, open, shed its scent, let you touch, taste, look about you, get the whole feel of it and understanding, after years of lying lost" (153). These passages vary from using the nature imagery to describe the casual discarding of a generation to the explanation of a difficult moment which unfolds understanding, finally, like a flower. In each of these cases, the text's reliance upon images of the land reasserts the presence of the feminine, contributing to the anxiety of its pervasive, abject, inescapable quality, but not offering an alternative embodiment for women apart from this anxiety and feminine-inscripted locale.

## NATIONAL BODY: ANOTHER EMBODIED STATE

The connection between the land and the nation emerges early in the novel as Clarissa remembers her youth in the city: she describes "such hosts of people; dancing all night; and the waggons plodding past to market; and driving home across the Park" (9). In the midst of the city and its frivolity emerges an image of the labor of the country. This passage reveals how the pastoral, feminine and, I argue, more primitive, land, whose produce the "waggons" bring to market, supports the civilized, masculine city. Mariana Torgovnick argues for a connection between the binaries of feminine/masculine with primitive/civilized: "the primitive was coded metaphorically as feminine, collective, and ecstatic, and civilization was coded as masculine, individualistic, and devoted to the quotidian business of the family, city, or state" (14). As the land is feminized, women's production is also implicated in supporting the city, the hub of the empire. The images of land and landscape become inherently connected to the national body in its concern with the people of the land and the identity which they create and project of their people and nation. As the character of Clarissa conjures images of the country, she, too, becomes implicated in the production of empire.[17]

The links between the physical place of the nation (geographical body) and the ideology of the nation (national body) have been well-documented by such critics as Ian Baucom who states that "Englishness has consistently been defined through appeals to the identity-endowing properties of place" and that "[t]he locale . . . serves as disciplinary and nostalgic discourse on English national identity by making the past visible" (4–5). For Baucom, place is essential in national identity as it grants a tangible materiality to national ideology. As I discussed with the geographical body, Samuel Hynes explains how after the World War I writers looked to "a lost rural England that had been simpler and more decent and, somehow, more English" (13). This sense of interwar Englishness, then, can be directly linked to the ideas of the English countryside, the place chosen to represent the English national ideal. This pastoral ideal has already been connected to feminine embodiment above via the character of Clarissa, and, with its connection to the national body, imperialism becomes another kind of inscription of and on the feminine body.

The idea of England operates on the idea of the feminine, specifically on the feminine as supplied by the pastoral, and which requires the protection of women as shown by Septimus' claim that "[h]e went to France to save an England which consisted almost entirely of Shakespeare's plays and Miss Isabel Pole in a green dress walking in a square" (86). Septimus' comment about his motivation for war implicates women as icons of Englishness that must be preserved. And, with the correlation between Miss Isabel Pole's green dress and Clarissa's green party dress (52), we see that Clarissa is also summoned as a feminine image of English identity. Septimus' comment also reveals the deep-rooted discrepancy between two bases of Englishness: whereas the male figure of Shakespeare represents intellectual and creative production, as indicated by his "plays," the female figure of Miss Isabel Pole represents a female figure performing, as indicated by her costume of "a green dress" (86) and her activity as "walking in a square" (86). Although in previous passages Miss Isabel Pole is credited as the teacher who introduces Shakespeare to Septimus, in this passage she is reduced to a description more suited to a character in one of his plays, complete with stage directions.

The character of Clarissa also reveals the nationalistic inscriptions upon women as she operates as a symbol for English national identity. Her sense of her "virginity" (31) connects her to ideas of English purity, both the purity of the English woman and the purity of English culture. In this, Peter's description of Clarissa's asexual coldness (8, 43, 49) becomes a positive feature in its indication of her sexual purity. Thus, absenting herself from her sexual body becomes useful in the patriarchal rhetoric of imperialism. The lack of the presence (here, read sexual) of the feminine body becomes another way in which women can avoid demarcation of the abject or impure feminine (both in the sense of promiscuity and of bodily expulsions).

Clarissa also operates as symbolic of nationalism through the conflation of her character with the queen. As the crowd watches the grey car move through the city, they "perceived instinctively that greatness was passing,

*The Shape of Modernism* 39

and the pale light of the immortal presence fell upon them as it had fallen upon Clarissa Dalloway" (18). So, Clarissa has been touched by the presence of what she thinks is the Queen. Upon hearing of the passing grey car, Clarissa thinks,

> It is probably the Queen, thought Mrs. Dalloway, coming out of Mulberry's with her flowers; the Queen. And for a second she wore a look of extreme dignity standing by the flower shop in the sunlight while the car passed at a foot's pace, with its blinds drawn. The Queen going to some hospital; the Queen opening some bazaar, thought Clarissa. (16)

As she thinks of the Queen, Clarissa, too, becomes dignified.[18] This is expanded on the next page as she thinks of the Queen giving a party that night: "And Clarissa, too, gave a party. She stiffened a little; so she would stand at the top of her stairs" (17) like the Queen. As Kathy J. Phillips argued, "Englishwomen become necessary to maintain the Empire not only as providers of sons but also as embodiments of an inspiring image" (227), and Clarissa provides exactly that image for her partygoers at the top of her stairs. In linking Clarissa to the queen, Woolf proposes Clarissa as an "inspiring image" and exposes her complicity with the work of empire.

Woolf underscores Clarissa's conflation with the queen by revealing Clarissa's sense of (creating) herself as a hub of society just as the queen is a hub of the empire. She describes the effort, the consciousness of this operation, as she puckers her lips in the mirror:

> It was to give her face a point. That was her self—pointed; dart-like; definite. That was her self when some effort, some call on her to be her self, drew the parts together, she alone knew how different, how incompatible and composed so for the world only into one centre, one diamond, one woman who sat in her drawing-room and made a meeting point. (37)

Here, Clarissa connects the performances of her body, drawing the disparate parts together, with the performances of her hostessing, making a meeting point in her drawing room, both of which demonstrate the performance of national identity, making a meeting point for the ideals and consciousnesses of the people "into one centre." This "one centre" becomes a microcosm of the center of the empire, London, as Clarissa brings together the Prime Minister, Ministers of Parliament, and socialites at her party. Clarissa considers herself responsible for making the meeting of the parts happen. As she can make the dispersed parts and presences of herself come together, she can make the dispersed parts of the world come together into one center, with herself at the hub. Her party making, then, becomes analogous to nation making as she operates as a figurehead and center for her small domain.[19] Although the symbolic work of women as national figureheads provide for more agency and action than in the feminine nature symbology, women, as demonstrated through Clarissa, still operate as images of a kind of feminine ideal, as icons of national and imperial identity.

Although Clarissa's imitations of nation making are effective in influencing her immediate community, Clarissa remains a figure(head) that is dressed and performed appropriately. As a young woman at Bourton, she begins her career as the center of activity and of consciousness, as active figurehead. Her reaction to social/sexual transgressions affects everyone, changes others' perspectives:

> They were talking about a man who had married his housemaid, one of the neighboring squires. . . . She had had a baby? He could see Clarissa now, turning bright pink; somehow contracting and saying, 'Oh, I shall never be able to speak to her again!' Where upon the whole party sitting round the tea-table seemed to wobble. (59)

Clarissa's reaction to the news of one woman's sexual activity concerns everyone. In fact, "Every one wobbled; every one seemed to bow, as she spoke, and then to stand up different. . . . Clarissa did frighten people" (59). Here, as Clarissa reacts, everyone reacts. She is a center for morality as well as for a national ideal as her presence ripples out to affect everyone in the room so that they stood up "different."

Although her participation in creating, embodying, and affecting national ideals grants her access to the patriarchal culture, within it she is more fully inscribed in patriarchy via nationalistic demarcations for women. Her complicity with such nationalism does not grant her any kind of escape from her feminine embodiment, but like her affiliation with the land, more deeply inscribes her as she fulfills the role of the English woman. In fact, Clarissa appears to have no way out of this inscription within nationalism. As I discuss below, other female models such as Sally, Miss Kilman, and Lady Bruton have failed to escape as well, suggesting that escape from nationalistic inscriptions on the feminine results only in ostracization.

First, Sally, whose character initially suggests possibility in her subversion of social rules and expectations, ultimately becomes complicit in nationalistic embodiments for women. She is described as wild in her youth at Bourton:

> she ran down the passage to fetch her sponge bag, without a stitch of clothing on her. . . . She stole a chicken from the larder because she was hungry in the night; she smoked cigars in her bedroom; she left a priceless book in the punt. . . . She accused Hugh Whitbread, of all people . . . of kissing her in the smoking-room to punish her for saying that women should have votes. . . . And Clarissa remembered having to persuade her not to denounce him at family prayers—which she was

capable of doing with her daring, her recklessness, her melodramatic love of being the centre of everything and creating scenes. (26–27)

Sally subverts social expectations of dress and behavior in her disregard for social conventions of modesty, femininity, and religion so that Clarissa calls her "reckless" and "melodramatic." Sally also subverts expectations of sexual behavior when she kisses Clarissa (52). Even upon marriage, Sally is associated with wildness as "she lived a very solitary life, in the wilds" (187) of Manchester. So, even though her wild status has been contained within marriage and highly productive maternity—she continually repeats that she has had five boys—she is still sequestered outside of the more *civilized* areas represented by London and Bourton and outside of the social echelons inhabited by Richard and Clarissa.

Her association with the land also changes from her youth where she "went out, picked hollyhocks, dahlias—all sorts of flowers that had never been seen together—cut their heads off, and made them swim on the top of water in bowls" (34), to her adult life where she grew "plants, hydrangeas, syringas, very, very rare hibiscus lilies that never grow north of the Suez Canal, but she, with one gardener in a suburb near Manchester, had beds of them, positively beds!" (190). Where in her youth Sally thwarts reproduction through her symbolic castration of the flowers' heads and thereby thwarts the decorative objectification of the feminine, she becomes a domesticator and naturalizer of foreign plants, imitating not only colonialism but female domination as well. Her wild activity has been contained into her role as complicit cultivator and breeder of the exotic.

Woolf reminds us here that the landscape of the countryside that is directly linked to national identity is made up of plants appropriated from other countries and domesticated in and for England. Significantly, with the purity of national identity at stake, its impurity is demonstrated to us through a character who claims to have "French blood in her veins" (33). Here Woolf alludes to the impurity behind English national identity that from the beginning to be English was to be a hybrid of conquerors.[20] As Susan Stanford Friedman states, "Britain, like all nations, has its own centers and peripheries, its history of internal conquest and colonization, its 'foreigners' and 'others' within national boundaries" (120). Through Sally's lineage, Woolf satirizes the concept of English purity and national identity,[21] but, through Sally's co-opted status, Woolf demonstrates how even the wildest of women must conform to the boundaries of patriarchy and imperialism.[22]

Miss Kilman's character further explores the ideas of women's complicity with nationalistic ideology as she operates as Clarissa's counterpart in the worlds of maternity and empire. The contrast begins as both Miss Kilman and Clarissa describe Miss Kilman's body as undesirable. As Miss Kilman and Elizabeth are about to leave for the Army and Navy Stores, Clarissa thinks, "She in touch with invisible presences! Heavy, ugly, commonplace, without kindness or grace, she know the meaning of life!" (125). For Clarissa, Miss Kilman's "heavy, ugly" (125) body restricts Miss Kilman's access to knowledge and spirituality as well as to society. In addition to Clarissa's criticism of Miss Kilman, Miss Kilman herself despises her body. Walking to the stores with Elizabeth, Miss Kilman thinks about "her unlovable body.... No clothes suited her. She might buy anything. And for a woman, of course, that meant never meeting the opposite sex. Never would she come first with any one" (129). Clearly, Miss Kilman believes that her body prevents her from being desirable and therefore never being granted access to the worlds of marriage and maternity.[23]

Miss Kilman is also politically undesirable as "they had turned her out because she would not pretend that the Germans were all villains" (124).[24] Thus, Miss Kilman, abject in body and ideology, is unable to participate in either marriage or empire and is thus unable to participate in the symbolic system.[25] The consequence of Miss Kilman's position is most clearly demonstrated in her attempt to make her way through the Army Navy Stores after Elizabeth's departure:

> she lost her way, and was hemmed in by trunks specially prepared for taking to India; next got among the accouchement sets, and baby linen; through all the commodities of the world, perishable and permanent, hams, drugs, flowers, stationery, variously smelling, now sweet, now sour she lurched. (133)

Miss Kilman, unable to participate in the "accouchement sets, and baby linen" (133) of marriage and maternity like Clarissa, and unable to support British nationalism in her German sentiments, is lost among the booty of both. Miss Kilman is simply kept hostage—she "los[es] her way... and was hemmed in by trunks" (133)—within these worlds and "the commodities of the world" (133), seeing the signs of patriarchy and empire, but unable to use them or participate within either system.

Third, Lady Bruton, who could have been a leader within patriarchy and imperialism had she been a man, who "should have been a general of dragoons herself" (105), instead relies upon men to carry out her ideas of colonial expansion. Lady Bruton bears "the reputation of being more interested in politics than people; of talking like a man" (105). As an alternative to being relegated to figurehead status, she is "a woman [who] could have worn the helmet and shot the arrow, could have led troops to attack, ruled with indomitable justice barbarian hordes and lain under a shield noseless in a church, or made a green grass mound on some primeval hillside" (180). She is essentially invested in England and empire as:

> she had the thought of Empire always at hand... so that one could not figure her even in death parted from the earth or roaming territories over

which, in some spiritual shape, the Union Jack had ceased to fly. To be not English even among the dead—no, no! Impossible! (180–81)

Specifically, she is interested in a "project for emigrating young people of both sexes born of respectable parents and setting them up with a fair prospect of doing well in Canada" (108). Despite all of these qualities, and the potential for undoing gender binaries, Lady Bruton is unable to write a letter to *The Times*, "feel[ing] the futility of her own womanhood as she felt it on no other occasion" (109). As powerful as Lady Bruton may appear, she is unable to carry out her plans. Even complete cooperation and leadership in imperialism and patriarchy, fails to provide a viable alternative for the place of the feminine in the national body.[26] Lady Bruton's failure to write a letter to *The Times* specifically depicts the failure of the feminine to access patriarchal language.

Instead, the feminine is continually re-inscribed, replicating women's status in promoting empire through the ideas of English purity, of national figurehead or imperial hub/center, and of replicating and reproducing for the imperial domain (the spreading of Englishness into other territories). Women's identities, multiply marked in their physical bodies, geographical affiliations, and national cooperation, find no recourse for identity apart from that purported by patriarchy and empire. It is left, then, to the textual body to provide an alternative to these deeply embedded embodiments of the body, land, and nation.

## TEXTUAL BODY: THE SHAPE OF MODERNISM AND THE FEMININE FORM

> It wasn't simply that something had been added to history; the *shape* of history had been radically altered.
>
> Samuel Hynes, *A War Imagined* (346)

"Altered" or alternative ways of imagining identity are inherently connected to experimentation with literary form as it acknowledges and creates space for alternative imaginings of language and culture and for the changes in, as Hynes suggests, "the *shape* of history." Simply, if there are alternate ways of writing, then there are alternate ways of thinking; if there are alternate ways of thinking, then there are alternate ways of constructing identity. Through her textual experimentation with the stream-of-consciousness form, Woolf gestures toward these alternate ways of constructing identity and creates a space for these new identities to emerge. According to Samuel Hynes, World War I affected British culture specifically in changing its *shape* or the way in which British culture was conceived or conceived of itself. The new postwar imagination also allowed for new ways of conceiving of the shape of modern literature as well.[27] Experimenting with literary form can thus be seen as a cultural by-product of living through the war and writing after it; it is another way of expressing the changing shape of the postwar culture. In this postwar culture, if the shape of narrative can change, then perhaps another way of looking at woman's *shape* or body is also possible. This postwar subjectivity can then be expressed in new shapes of narrative and in new possible identities for women. I argue that these new shapes of narrative and identity are precisely what *Mrs. Dalloway* attempts to express through its experimentations with stream-of-consciousness form.

First, to delineate this convergence of narrative experimentation and identity formation, which signals a radical political movement within textual experimentation as well as a radical shift in narrative style, I want to review the connection between narrative and identity creation from my introduction. Specifically, I consider here Susan Stanford Friedman's explanation of the effect of narrative on identity:

> . . . identity is literally unthinkable without narrative. People know who they are through the stories they tell about themselves and others. As ever-changing phenomena, identities are themselves narratives of formation, sequences moving through space and time as they undergo development, evolution, and revolution. . . . Narrative texts—whether verbal or visual, oral or written, fictional or referential, imaginary or historical—constitute primary documents of cultural expressivity. Narrative is a window into, mirror, constructor, and symptom of culture. Cultural narratives encode and encrypt in story form the norms, values, and ideologies of the social order . . . around which institutions of gender, race, class, and sexuality are organized. (8–9)

If narrative contributes to, if not constructs, identity through its operations as "window into, mirror, constructor, and symptom of culture" (8), then the construction of not only new narratives but new forms of narrative can be seen as creating new forms of identities, or, at least, of creating new possibilities for new identities. As examples of "cultural expressivity," these narratives reflect the changes of the culture as well as the identity politics—the "norms, values, and ideologies" and the "gender, race, class, and sexuality" (8–9)—of the author. Narrative, then, suggests at once both finality in its mirror image "reflect[ion]" and process in the changing, developing nature of experimental narrative.

As such, in *Mrs. Dalloway*, Woolf both documents the "norms, values, and ideologies of the social order" and demonstrates their possible "development, evolution, and revolution" as she creates alternative possibilities for the social order. As we see Clarissa collecting and constructing herself in the mirror (37) in preparation for her party and in acknowledgement that she will collect all of these people together, so Woolf, too, collects and mirrors the people of a traditional social order in *Mrs. Dalloway*. Richard,

Hugh, Lady Bruton, the Prime Minister are all representatives of a Georgian society that is evaporating. Woolf, too, heralds the evolution and revolution of this society through her representations of the younger Sally, Miss Kilman, and Septimus. Woolf shows us that this society is made up not only of the politicians and the gentry but also of those used up, abused, and discarded by the workings of this society. Through her inclusion of these characters, Woolf more fully documents the makeup of her postwar society and how it is evolving.

Experiments in narrative, though, do more than just mirror the social order and chart its potential trajectories; they also interact with and affect that social order. As Rachel Blau DuPlessis argues, "Any literary convention—plots, narrative, sequences, characters in bit parts—as an instrument that claims to depict experience, also interprets it. No convention is neutral, purely mimetic, or purely aesthetic" (2). Specifically, literary conventions are producers as, she explains further:

> narrative structures and subjects are like working apparatuses of ideology, factories for the "natural" and "fantastic" meanings by which we live. Here are produced and disseminated the assumptions, the conflicts, the patterns that create fictional boundaries for experience. (3)

DuPlessis extends Stanford-Friedman's ideas about narrative as reflection to argue that it is not "purely mimetic" (2) of culture but also an interpreter and producer of culture.

In *Mrs. Dalloway*, the "fictional boundaries for experience" that DuPlessis discusses are here porous and loose as the narrative moves across temporal, physical, and psychological boundaries. When the grey car passes through London and into the gates of Buckingham Palace, we travel through the consciousnesses of the onlookers:

> So Sarah Bletchley said with her baby in her arms, tipping her foot up and down as though she were by her own fender in Pimlico, but keeping her eyes on the Mall, while Emily Coates ranged over the Palace windows and thought of the housemaids, the innumerable housemaids, the bedrooms, the innumerable bedrooms. Joined by an elderly gentleman with an Aberdeen terrier, by men without occupation, the crowd increased. Little Mr. Bowley, who had rooms in the Albany and was sealed with wax over the deeper sources of life but could be unsealed suddenly, inappropriately, sentimentally, by this sort of thing—poor women waiting to see the Queen go past—poor women, nice little children, orphans, widows, the War—tut-tut—actually had tears in his eyes. A breeze flaunting ever so warmly down the Mall through the thin trees, past the bronze heroes, lifted some flag flying in the British breast of Mr. Bowley and he raised his hat as the car turned into the Mall and held it high as the car approached; and let the poor mothers

of Pimlico press close to him, and stood very upright. The car came on. (19–20)

Through the vehicle of the grey car, Woolf slides from Sarah Bletchley's consciousness to Emily Coates' to an "elderly gentleman['s]" to Mr. Bowley's consciousness, not just describing each character but entering into each character's mind and expressing their observations. We move from Sarah's fireside thoughts to Emily's concern about the housekeeping to Mr. Bowley's patriotism. Although their consciousnesses stay contained within their bodies, the narrative does not, as it slides easily from one body's consciousness to another. In this way, Woolf's text bursts the boundaries of form and of consciousness as well as body, enacting the feminine abject by crossing borders of bodies and minds. Woolf shows that the psyche, like the feminine, like empire, cannot be contained within one mind, body, nation, or sentence. Furthermore, as DuPlessis states that "[t]o change story signals a dissent from social norms as well as narrative forms" (20), we can see Woolf's experimentation with form in *Mrs. Dalloway* as a "dissent" against society despite the apparent traditional representations of the women within the narrative itself. The text of *Mrs. Dalloway*, then, operates contrarily from its narrative and criticizes the behavior of the characters and the ideologies it represents and performs.

Experiments with narrative, then, are linked not only to the construction of identity in general but specifically to the development of new gender identities. Rita Felski states that: "If our sense of the past is inevitably shaped by the explanatory logic of narrative, then the stories that we create in turn reveal the inescapable presence and power of gender symbolism" (1). The fact that experimentation with these new narratives emerged during this interwar period suggests the anxiety around issues of the feminine as well as new possibilities for women's identity and subjectivity. As Maroula Joannou explains, "Much writing between the wars is concerned with the expression of cultured and gendered identities in ways appropriate to the new social conditions in which women found themselves" (191). If Woolf's experimentation with form is also an experimentation with creating new possibilities for identity, these possibilities inherently include new identities for women.

In accordance with women's "new social conditions," Woolf provides new textual conditions which mirror, document, and criticize the traditional gendered identities for women as they create new possibilities and places for new gender identities to emerge.[40] The boundlessness Woolf creates in the text contrasts the ways the activities of traditional, patriarchal language are reenacted and represented through the characters, specifically through women's bodies and identity; Clarissa comments on the language Peter has given her, for example: "She owed him words: 'sentimental,' 'civilized'; they started up every day of her life as if he guarded her" (36). Even years later, Clarissa acknowledges Peter's (and, I suggest, patriarchy's) guarding of her through language into a specific kind of feminine identity which in turn becomes useful for the ideologies of patriarchy and nationalism as they subsequently use this language to control female identity and subjectivity. Woolf criticizes the ways in which language can "guard" women and create feminine identity—here Clarissa as "sentimental" and "civilized."

We also see Woolf's criticism of the effects of patriarchal language on women's identities as Hugh and Richard are called upon to help Lady Bruton write a letter to *The Times*. Despite Lady Bruton's warrior-like presence in the society of the novel, Hugh is the one shown to be "carefully writing capital letters with rings round them in the margin, and thus marvelously reduced Lady Bruton's tangles to sense" (110). As Hugh outlines Lady Bruton's letter into "sense," he pares away the excess of her "tangles," and encloses each of her ideas with a circle. The language implies not only Hugh's reconstruction of her language but also his elimination and containment of her excess feminine, read bodily, tangles as well. Lady Bruton instigates ideas and commands others to help her but cannot appropriately organize her ideas into the patriarchal language required of a letter regarding government machinations. It is as if Lady Bruton sees no other linguistic option than to enlist patriarchy for her message. Instead, though the letter is regarding Lady Bruton's plan to establish young couples in Canada, demonstrating her complicity and instigation of the expansion of empire, it is nevertheless contained within the appropriate patriarchal language that Hugh performs for her.

At the same time, Woolf criticizes the use of such contained and appropriate language and the institutions that rely upon it as a kind of parasitic relationship. The portrayal of Hugh as a kind of buffoon and lackey of the royalty undermines his position as a herald of linguistic order and reason. Thus, the text criticizes this kind of masculine containment of language as well as those who attempt to contain it. Here, we see Woolf's critique of such language that operates on patriarchal structures and that, in turn, contributes to their oppression of women and women's bodies, as she attempts to create new bodily metaphors in and a new bodily form of the novel.

As in the example of the grey car, Woolf's textual experimentation with the stream-of-consciousness form allows for the narrative to incorporate experiences outside the acceptable social norm: the working class woman watching the grey car, or the lesbian sexuality and physicality of Clarissa remembering Sally's kiss. The experimental form of the text accommodates and validates these identities through their inclusion in and incorporation into the text. Unlike the linguistic performances of Hugh, which try to eliminate and conform these moments of excess and abject (read feminine) language, the text of *Mrs. Dalloway* not only presents but foregrounds these moments. The inclusion and embracing of experimental textual form, as in stream-of-consciousness, and of figures of social subversion, as in the working class women and Sally Seton's youthful transgressions, serve to create a text in opposition to the kind of sense making of Hugh's patriarchal text as represented by his letter editing.

In addition, Woolf's experimentations must work against the precedent set in both fin de siècle and modernist writing.[41] Historically, though, the figure of the woman in modernism is inherently troubled both as a figure of the traditional paradigms of the past and as a representation of a new, dangerous modernism. As Rita Felski documents in *The Gender of Modernity*, in the late nineteenth century, "[w]oman is aligned with the dead weight of tradition and conservatism that the active, newly autonomous, and self-defining subject must seek to transcend. Thus she functions as a sacrificial victim exemplifying the losses which underpin the ambiguous, but ultimately exhilarating and seductive logic of the modern" (2). Besides establishing woman as that which must be transcended, Felski goes on to argue that: "[t]hus in the early twentieth century the figure of the New Woman was to become a resonant symbol of emancipation, whose modernity signaled not an endorsement of an existing present but rather a bold imagining of an alternative future" (14). Although the female characters in *Mrs. Dalloway* do not act as "resonant symbol[s] of emancipation," but more often as the "tradition and conservatism" of the woman of the fin de siècle, Woolf does signal the "bold imagining of an alternative future" in the experimentation with form and the possibilities it holds for literature and women's identities.[42]

Thus the shape of women's identities is inherently caught up in the shape of modernism, specifically in the modernist text and the anxieties produced by and contained therein. As Rita Felski notes, "[i]ncreasingly, images of femininity were to play a central role in prevailing anxieties, fears, and hopeful imaginings about the distinctive features of the 'modern age'" (19). These "anxieties, fears, and hopeful imaginings" were specifically located in one form of modernism: the masculine text of the imagist poem. Leslie Heywood describes this form of modernism as "anorexic." To extend my analysis of Heywood's ideas from the introduction, I begin by exploring Heywood's argument that the attempts of certain male modernists to "construct an elite community" (61), to create "individualism" that "wants beyond all things to be different, to stand out as superior" (61), that often "involves the renunciation of the feminine" (62), and the "negation of the body" (63), manufacture "a creativity made possible by an expurgation of the flesh as female" (63). Specifically, she sees these ideas manifest through "the commonplace ideals of modernist texts: clean form, the emergence of art through the formal technique of cutting, and the isolation of the artist from the mass consciousness of the modern world" (64), create what she calls an "anorexic" form which parallels the denunciation of the fleshy female body and its maternity:

> in this trope the female body is consumed in order to give birth to the male body as text. This is specifically modernist because the privileged term here is not the *spirit* but the *male body* as *created through words*—the "hard body" of the imagist poem, the "extinction of personality,"

the insistence on purification, dissection, cutting to arrive at the work of art. (69, italics in original)

Clearly, this is a form practiced and encouraged by Pound and Eliot, but not by Woolf. This is one of the many forms of modernism that Woolf rejects and refuses to explore, choosing instead the boundless form of stream-of-consciousness explored by other modernists such as James Joyce and Dorothy Richardson.

In this choice and production of form, Woolf creates the possibility for women's identity to not be contained or determined by her physical body or by the machinations of patriarchy. Although Woolf meticulously edited (or "cut") her work, her texts, as seen with the emergence of *Mrs. Dalloway*, are not "anorexic" in form. The form of *Mrs. Dalloway* is instead both a critique of this modernist (anorexic) aesthetic which denies the feminine and the experience of the feminine abject in its crossing of boundaries through stream-of-consciousness.

In addition to criticizing the "anorexic" modernist aesthetic that Heywood discusses, *Mrs. Dalloway* also criticizes the foundations of this modernist aesthetic in its eradication of the feminine. Rita Felski argues that "the modern is predicated on the absence of the Other and the erasure of feminine agency and desire" (17). This "erasure" contributes not only to modernism's repudiation of the feminine that Heywood discusses, but also to the necessity for writing the feminine back into modernism by artists such as Woolf. As Felski later explains, "[t]hrough its articulation of repressed truths, the fractured text in some sense challenges, undermines, or otherwise calls into question the mystificatory discourses of a bourgeois/patriarchal order" (26). Although Felski does not speak here of the "fractured text" as created by only women modernists, her argument contains within it the effect of modernist texts created by Woolf and others. Later, Felski specifically associates modernist experimentation with the feminine when she states that:

> This refusal of traditional models of masculinity took the form of a self-conscious textualism which defined itself in opposition to the prevailing conventions of realist representation, turning toward a decadent aesthetic of surface, style, and parody that was explicitly coded as both "feminine" and "modern." Loosening itself from the body of woman, femininity was to become a governing metaphor in the fin-de-siècle crisis of literary representation, linked to an aesthetic definition of modernity that emphasized, with Nietzsche, the undecidability and opacity of language and the omnipresence of desire. (90)

The version of modernism that Felski examines utilizes the feminine as a way to create a new form, a new form in which was embedded the anxiety or "crisis" of the feminine as it was emerging at the beginning of the twentieth century. Woolf deploys these modernist strategies through her use of stream-of-consciousness which "loosen[s] itself from the body of woman" and its inscriptions in order to demonstrate women's intellectual interiority and subjectivity.

The text also demonstrates the crisis of the feminine through the insistent reappearances of Clarissa in the text. This crisis is particularly manifest through Peter's anxiety about seeing Clarissa. As I have already argued, Clarissa represents, at least for Peter, an ideal of English landscape and national identity which he desires to be solid and contained both physically and ideologically, but which is instead inescapable in its continuing fluid presence and re-emergences. The last passage of the novel most clearly demonstrates Peter's anxiety:

> What is this terror? What is this ecstasy? He thought to himself. What is it that fills me with extraordinary excitement?
> It is Clarissa, he said.
> For there she was. (194)

For Peter, Clarissa is both a "terror" and an "ecstasy." She is both that which he fears and that which he desires. The text belies Peter's desire for a contained femininity by demonstrating Clarissa's unavoidable feminine presence as she continually reappears in Peter's consciousness and physical reality.

But Peter's consciousness is not the only place that the figure of Clarissa reasserts itself; she also continues to reappear in the text as "there she was" (76, 194). In this way, the text again shows how Clarissa, repressed and invisible in her physicality, is present in her physical ideology. Her body does exist. It is present, just as the abject feminine does exist and is present, and this is exactly what is anxiety producing about it. In the text's reassertion of her presence, it demonstrates that the feminine presence and, I argue, its emergence in the modernist narrative, is unavoidable.

The assertion of the feminine through a physical presence presents hazards to the establishment of women's subjectivity apart from their bodily inscriptions. In contrast to Felski's argument that experimental form operates liberatorily for women writers, this same experimental form can be seen as a kind of rejection or repudiation of the (feminine) body. Patricia Moran sees that Woolf "describe[s] textuality and technique as a means of escaping from the confines of the body, and the necessity for escape seems to derive in part from contempt for its femaleness" (17). I concur with Moran that the body Woolf is trying to escape is the patriarchally defined feminine body. Incorporating both Felski and Moran's positions, I argue that part of Woolf's textual experimentation was a creation of a new kind of feminine form which would not be repudiated and would instead show the text as an alternative to the both/and trap of abject femininity encoded on the female body.

Unlike Clarissa's body which is described as cold, hard, and impenetrable, the text of *Mrs. Dalloway* does not imitate the cold, hard, anorexic form of the imagist poem that Heywood discusses. Although Clarissa's body and psyche withdraw from the sexuality of Clarissa's contact with women (such as in the match in the crocus passage 32), the text does not withdraw from women's bodies but continues to represent them and to explore their interiority.

As Woolf changes elements of traditional narrative through the stream-of-consciousness form, she also attempts to change the ideology from which they come. As Rachel Blau DuPlessis explains, "A writer expresses dissent from an ideological formation by attacking elements of narrative that repeat, sustain, or embody the values and attitudes in question" (34). The effect of narrative on identity can also work in reverse as later DuPlessis explains that, "trying to make fiction talk about women and their concerns, especially when a woman is the speaking subject, may necessarily lead to a critical transformation of narrative structures" (56). Within the creation of new gendered identities in fiction, narrative experimentation becomes an obvious recourse if not a requirement.[44]

In *Mrs. Dalloway*, Woolf's experimentations let the woman be the "speaking subject" and transform the narrative through its exploration of the characters' inner monologues. Although Woolf includes the inner workings of male characters' minds, especially Septimus, the portrayal of women's psyches demarcates the creation of a specific kind of identity for women, one which transcends the boundaries of women's physical, geographical, and national demarcations. Whereas the exploration of male characters' minds such as Peter's serve to criticize Peter's chauvinism, the exploration of the minds of Septimus and the female characters serves to reveal the subjectivity of previously unexplored figures. Woolf does not just create a room of their own for women; she creates a new narrative imaginary in which these characters think, feel, and live out their lives, each part of which she attempts to explore and articulate.

It is as if Woolf creates the space or the shape of women's identities yet to emerge. It is the outline of their possibility that has as yet to be filled in with the details of this new woman's experience. I explore the nuanced shading in of these new identities in the subsequent chapters' concern with the further textual experimentation of Woolf and Olive Moore. Their construction, during the 1930s for Woolf and Moore, grants a further look at the possibilities for new shapes of the modernist text and modern identities for women.

## 2 Exposure and Development
### Re-Imagining Narrative and Nation in the Interludes of Virginia Woolf's *The Waves*[1]

The popular nineteenth-century expression, "the sun never sets on the British Empire," encapsulates the established association of the sun with the reach of the empire and with the mission of British imperialism.[2] This mission included "images that show the natives being freed from despotic rule, raised from their ignorance, and saved from cruel and barbarous practices. These vignettes tell of the civilizing mission, which is primarily a story about the colonizing culture as an emissary of light" (Sharpe 100). The story of imperialism includes the story of "the colonizing culture" representing and bringing "civilizing" light to the "natives." In addition, as Gayatri Spivak reminds us, "imperialism, understood as England's social mission, was a crucial part of the cultural representation of England to the English. The role of literature in the production of cultural representation should not be ignored" (269).[3] The story of imperialism then, not only instructs the colonized but also instructs the English, justifying imperialism, and contributing to the shape of English national identity and narrative formation.[3]

*The Waves*, widely regarded as one of Virginia Woolf's most experimental texts, attends to national identity as well as textual experimentation. Specifically, the nine interludes of *The Waves*, often neglected in criticism of *The Waves*, are deeply concerned with the politics of empire, which "resonate through the interludes . . . their images replay ruling-class expectations of mastery and fears of turbaned, armed warriors assaulting their shores" (Scott, *Refiguring* 31).[5]

In their essential function, the interludes of *The Waves* show the movement of the sun, from rising in the East to setting in the West, fixing and moving the reader's gaze from the east, a site of expansion and empire-making, to the West, the site of the British homeland.[4] Here I refute Jane Marcus' germinal argument that *The Waves* "emphatically dramatizes the very historical moment in which the sun does set" (155). In fact, the light of empire is not extinguished by any means.[5] Instead, the interludes reveal how, like their ongoing solar and oceanic cycles, the imperial impulse continues—and, at this moment of anxiety about the future of the empire, continues in the homeland as well as in the colonies.[6]

Imperial colonization enacts violence ideologically by reducing its subject to an object and by placing it within the realm of the Other. Imperial colonization enacts violence materially by subjecting that colonized subject/object to the position of the Other through physical and political domination (see footnote 4). Considering these effects of objectification, the colonized space and the feminized space operate comparably, then, in the ideology of imperialism which requires that each occupies the place of the Other in opposition to the dominant (colonizing and/or patriarchal) force of empire. Thus, in *The Waves*, it is not surprising to find the incorporation of feminine images in the representation of the colonized. What is surprising is the use of feminine images to also represent the imperial project itself. It is these two intertwined depictions of the feminine within imperialism—the subjugation of the feminine as it is relegated to the status of the colonized and the utilization of the feminine to further the cause of imperialism—that I propose to unravel in this essay and that I argue the interludes of *The Waves* also seek to expose and resolve.

As I explore at length in the first section of this chapter, *The Waves* utilizes the imagery of the sun to demonstrate the effects on representations of the feminine, here used to denote the companion to the monolithic term *patriarchy*, in both the imperial project in general (in its use of images and bodies of women to promote and extend the empire) and colonization in particular (in its inhabitation of feminized spaces). As the sun of the interludes, at first anthropomorphized as a woman, comes to invade feminized spaces in the novel, the feminized subjects, be they women's bodies or the domestic spaces of the garden and home, become objectified through the aggression of the sun which, I argue, essentially operates as an imperialistic and patriarchal figure in the interludes.

In general, I argue that the identity configurations of the female subjects, both produced by and performed for patriarchal imperialism, are critical to national identity and, therefore, to imperial ideology. As Kathy Phillips argued, "The attitudes that determine the pecking order at home also fix the hierarchical oppressions of the Empire" (182). The equation also works in reverse: the same attitudes, hierarchies, and, one could say, stories, are repeated at home as they have been played out in the colonies.[7] These stories of empire, as told by the interludes of *The Waves*, reveal the "hierarchical oppressions of the Empire" (Phillips 182) and their effects on women, the land, the domestic space of the home, and on narrative construction.

In addition, I argue specifically that *The Waves* also reverses this position of the objectification of women in the service of empire in its reshaping of imperial and modernist tropes of enlightenment and in its textual experimentation. *The Waves*' portrayal of the imperial project and its effects on the homeland in its use of gendered bodies does not preclude all possibility of locating a new shape of identity subjectivity for women. Instead, I concur with Tamar Katz's reading of modernist textual experimentation:

> Modernist experiments in narrative form often take as their goal the reshaping of narrative to a newly-envisioned subjectivity. Stream-of-consciousness, impressionism, point-of-view narration—a range of narrative strategies offer the perceptual processes of the subject as the real story, and in doing so raise the question of just what shape subjectivity might possess (232).

I argue that Woolf's textual experimentation not only questions "what shape subjectivity might possess," but also attempts to propose a new shape of female subjectivity through a new textual form which re-imagines narrative construction and, with it, national identity and the feminine inscriptions upon which it relies.

The tension between these two impulses of exposing and proposing emerges early in the first interlude in the image of the sun as a woman shining a lamp: *"as if the arm of a woman couched beneath the horizon had raised a lamp"* (7). Although it is tempting to propose that Woolf illuminates a feminist presence in the novel through this imagery of a female sun, I argue that the lady with the lamp *does not* operate as a feminist figure, controlling the solar cycle, but instead is a figurehead for the sun and a tool of imperialism.[8] Viewed this way, the lamp may be interpreted as the light of empire extending from the horizon to the home. As I will argue, this imagery of the light becomes increasingly violent and militaristic throughout the interludes, extending the effects of empire and its violence onto the domestic spaces of the homeland. Through both the narrative's reclamation of the imagery of enlightenment and shadow, and through the form of the text's experimentation in the interludes then, Woolf attempts to extinguish imperialism's domestic gaze and reclaim language which has been in the service of empire. I, therefore, take the paradoxical position that *The Waves* creates at once an alliance between the feminine and nature through the imagery of the sun and a simultaneous critique of that alliance. This position proves productive because of the way Woolf reveals how the feminine, through this imagery, is portrayed as complicit in the work of empire.

As if in response to patriarchy's employment of images and bodies of women, *The Waves* also concerns itself with creating a new kind of textual space or "cultural project" that "consists . . . in offering the possibility of *different* modes of subjective positionings in language beyond the pretty fictions of the patriarchal order" (Paccaud-Huguet 230).These "subjective positionings" include identity formation at both the national and textual levels: the text challenges empire as a basis for national identity and challenges patriarchy as a basis for narrative. To that end, *The Waves* disrupts patterns of narrative and form to create not only new stories but new ways of telling stories through its imagery of light and shadow and through its structure of cycle and disruption.

This chapter, then, proceeds to argue for *The Waves*' exposure of imperialism's annexing of female imagery and its subsequent development of alternative feminine representations. I do so by considering, first, how the feminine is inherent in the work of empire and how the interludes of *The Waves* both expose and undermine that relationship; second, how imagery of the feminine converts into masculine or androgynous imagery in displaying the activities of imperialism, specifically dislocating the feminine from an active role to passive one; and, third, how the textual experimentation of the interludes contributes to both the revelation and disruption of these relationships.[9] To that end, I argue that Woolf here deploys her experiments with narrative and form to recover the image of the feminine from its uses by imperialism and to simultaneously create a space in which that feminine can live outside of the reach of empire and its violence.

## GENDERED IMP(ERIA)LICATIONS: WOMEN'S BODIES AND THE LIGHT OF EMPIRE

During the interwar period, the imperial project utilized women in its efforts to both produce citizens and represent national ideologies.[10] After the war, women's bodies facilitated establishing definitions of self and other as well as (re)produced national subjects as they are "cultural[ly] appropriat[ed]"(Moran 149) by and for patriarchy and imperialism through their "corporeal identification" which marks them as "implicitly incompatible with the spiritual aims of citizenship."[19] Through the machinations of patriarchy and imperialism, then, women's bodies, marked as pure and as purely bodies, become vessels for the production of citizens and for the symbolic representation of imperial ideology. In the colonies, the role of women was to provide an "attachment to the mother country" by making colonies which were "peopled with loyal British women as well as British men. . . . Without that home-life settlers [would] bring with them none of the peaceful influence" (Thane 31). Women were both essential and essentialized in the project of empire by representing and recreating the homeland in the colonies. For women to provide this "attachment to the mother country," they must already portray an established representation of the mother country. Their identity, as Jane Garrity argues, "arises from the ability to reproduce conventional models of British womanhood—models which, whether generative or purely sexual, are dependent on some valorization of an essentialized female body" (260). Both physical and national identifications then, mark women's bodies and demarcate women as signifiers of nation and empire.

In *The Waves*, the light of imperialism fixes its gaze on the bodies and identities of women as a site of tenuous national identity and imperial domination. As *The Waves* also criticizes imperialism's use and determination of female identity, it reveals deeply established inscriptions of the feminine in the work of empire. I argue that in the interludes of *The Waves* the image of the sun as the lady with the lamp exposes these implications of imperialistic demarcations for women.[11] Through the lady with the lamp, the woman's body heralds not only the sun and the light of Empire, it also calls forth other symbolic representations that inscribed women's bodies, namely maternity, purity, and domesticity. From the first interlude, the body of the lady with the lamp is employed in the work of imperial enlightenment as the bearer of the light which spreads from the horizon to the home:

> *Behind [the horizon], too, the sky cleared as if the white sediment there had sunk, or as if the arm of a woman couched beneath the horizon had raised a lamp and flat bars of white, green and yellow, spread across the sky like the blades of a fan. Then she raised her lamp higher and the air seemed to become fibrous and to tear away from the green surface flickering and flaming in read and yellow fibres like the smoky fire that roars from a bonfire.* (7)[12]

Demonstrating both agency and complicity, this passage shows how the woman is both powerful in her ability to raise the lamp of the sun, changing the colors and texture of the air, sea and sky, but also an agent of a power outside herself (i.e., the lamp). Her body, specifically her arm, is used to hold up the lamp whose light shines on the waves, the beach, the garden, and the house, and thus extends the light from the horizon to the home.

Jane Marcus persuasively refers to this arm as "the mighty white arm of empire and civilization" (159), placing the agency of empire in the body of the woman itself and extending the symbolism of solar enlightenment specifically to imperial activity. Although I agree with Marcus' correlation between the lady/sun and empire, I argue that the lamp itself, not the woman's arm, contains the light and thus represents imperial enlightenment. The woman's arm, only a tool for holding the lamp, situates the body of the woman as a manipulated figurehead lacking agency of her own.[13] In the interludes, broadly, I suggest the woman's body becomes the tool for spreading the light of empire, and her status as imperial instrument indicates that *The Waves* perceives women in an inextricable and subordinate relation to imperialism.

Some critics have characterized this feminized sun as a herald of a new, feminist space. For example, Madeline Moore sees that "[i]n the first prologue prior to the children's birth, the creative force of nature is anthropomorphized as a great mythic woman who is the source of all creation. She is the symbolic figure out of which Woolf establishes a cosmogony in *The Waves*" (228–29). For Moore, the lady with the lamp becomes a powerful protofeminist and the basis for the entire "cosmogony" of *The Waves*. Moore's analysis ultimately essentializes women as earth mothers and as producers (and reproducers) of nature, platonically reducing them to a lesser status than the thinking man. Specifically, by associating women with nature, Moore's reading reduces women to a less-civilized, utilitarian, and/or iconographic status rather than proposing equality or alterity for women, and therefore falls short of locating an alternative to patriarchal forms and stories, including mythic ones.

In contrast, I align my argument with Jane Goldman's which states that the sun in *The Waves* is "predominantly patriarchal," demonstrating women as the "enslaved functionary of the patriarchal order" and as "appropriating the icon of masculine subjectivity (the sun)" (189). To this I add that Woolf preserves the essence of the sun's patriarchal position in order to criticize the use of women as figureheads of patriarchy and imperialism.[14] As the sun's gender changes throughout the interludes, its "patriarchal" position is ultimately revealed.

Throughout my argument in this section, I trace three progressions in the interludes: the progression of the sun's gender from feminine to androgynous, the progression of the sun's characterization from feminine to primitive, and the progression of the imagery of the sun from feminine light to feminine darkness. First, the sun's gendered physicality, first seen in the image of the lady with the lamp, devolves by interlude three into that of a girl. Eventually, the metaphor of *"The girl who had shaken her head and made all the jewels, the topaz, the aquamarine, the water-coloured jewels with sparks of fire in them dance"* (73) in the third interlude regresses further into an androgynous *"it,"* staging the continued evolution of the sun into an ungendered and violent entity. The fourth interlude abandons the feminine imagery of the sun so that it no longer *"couch[es] on a green mattress"* or *"dart[s] a fitful glance through watery jewels."* Instead, the sun, now directly *"bare[s] its face"* and *"look[s] straight over the waves"* (108). Although Woolf actively promotes androgyny in other texts, namely *A Room of One's Own* (*Room*), in the interludes of *The Waves*, I argue that the seemingly androgynous "it" enacts violence when associated with imperialism and is therefore a place holder for patriarchy.[15] This, then, is not the kind of idealized social and/or authorial androgyny Woolf advocates in *Room* but a gradual unveiling of the patriarchal forces behind the feminine figurehead of imperialistic enlightenment.

Paralleling this progression to gender neutrality is a simultaneous devolution of the light from feminine to primitive, in both the text's use of *"lances"* (108) in the fourth interlude and its conversion of the lady with the lamp into *"turbaned men with poisoned assegais"* in the third and fourth interludes (75, 109). The sun thus moves from a feminine icon of enlightenment to a now specifically masculine stereotype of the primitive warrior. As I cited in the previous chapter, Mariana Torgovnick asserts that "the primitive was coded metaphorically as feminine, collective, and ecstatic, and civilization was coded as masculine, individualistic, and devoted to the quotidian business of the family, city, or state" (14). In this definition, the masculine governs the civilized state and empire, each inhabited by the primitive feminine. Torgovnick further argues that this "fascination with the primitive . . . can express itself in a variety of ways: negatively—for example, as fear of the primitive or as a detour into violence—and positively, as admiration for the primitive, conceived to be the conduit of spiritual emotions" (7). The association of woman with the negative expression of the primitive—with violence—is exactly the kind of detour at play in the interludes of The Waves.[16] Although the solar imagery abandons the mask of the female figurehead, the evolution of the imagery as well as the common association of women with the primitive as outlined by Torgovnick, suggest a continued interchange between the feminine—which is at once both the pure English rose and the primitive savage—and the imperial project. This association reveals not only the appropriation of women's bodies for the spread of imperialism through the lady with the lamp, but also the inherent violence involved in this act.[17] Significantly, the etymology of "couch" used in conjunction with the lady with the lamp in the interludes reveals additional violence. Although in The Waves it denotes to "lie or lay down," it also connotes its other definitions—"to lie in ambush" and "to lower a lance into position for an attack"—further suggesting the ambiguity of women's involvement in empire and war in the interludes.

This devolution into the primitive also reveals the paradoxical position of women in empire as passive symbols rather than active agents in empire making, conveniently manipulating and adapting the images of women to advance the cause of empire by portraying it as in need of containment.[18] In the fifth interlude, we see the sun more explicitly connected to the work of empire:

> *It was no longer half seen and guessed at, from hints and gleams, as if a girl couched on her green-sea mattress tired her brows with water-globed jewels that sent lances of opal-tinted light falling and flashing in the uncertain air like the flanks of a dolphin leaping, or the flash of a falling blade.* (148)

The *"water-globed jewels"* in this passage connect the sun to sea exploration, empire building, and the booty of each, decorating the female figurehead with imperial activities which she then carries and carries out. By the end of the description, these *"jewels"* are connected further to violence as they *"sent lances"* like *"the flash of a falling blade."* Through the solar imagery, the interludes of The Waves reveal how the ideology of empire creates a false alliance between the feminine and nature and uses that alliance to further its imperial goals. The imagery of the sun also exposes patriarchy as hidden behind feminine representations, making the image of the lady with the lamp a kind of Trojan horse, appearing at first a benign girl but eventually revealed to be accompanied with the violent *"lances"* and *"blades"* of warfare. The conversion is complete as what once were the lady with the lamp's *"blades of a fan"* (7) in the first interlude become in the fifth interlude *"a falling blade"* (148) of the warrior's lances.

Although the increasing gender neutrality of the sun may appear to create an androgynous space in the interludes, the association of that space with primitive and violent, militaristic imagery proves destructive for women and the images of them used to advance the light of empire. Its disturbing depiction of the woman's body as a tool for spreading the light of empire takes on not only the activity of empire per se, of enlightenment, but also its violent attitudes and patriarchal behaviors through the imagery of the sun's militarism in stereotypical savages with spears and assegais and of the war machine of cavalry. Thus, the images and bodies of women are implicated through the imagery of the sun to be complicit agents of empire and its violence, albeit unwitting ones. In contrast to the episodes, where the characters are working to distinguish themselves in their gendered, national, and vocational identities, the interludes develop a dissolution of these same identities as the sun becomes gendered neutral and then masculine, for example. The violence of the waves, at its height in the fourth interlude (108–10), preceding Percival's departure for India, continues in the fifth and sixth interludes, after Percival's death. In this way, the violence of the waves replicates the activities of empire, continuing its crashing upon and through the colonies even after the dream of imperialism has died.[19] Kathy Phillips suggests that "[r]eferences to imperialism and militarism often occur together because, once a country accepts the need for colonies, it must rely on force to put down local rebellions and fend off other European nations" (225), asserting the inexplicability of colonialism, read here as an extension of imperialism and violence.

In addition, as the solar imagery becomes gender neutral, and the façade of the feminine is abandoned, the light of the sun increasingly invades the domestically coded home and homeland. From the first interlude, as the light touches the house, it "*sharpen[s] the walls of the house, and rest[s] like the tip of a fan upon a white blind and ma[kes] a blue fingerprint of shadow under the leaf by the bedroom window*" (8). Here, the light is figured as necessary as the house and "*all within*" is still "*dim and unsubstantial*" and in need of enlightenment. In the second interlude, as the sun lays "*broader blades upon the house*" (29), the sharpness of the light in the first interlude becomes "*blades*," so that what in the first interlude seems like a neutral sharpening here becomes a tool of violence. In the fourth interlude, where the light has devolved from feminine to neutrality, it now "*[falls] in sharp wedges inside the room*," reasserting the violence of the light's imagery: "*A knife looked like a dagger of ice*" (110)—and conjuring the imagery of the warriors' "*lances*" and "*assegais*." The imagery of the sun, as "*sharp*," "*blades*," "*a knife*," and "*a dagger*" (29, 110), thus appears to invade and attack the house, revealing how imperial violence comes to bear on the home of the homeland. Nearly every interlude's description moves from the horizon to the house, moving the imagery of violence from the distant sites of colonization into the supposed havens of domesticity in the homeland and enacting the effects of imperialism on the colonizing country as well as on the colonized.

The third progression follows the transformation of the imagery of the sun from feminine light to feminine shadow. As the light strengthens, it contributes to the creation of its opposite, darkness, and with it creates a greater distinction between light and dark, self and other, masculine and feminine. In the fourth interlude, *"as the light increased, flocks of shadow were driven before it and conglomerated and hung in many-pleated folds in the background"* (110). Here, the shadows become cloth like, and are gendered feminine, as the light drives it/them out of view. With this feminizing of the shadows, the unmasking of the sun as masculine is complete. Furthermore, the sun's striking *"straight upon the house"* with *"sharp-edged wedges of light"* in the fifth interlude is even more of an attack on the *"dark windows . . . of impenetrable darkness"* (150) of the feminized home. The light of empire is locked out of the house, unable to penetrate the feminine, domestic sphere still described here as *"darkness."* The inscription of the feminine as uncivilized or savage, evidenced earlier in the imagery of the sun, here becomes displaced in and converted into the shadows of the domestic sphere. These feminized shadows now become the target of the imperial light's pursuit and violence, a threat that must be extinguished although created by that selfsame light. Ultimately, in the sixth interlude, as the *"[l]ight driving darkness before it split itself profusely upon the corners and bosses; and yet heaped up darkness in mounds of unmoulded shape"* (166), the light pursues but cannot eradicate the darkness or shadows.[20] The transformation of the activities of the sun from bearing the feminine light to attacking the feminine darkness exposes both the masculinist basis of imperial activity and the effects of that activity on the feminine, be that representations of women's bodies or the feminized space of the home.

All three progressions—from feminine to androgyny, from feminine to savage, and from feminine light to feminine darkness—work to expose the violence inherent in imperialism. As I argue in the next section of this chapter, through the use of feminine imagery, the interludes also expose how this violence first utilizes the feminine façade and then abandons it when attacking the feminized, domestic spaces of the homeland.

As if in response to the invasion of the light, the imagery in the interludes of *The Waves*, having exposed these representations of women as both light and shadow, reverses itself and reclaims the image of feminized darkness. In the closing interludes, the image of the lady with the lamp, tainted with imperialist ideology and practice, is revealed as no longer useful for women. Woolf instead reclaims the ideology of women as dark or unenlightened (primitive) by here refiguring the imagery of shadow in the interludes as a space of alterity for female subjectivity. The descriptions of shadow and darkness used throughout the interludes, by the eighth interlude, encompasses all of the landscape of the interludes:

*As if there were waves of darkness in the air, darkness moved on, covering houses, hills, trees, as waves of water wash round the sides of some sunken ship. Darkness washed down streets eddying round single figures, engulfing them; blotting out couples clasped under the showery darkness of elm trees in full summer foliage. Darkness rolled its waves along grassy rides and over the wrinkled skin of the turf, enveloping the solitary thorn tree and the empty snail shells at its foot. Mounting higher, darkness blew along the bare upland slopes, and met the fretted and abraded pinnacles of the mountain where the snow lodges for ever on the hard rock even when the valleys are full of running streams and yellow vine leaves, and girls, sitting on verandahs, look up at the snow, shading their faces with their fans. Them, too, darkness covered.* (237)

Here, the antithesis to the lady with the lamp, the *"girls, sitting on verandahs . . . shading their faces with their fans"* (237), emerges as an alternative to embracing the light and work of empire. Instead of being invaded by the militaristic sun, the girls are protected by darkness and shield themselves from the imperial solar gaze; instead of being light bearers, emanating or carrying the light themselves, the girls are shadow seekers, refusing to participate in the work of enlightenment. The language of darkness with its implied femininity and subjection of the feminine, inherent in the ideology of empire, changes in the interludes to a language of possibility and freedom, defying the trope of darkness as savagery or ignorance and converting it instead into a means of protection from the light of empire. Like the house in the interludes which is shuttered away from the light—containing *"still denser depths of darkness"* (150)—the girls, rather than cloistered from incorporation into the imperial project, are posed to see a world without the harsh light of empire and free from the violence and inhabitation of the imperial sun.

With the setting of the sun, Woolf temporarily extinguishes the light of empire and it's co-opting of the imagery and labor of women. In doing so, she proposes the darkness as a place of possibility for a new female subjectivity to emerge. Just as Woolf proposed removing the Angel in the House, described in The Pargiters as "the woman that men wished women to be" (qtd. by Hussey 219), she here proposes removing the woman as bearer of imperial enlightenment, the Lady with the Lamp. As the cyclical nature of the sun promises that it will return, Woolf prepares for a new image of woman, resistant to the light of empire and its violence, to replace the iconic lady with the lamp. In the face of the oncoming darkness, the imagery of the girls shading themselves from the light, rather than triggering ignorance or danger, presents a conscious refusal to be touched by or to be bearers of the light of empire. Through these girls the text suggests that future generations may not embrace the light of imperialism, may not engage in the work of empire. In addition, the girls *"look up at the snow,"* focusing on an element that resists the potency of the imperial sun and directing their gaze upon a symbol of resistance. Whereas the lady with the lamp, the *"woman couched,"* conducted light, these girls refuse to look at it, and in turning from it, turn also from the inscriptions of imperial enlightenment on female subjectivity that accompany it.[21]

## HARNESSING THE SEA AND LAND: DOMESTIC IMPERIALISM AND THE CYCLES OF NATURE

Throughout *The Waves*, as the sun moves across the sea and land, it moves from the horizon, a site of imperial expansion, toward the English landscape and the domestic spaces of the English garden and home. As it does so, the imagery of the sun, in its variously gendered and imperial manifestations, incorporates the spaces of the English homeland into the imperial project. In addition, just as the imagery of the sun becomes androgynous and increasingly violent, the language of the waves incorporates these changes and extends the violence of the solar imagery from the horizon of imperial expansion to the sites of the domestic homeland: the garden and house. In this section, I proceed by first documenting the progression of the waves from feminine to masculine and back to feminine, demonstrating the increasingly violent rhetoric and imperialistic language of the waves. I then follow this imagery as it extends from the waves to the birds in the garden and onto the pastoral landscape of England. The landscape, rather than taking up imperialistic rhetoric instead becomes, like women's bodies, the figure on and in which imperial ideology is manifested in its appearance and production for empire. Finally, I argue that the text poses a reversal through its use of natural tropes which, in their cyclical nature, operate outside of the bounds of humanity and imperialism.

The English sea and landscape, categorically seen as femininely encoded properties, easily assimilate into the ideology of imperialism and its use of the feminine, as already witnessed in the first section of this chapter. Although these locations may also herald feminine alterity, *The Waves* reveals that these spaces conveniently serve as additional tools for patriarchy and the imperial project, extending the use of feminine imagery from women's bodies to the geographical body. The sea, marked as a "medium of connection and imperialist expansion," as Margaret Higgonet suggests, also figures "as a scene of evasion and exile" (11). These combined and contradictory characteristics of the sea as both feminine and masculine situate it metaphorically as an ideal medium to relay the contradictory characteristics of the sea in *The Waves*. The sea is initially feminized and then, like the sun, becomes increasingly androgynous and violent. In addition, extending her own criticism from the sea to the land, Higgonet proposes that "Freudian readings in which the land stands for the female sexual organs can be reversed, letting the woman stand for the land" (11), suggesting that woman and the land become both synonymous and synecdochical. The feminizing of the land continues the extension of the feminine and imperialism from the light of the sun, not only figuring the land as a site of conquest, but also by figuring women as inert and passive objects within both geographical and national configurations. As Anne McClintock suggests, women are "[l]inked symbolically to the land," and this connection "relegate[s women] to a realm beyond history and thus bears a particularly vexed relation to narratives of historical change and political effect" (31), placing women in a disabled position and in an anachronistic space outside of active participation in patriarchal and imperial endeavors.

In *The Waves*, the images of the waves themselves summon culturally inscribed feminine representations. As Patricia Moran argues, the waves serve as one of the ways "Woolf . . . drew upon a cultural repertoire of metaphors for femininity . . . to describe variously 'feminine' modes of consciousness, women's bodies, or the dynamics of women's relationships" (17).[22] Even Woolf's choice of emphasis on the waves implies that the sea and, I argue, the landscape, are already defined as feminine spaces. As I show, at the beginning of the interludes the sea, like the sun, is feminized but becomes progressively more associated with masculine and military imagery, with turbaned warriors and the beast stamping, creating an increasingly masculine and violent depiction of the waves: this violence continually moves from the horizon to the homeland with each crash of the waves. Anca Vlasopolos argues that "the opening toward the sea that seemed to offer possibilities of renewal in Austen becomes for Woolf and Chopin merely another man-shaped vista" (80), and I suggest, too, that the shift from feminine to masculine associations in the solar and oceanic imagery of *The Waves* allows for the progressively violent language of imperialism borne out by the waves.

This violent language of imperialism, as evidenced through the description of the waves' expansion from the horizon to the house, also demonstrates the consequences of imperialism on the places it inhabits: the inherent violence of colonization. As military imagery rages throughout the interludes, increasing as the sun becomes gendered neutral; it takes the form of spears and assegais and the war machine of cavalry, exposing the violent military presence inherent in imperialism. Throughout most of the interludes, though, violent military imagery plays out on the beaches, gardens, and houses of the femininely gendered homeland throughout the interludes, rather than the colonies.

The waves extend the violent and militaristic language of the sun from the horizon inland, thereby operating as the physical and metaphorical transporter of the language of the solar imagery. Initially, in the first interlude, the waves figure as feminine as a *"grey cloth"* (7) that, as they break on the shore, *"[sweeps] a thin veil of white water across the sand"* (7). In the second interlude, the waves become*"[b]lue waves, green waves swept a quick fan over the beach"* (29). In the third interlude, *"Light almost pierced* *the thin swift waves as they raced fan-shaped over the beach"* (73). In light of the fans used by the girls on the verandah in the penultimate interlude, these fans arguably suggest the waves here as feminine. The feminizing of the waves fades quickly into increasingly masculine and violent discourse.

The imagery of the waves does not just become increasingly masculine, or even just increasingly violent, it expresses specific militaristic violence, incorporating the inherent violence in imperialism.[23] Later in the third interlude, the militaristic imagery of the waves emerges in the sea holly's *"mailed leaves,"* *"blue as steel,"* and the *"[l]ight almost pierc[ing] the thin swift waves as they raced fan-shaped over the beach"* (73), and, at the beginning of the fourth interlude, in the cavalry's *"horses' hooves"* and the colors of *"steel"* as well as the savage imagery of *"lances and assegais"* (108). Here, the militaristic imagery combines with mechanic imagery so that the steel, initially referencing implements of war, segues into the *"energy, the muscularity of an engine which sweeps its force out and in again"* (108).[24] In the last paragraph of the fifth interlude, the waves *"br[eak] and spread their waters swiftly over the shore. One after another they massed themselves and fell"* (150), signaling armies falling on their enemies, spreading over the terrain.[25] The last sentence of this interlude, *"The waves fell; withdrew and fell again, like the thud of a great beast stamping"* (150), introduces Louis's beast to the interludes, as the war imagery of armies falling and falling again like waves upon their enemy is now compared to a beast pawing and preparing to charge.[26] The text here reveals the beast of imperialism's requirement for war and its violence, and criticizes the uncivilized, bestial nature of imperialism.

The waves' metaphorical activity extends from imperialism to colonization as it uproots rock and land, inhabits new places, and establishes new colonies of water. At the end of the sixth interlude, the waves *"massed themselves, curved their backs and crashed. Up spurted stones and shingle. They swept round the rocks, and the spray, leaping high, spattered the walls of a cave that had been dry before, and left pools inland, where some fish, stranded, lashed its tail as the wave drew back"* (166). The colonization by the waves is a violent one as they *"crash," "spray,"* and *"spatter,"* demonstrating the requirement of violence in establishing empire in the colonies in which *"some fish, stranded, lashed its tail."* This portrayal of colonization concludes in the abandonment of the colonies in the seventh interlude: *"The waves no longer visited the further pools or reached the dotted black line which lay irregularly marked upon the beach. The sand was pearl white, smoothed and shining"* (182). As the metaphorical colonies of the *"pools"* are abandoned, even *"the dotted black line"* separating the two territories of sea and land is also abandoned, foretelling the eventual abandonment of the British colonies as well.

The imagery of shadow that I discussed in the first section of this chapter reintroduces the feminine into the imagery of the waves. With the sinking of the sun in the ninth interlude, the absence of light creates a lack of definition and clarity on the horizon: "*Sky and sea were indistinguishable*" (236). The waves themselves though, continue: "*The waves breaking spread their white fans far out over the shore, sent white shadows into the recesses of sonorous caves and then rolled back sighing over the shingle*" (236). The waves, again feminine with the use of the fan imagery, travel far and spread their now-white-shadow presence. With the feminization of the waves, the imagery returns to describing expansion and exploration, abandoning the violence of the previous passages. But, in the final line of the novel, "*[t]he waves broke on the shore*" (297), the text brings us back to the beach and to the violence inherent in the waves' activity of breaking, suggesting that the waves' cycle is endless and undeterred by humanity. As it acts metaphorically for empire, it suggests, too, that the imperial project also continues its violence.

The language of violence established with the waves extends toward domestic spaces as it moves to the garden with the description of the birds and, in this, suggests the invasion of the imperial gaze into the English landscape and nature. The imagery of the birds replicates the progression of the waves into violence. In the third interlude, the birds in the garden sing "*together in chorus*" (73) and swerve "*all in one flight*" (73) as the cat approaches, bringing "*fear*" and "*apprehension of pain, and joy*" (73). Unified against a common enemy, they also sing "*emulously*" or in the spirit of rivalry, "*as they chased each other, escaping, pursuing, pecking each other*" (74), indicating the changes toward violence in this interlude. When, in the seventh interlude, the birds "*swooped and circled high up in the air. Some raced in the furrows of the wind and turned and sliced through them as if they were one body cut into a thousand shreds. Birds fell like a net descending on the tree-tops*" (182), their activity is described as uniform, until it is "*cut into a thousand shreds.*" Again, the use of the word "*fall,*" along with their uniform movement and shredding, conjures military violence as the birds descend to occupy the trees. The birds, like the waves, also operate as carriers of imperialist language and imagery, migrating the imagery of the sun from the waves to the land and the garden.

Beyond these images of violence in the waves and birds, which implicate the nature of the homeland in the work of empire, the landscape itself is also harnessed into the imperial project in its appearance and production. In its appearance, the landscape reveals how it is manipulated, groomed, and corseted like a body, continuing its feminization as well as its history of colonization. In its production, the landscape reveals its support of the empire, whether complicit or coerced. The imagery of the landscape incorporates the imagery of the sun and waves, utilizing militaristic if not violent descriptors, thus exposing the imperialistic demarcations within the feminine of the English landscape.

The imagery of the landscape, or its appearance, reveals how the hand of empire is at work in the cultivation and presentation of the English landscape. In the fourth interlude, the imagery appears to change from violent waves to peaceful pastoral as the sun enters the "*cornfields and woods,*" "*rivers,*" and "*lawns,*" but the language of military violence follows these initial idyllic descriptions. I cite the passage entire, beginning with the description of the waves:

> [The waves] fell with a regular thud. They fell with the concussion of horses' hooves on the turf. Their spray rose like the tossing of lances and assegais over the riders' heads. They swept the beach with steel blue and diamond-tipped water. They drew in and out with the energy, the muscularity of an engine which sweeps its force out and in again. The sun fell on cornfields and woods. Rivers became blue, and many-plaited, lawns that sloped down to the water's edge became green as birds' feathers softly ruffling their plumes. The hills curved and controlled, seemed bound back by thongs, as a limb is laced by muscles; and the woods which bristled proudly on their flanks were like the curt, clipped mane on the neck of a horse. (108)

The progression of the passage, from the waves falling "*with the concussion of horses' hooves,*" to the sun falling on "*cornfields and woods,*" to the birds' "*plumes,*" and the repetition of the horse imagery in the woods "*flanks*" and "*mane,*" clearly demarcates the transference of military imagery, via cavalry, from the waves to the land. The repetition of forms of "fall" throughout the passage mimics language of armies falling on or attacking their enemies.[27] In addition, the hills are "*curved and controlled*" (108), extending the idea of cultivation. Specifically, as the hills "*seemed bound back by thongs*" (108), the passage connotes an unnatural corseting in order to produce but also to appear or perform in a certain way. In this description the landscape figures as important, and like a body, in both its appearance as well as its production, and, like women's bodies, the land is important in what its image signifies as well as in what its production yields. I argue that this image serves to represent and contribute to the national and imperial ideologies.

The body of the land, therefore, figures as inherently caught up in the representations and activities of empire. As it is compared to a natural construction of the body, "*as a limb is laced by muscles*" (108), the imagery connotes that the binding of the thongs is as natural as the lacing of muscles on a limb. Both the binding and the lacing conjure Roman imagery, of sandals and bare, muscular bodies, suggesting bodies that are beautiful and useful, and recalling the body of another great empire. The bodies operate like women's bodies, in that they are configured to conform to an image that appropriately represents the homeland to the empire and vice versa.[28] The signaling here of the Roman empire reminds us that England, too, was once a colony, that its history is based on its own colonization, and like many of the colonies, it in turn re-enacts colonization on its own and on other groups.[29] From its inception, England operates within and identifies with the acts of empire, and these images assert the text's critique of empire's continuance and its violence, in light of the cycles of imperialism and colonization throughout English history.

In the interludes of *The Waves*, the history of imperialism emerges as both inscribed upon the landscape and produced by it. The hills and the woods of the fourth interlude, compare to the flanks and mane of a horse—"*the woods which bristled proudly on their flanks were like the curt, clipped mane on the neck of a horse*"—and conjure the horses of the warriors from the beginning of the paragraph: "*[The waves] fell with the concussion of horses' hooves on the turf. Their spray rose like the tossing of lances and assegais over the riders' heads*" (108). In this case, not only are the waves and the sun—the areas of the sea and horizon—constructed through military imagery, but the pastoral landscapes of England are also included and, therefore, implicated in the same imperial project. The text points out that the imperial gaze incorporates the entire homeland including the pastoral countryside.

The later interludes demonstrate the land's status as used and used up by the necessities of the imperial project. As the light of the sun penetrates the garden, it causes production to the point of abundance and eventually wastes. In the fifth interlude, the sun "*beat[s] on the orchard wall, and every pit and grain of the brick was silver pointed, purple, fiery as if soft to touch, as if touched it must melt into hot-baked grains of dust. The currants hung against the wall in ripples and cascades of polished red; plums swelled out their leaves*" (149). The light penetrates through "*the grey-blue clouds*" and onto the landscape, giving the appearance to the bricks that they are temporary and on the verge of collapsing "*into hot-baked grains of dust.*" The light on the plants makes them ripe to bursting. The harshness of the light, which "*beat[s] on the orchard wall,*" demonstrates the effects of imperial activity on the domestic sphere of the homeland. Bringing home the bounty of imperialism destroys the produce of the homeland and the home.

Eventually the pastoral homeland, full to overflowing, reveals not only the land's participation in the production for empire, but also the waste inherent in that production. In the sixth interlude, the description of the trees, whose "topmost leaves . . . were crisped in the sun" (165), reveals the imperial sun as scorching and destructive. In the ninth interlude, the trees, shaking, send leaves *falling* to the ground where they wait "dissolution" (236) or decomposition into waste. By the end of the interludes, everything from the horizon to the hearth has been touched by the light of empire and changed, deformed, and destroyed in the process.

The final interlude, "*The waves broke on the shore*" (297), shows that the cycles of ocean and land will continue despite the activities of man and empire. These cycles continue, as Sue Roe argues, "While the characters go about their business in the material world which they construct and subject to question, the organic world ascertains its own rhythms, which are sustained, come what may"(183–84).With the inclusion of "*broke*" in the language of this final sentence the imagery hearkens back to the violence witnessed throughout the interludes, promising cycles of violence and war.

Despite the text's imperial language of dominance, invasion, and violence in the imagery of nature and the sun's activities on and in the homeland, the text also poses a reversal to this imagery through the use of solar and oceanic elements which operate cyclically. Nature's cycles, which mostly operate outside of human intervention and existence, counter these representations of the homeland as tools of empire. Through the continuation of the solar and oceanic cycles that operate outside the influence of humanity and its imperial activities, nature resists performing as a symbol and producer for empire. In fact, as Susan Lorsch argued, the interludes of *The Waves* operate outside of human activity: "Obviously people do inhabit this place . . . but Woolf is careful to capture this natural setting in their absence" (195). The solar and oceanic cycles not only continue endlessly but continue despite human contact. The sun does not set forever on the empire or on England but promises to continue. As the sun can be associated with the imperial project, it promises the continuation of imperialism. As the sun and waves stand for forces that operate outside and/or beyond human machinations, they promise the continuation of nature and space that is undaunted by the empire and its violence, and therefore, the possibility of other spaces and roles for men, women, nations, and narrative.

Through the dominance of nature throughout the interludes, and especially through the presence of the interlude's voice in the novel's final line, Woolf creates a text in which the activities of mankind are secondary to those of nature, and therefore, counters empire with the portrayal of an alternate world in which empire is not dominant. The interludes are, in fact, dominated by nature only, suggesting "the powerlessness of human life before the final authority of nature."[50] As I argue in the following section of this chapter, Woolf creates in *The Waves* a text that operates outside of the "narrow bounds of [the] social realism" of humanity, revealing "its politics . . . in its refusal of the imposing categories of past narrative and past society, its dislimning of the boundaries of the self, the nation, the narrative" (Beer 76). By foregrounding nature in the interludes, *The Waves* provides a space in the novel that moves in and out of mankind, criticizing man's activities in narrative and nation and continuing on despite them.

## TEXTUAL OCCUPATION: PUSHING WORDS TO THEIR LIMITS AND ACROSS THE MARGINS

The textual experimentation of *The Waves* likewise exposes similar concerns about empire as those witnessed through the solar and oceanic imagery of the interludes. Just as the imagery of the sun exposes the strategic use of images of women in the imperial project and the violent ramifications of this practice on the feminine, *The Waves* employs a linguistic practice that has a penetrating presence, demonstrates a two-way movement of hybridity, and reveals an anxiety about ending and continuing, further exposing the text's concerns about the practices and effects of imperialism through its narrative construction.[31] *The Waves* as a visual text tries to fill its entire world by filling all the blank spaces on the page. Its dense, blocky form, found most clearly in the later episodic chapters, extends the textual experimentation of Woolf and others beyond that seen in Woolf's earlier works. This attempt to fill the page can be seen to represent the imperial impulse to fill the blank spaces on the map.[32] The increased occupation of the margins of the text as the narrative progresses parallels and pictures the heightened imperial activities in the 1930s (see footnote 6) as well as the heightened anxiety about the continuation of empire. In addition, as I argue in detail below, the incorporation of interludic language into the episodes, depicts an impulse toward "literary hegemony" on the part of Bernard in particular and the episodic narrative in general.[33] If, as Simon Gikandi argued, "the imperial map of the world was to thread its way into the cultural products of the West and become a vital part of its 'texture of linguistic and cultural practice'" (5), *The Waves* reflects the violence of its cultural practice, a practice which attempts to push out all other voices and into all other spaces. In this way, *The Waves* can be seen as a text which exposes the practices of imperialism in its physical construction of a visual monopoly of the words on the page.

*The Waves* betrays its deep anxiety not only about the empire's dominance but also about its future. National cultures, as Anthony Easthope claims, "are . . . reproduced through narratives and discourses" (12), and so the national culture reproduced through *The Waves* is one of intense anxiety about its position in the world, both nationally and textually, demonstrated most clearly through the imperialist "hero" (123), Percival, who dies from being thrown from his horse or because "[h]is horse tripped" (151), turning the activities of imperialism into a farce. In the interludes of *The Waves*, this anxiety emerges through concerns about hybridity and conclusion, both concerns of this later stage of imperialism as well.[34]

The hybridity of the text is evidenced in the cross-pollination of interludic and episodic languages. In the fifth interlude we hear the echo of Louis' beast from the episodes: "*The waves fell; withdrew and fell again, like the thud of a great beast stamping*" (150). The language of the interludes is in turn taken up by the episodes. At Percival's dinner, Rhoda's remarks incorporate interludic imagery of "birds' wings," a "white arm," and "the sea" (139). Rhoda alludes to several of the tropes of the interludes, but in many sites of the episodes, the exact language of the interludes mingles with the narrative. Bernard's soliloquy in the last episode serves as the most striking example:

> Day rises; the girl lifts the watery fire-hearted jewels to her brow; the sun levels his beams straight at the sleeping house . . . the house is whitened; the sleeper stretches; gradually all is astir. Light floods the

room and drives shadow beyond shadow to where they hang in folds inscrutable. (291–92)

The specific interludic language of the girl's watery jewels and the house's folds of shadow suggest a violation of the boundaries of the established form and create a hybridized discourse between the episodes and interludes. In Bernard's final monologue, as Patrick McGee states, "the voice of the interludes . . . [n]o longer italicized, no longer safely confined to the margins . . . erupts from within the discourse of the imperialist subject" (638). The narrative of *The Waves* moves beyond the textual borders demarcating interlude and episode and threatens the purity of narrative with hybridity. As McGee continues, "if Bernard's final monologue is *explicitly* contaminated by the voice of the interludes that are supposed to frame it, then the entire set of monologues, by virtue of the abstractness of Woolf's style is *implicitly* contaminated by such a frame" and "this instability of the frame is also an instability of the center" (639). McGee's analysis utilizes the language of hybridity in its concern about contamination and the resulting unsettling of identity, in his analysis of narrative identity, and, in postcolonial theory such as Bhabha's of national and imperial identity. Thus, again, the two activities of narrative construction and national and imperial identity construction and maintenance intertwine in the novel and prove their co-reliance. It is at this moment of greatest textual hybridity that the narrative of the text becomes the most resistant, demonstrating in Bernard's final cry of defiance—"Against you will I fling myself, unvanquished and unyielding, O Death!" (297)—all of the anxiety about the return of the empire to the homeland, the encroaching contact with the other (narrative), and the desire for continuance.

The interludes develop these concerns about continuance and hybridity when the light, upon invading the domestic space of the house in the fourth interlude, creates ambiguity and monstrosity: "*A jar was so green that the eye seemed sucked up through a funnel by its intensity and stuck to it like a limpet*" (110). In this example, the sun of empire does not enlighten or civilize the domestic; it creates freakish hybrids and monsters, its violence proving destructive to the purity of the domestic and indicating the anxiety of imperial decline and of contamination.[35] Once the light enters the house in the sixth interlude, the language becomes inundated with violent military imagery: "*The blind hung red at the window's edge and within the room daggers of light fell upon chairs and tables making cracks across their lacquer and polish. The green pot bulged enormously, with its white window elongated in its side*" (165–66).[36] The red of the blind conjures the blood and violence of war, but also the *"daggers of light"* that *"fall"* upon the symbols of domesticity—chairs and tables—and cause cracks in their polish. Here, I further propose that the *"lacquer and polish"* and *"green pot"* infer the spoils of empire brought home from the colonies, merging the feminine and the colonized in the same space and representing the presence of the colonies in the homeland. The translation of the imperial impulse onto homeland domesticity is secured through the symbols of the colonies, exposing the anxieties about bringing the empire into the home and its potential contamination.

Yet, *The Waves* reverses or answers this position of anxiety through its textual form which, as the interludes break up the chronicle of the chapters, demonstrates the possible disruption of the traditional patterns and stories of narrative and nation. The episodes of *The Waves*, while enacting a break from traditional narrative form, still progress systematically from childhood to old age and death. With the addition of the interludes, *The Waves* strays further from traditional narrative form by breaking the pattern of beginning, middle, and ending, and interspersing the stories of the lives of the characters with a separate narrative of the ongoing solar and oceanic cycles. Although the lives of the characters continue to play out the sequence of traditional narratives (albeit in a very nontraditional narrative form), this narrative is interrupted by a static, continuous story of the sun, as Patricia Laurence suggests by "arrest[ing] the linear sequence of writing by using the techniques of simultaneity through the use of spaces of silence like the interludes of nature" (180).[37]

The use of both "poetic language and experimental structure" in the interludes enacts what Jane Marcus terms *anti-imperialist radical politics* that liberate the image of woman from the confines of collaboration with the imperial project (Marcus 155). By re-imagining women's affiliations with nature through the shadows of possibility rather than through the light of empire, the interludes "suggest the end of writing and the end of a certain kind of culture" based on the hierarchies of patriarchy and imperialism as reinscribed through narrative (Marcus 155). The interruption of traditional patterns of narrative in *The Waves* "resist[s] not only authoritative narratives that use words to define and communicate thoughts and feelings but also the very hierarchically-structured patriarchal culture that relies upon and uses these words to dictate to, define and dominate women" (Burford 269). The interludes, then, despite revealing the power of patriarchy and empire through their imagery of the sun, the waves, and their violence, paradoxically serve to disrupt the patriarchal and imperialistic episodes, creating a textual alternative that resists conventional narrative progression and creates a place in the text that exists outside of traditional forms and their hierarchies.

Woolf's experimentation with textual form, then, is also an experiment with spaces of personal and national identity, an attempt to find a place where different kinds of stories and nations may be created and enacted without the threat of dissolution or destruction. Woolf accomplishes this by creating not only an experimental narrative form, but by interspersing the narrative of the episodes with an alternate story in the interludes. In this alternate space, the cycle of the sun promises that the story of the interludes will continue and can, in fact, continue free of humanity's imperialism and language of violence, domination, and inhabitation. In this alternate space, too, not only can the imperialistic language be reclaimed and reworked, but imperial ideology, too, can be refigured.

## EXPOSURE AND DEVELOPMENT: THE OLD EMPIRE AND THE NEW WOMAN

Thus far, I have shown how the interludes expose the machinations of imperialism and its effects on women and the feminine through the confiscation of the female figure as a representation of imperial ideology and practice and the extension of the inherent violence involved in these practices upon the feminine other of the colonized as well as on the feminine sites of the homeland. Eventually and simultaneously, as the shadow imagery replaces the attempted enlightenment of the imperial sun, the textual experimentation also refigures imperial ideology through its practices of hybridity and disruption, experimentation and alterity. Thus, the exposure of imperialism's ideological and practical apparatuses lays juxtaposed with the development of future subjectivities of the feminine and of narrative as a kind of post-occupation reconstruction of the text.

In the third interlude, as the light of the sun enters the house, the furnishings appear to meld into one another so that they are both *"separate"* and *"inextricably involved"* (75). Likewise, the text of *The Waves*, comprising two separate but connected narratives and narrative strategies in the interludes and episodes which operate independently and interconnectedly, replicates the text's ideological tensions through its material form. Woolf's positioning of these two textual formats of the episodes and interludes in juxtaposition and dialogue with each other foregrounds the tension between the imperial impulse to colonize and the possibility of a new story beyond imperialism. With the conclusion of the interludes, as the shadows encroach upon the girls on the verandah, the interludes present a scene with the potential for the playing out of new narratives. If, as Torgovnick argued, "In its most generalized sense, 'primitive' refers to a posited but ultimately unknowable original state" (4), then I propose that Woolf deliberately points back to a supposedly primitive or dark place outside the light of imperialism, a place with other and undiscovered alternatives for the stories of women and nation. In order to develop feminine subjectivity and narrative, Woolf seeks to begin in an imagined prehistory, in a time and place that exists prior to or outside the inscriptions of the feminine developed by patriarchy and imperialism.[62] In this way, the interludes act as preludes, preparing the scene and creating anticipation for a new woman to speak on this stage still set in darkness.[63]

The final line of the novel, "*The waves broke on the shore*," could be read as a continuation of the language of imperialism in its reference to the imperial and militaristic activities of the sun and with that the promise of imperialism's continuation. As part of the interludes, though, it can also be read as a *break* with the tradition, ideology, and language of empire. Just as Woolf reclaims and refigures the language of darkness, she, in this final interlude, refigures imperialistic language of violence by turning it upon itself. Thus, *The Waves* concludes with the newly redefined darkness which offers new possibilities for women and the text to develop away from the light of empire.[64]

# 3 Modernist Con(Tra)Ceptions
## Re-Conceiving Body and Text in Olive Moore's *Spleen*

The tensions between the reality of imperialism's consequences for women and the possibilities of new stories beyond imperialism's gaze posed by Virginia Woolf in *The Waves* herald the tensions that Olive Moore poses in *Spleen* between the realities of female identity and embodiment essentialized in maternity, and the possibilities of new hybridized identities and embodiments through physical and textual (re)production.[1] Moore extends Woolf's refiguring of the feminine and the text in an attempt, as my title suggests, to *re-conceive* of the ways in which the feminine body and text are both imagined (or conceived) and created (or reproduced). In each reconception, Moore presents a complex, conflicted, and critical position on the feminine as located in women's bodies, feminized land and nations that serves to both expose the essentialized identifications of the feminine and the contrary positions that the modern woman must then embody and perform. Moore also proposes, in a near reversal of her critique, new hybridized identities of body, land, and text that seek to undermine the essentialized notions of the feminine by incorporating them within traditionally masculine conceptions of intelligence and literary production, moving from an image of a headless woman to a text which, I suggest, embodies both feminine and masculine textual experimentations. Moore complicates this position of possibility through her subtle and vitriolic critiques of women's lives and their complicity with maternity and patriarchy, as well as through her protagonist, Ruth, who is an ambiguous and uneasy representative of Moore's attempts at a gender identity hybridization that incorporates both the male sphere of the mind with the female sphere of the body. In doing so, Moore (ex)poses—or both presents and reveals—the tensions between her criticism of female embodiment and its consequences of maternal servitude, and her creation of a new modernist textual embodiment that operates beyond gender identifications and inscriptions. Her critique of the new modern woman belies any attempt at utopian fantasy. Instead, the narrative refuses to offer any substantive possibility of new identities for women outside of that of an author's (Moore's) own textual experimentation.

Olive Moore published four books in rapid succession between the late 1920s and early 1930s—*Celestial Seraglio* (1929), *Spleen* (1930), *Fugue*

(1932), and *The Apple is Bitten Again* (1934)—then disappeared from the London literary scene. Today we know very little of her life prior to and/or following her brief literary career. She was part of the Charles Lahr Red Lion Street circle, a literary and political meeting place in Lahr's Holborn bookstore. In addition to writing novels, she was a staff writer for the *Daily Sketch*. Per her description, prior to the publication of *Spleen*, she traveled to the States where the manuscript of *Spleen* was burned in a hotel fire, requiring her to rewrite it from memory.[2] We have recently discovered that she was married to the sculptor, Sava Botzaris, and we believe she died sometime prior to the 1970s, place unknown.[3] As of this writing, only one manuscript of her novels is known to survive; the Dalkey Archive Press has reprinted the books from their previous printings.[4] Moore's writing, at once both dense and fragmented, fuses the textual experimentation seen in other British women modernists, such as Virginia Woolf and Djuna Barnes, with the high modernist ideals of a literary and spiritual tradition represented by T. S. Eliot and Ezra Pound that I flesh out in the last section of this chapter.

*Spleen*, Moore's second novel, centers on an Englishwoman, Ruth, who marries quickly after her father's death and then is shocked by her subsequent pregnancy.[5] The novel opens on the island of Foria, off the southwest shore of Italy near Naples, where Ruth, after leaving her husband, Stephen, behind in England, exiles herself upon learning that the newborn child, Richard, is mute and deformed.[6] This exile of Ruth and Richard to Foria is figured as both an escape and a punishment and is complicated by Ruth's determined daytime neglect of and nighttime duty to the care of Richard as well as her changing conceptions of him as he reaches physical puberty. Ruth spends twenty-two years on the island until her husband dies and she returns to England to settle what is now her estate. Moore fills in these long, hot years in Italy with flashbacks to Ruth's childhood with her father, her marriage to Stephen, her camaraderie with his sister, Dora, her relationship with an Alsatian man in Italy, Uller, and her encounters with the Forians. The novel ends in London, shortly after Ruth's proclamation that Sharvells, now her estate, will not be made into a golf course as the solicitor suggests, but will be refashioned into a charity holiday home for poor children. It is understood that following the settling of the estate Ruth will return to Italy.[7]

*Spleen* moves quickly beyond a remaking of the body or land's façade from Ruth's attempts at a new creation through her maternity to Moore's attempts at a new creation through her textual experimentation. These projects of protagonist and author occur simultaneously; they even occur simultaneously in the character of Ruth. As Ruth struggles to re-conceive of female embodiment and identity within maternity, she also consciously attempts to break the litany of life for women: "Birth. Adolescence. Marriage. Birth. Old Age. Death" (126). To do so, she must confront the resulting deformity of her child and her self-imposed exile, alluding to the exilic status of the modern female artist as well. Moore's re-conceptualization of the body's (re)production through maternity signals her re-conceptions of textual production through textual experimentation; by re-imagining the female body through maternity, Moore begins to reimagine how to tell the story at the same time. These two separate ventures not only coincide with and parallel each other, but new physical and textual embodiments emerge from the same point of conception: female reproduction and textual production must move beyond the ideologies of patriarchy to imagine and create new female identities and narratives.

Through Ruth's re-conceptions, Moore ultimately argues for a complicated new form of merged identity which moves beyond entrenched and essentialized embodiments of femininity and maternity but still remains firmly rooted in the body, land, and literature. Moore does not argue for a remaking of the female body in man's image, but for what Luce Irigaray describes as a "jamming [of] the theoretical machinery itself, of suspending its pretension to the production of a truth and of a meaning that are excessively univocal" (78), where that production and meaning are "univocal" in being either unambiguously male or female. Rather than discarding the female body in favor of the male mind, for example, Moore proposes that the body can be re-conceived as a new configuration of the modern subject, especially of the female modern subject, which is a hybrid of both female body and male mind. It is not the female body itself, then, which Moore wants to re-conceive, but the way in which the body itself is culturally conceived. As I discuss later, Moore attempts to strip away the cultural presuppositions of the feminine as body by insisting on the presence of the intellect in women. In all of these considerations, Moore suggests hybrid physical and ideological manifestations of each (physical, geographical, and textual) body so that one is not "univocal" in body or mind, complicating both the mind/body binary and the male/female binary at once by suggesting something beyond each category yet including each in a new configuration.

Through these processes of critique and hybridity, Moore exposes the etymological history of conceiving and conception in the multiple re-conceptions of the body and the text that she attempts in *Spleen*. To conceive was first used in the thirteenth century in exclusive relation to the body, specifically with pregnancy, or "to take to oneself." In the fourteenth century, it became associated with the conceiving of an idea, or to "take into the mind," and in the sixteenth century, to "formulate with words."[8] In *Spleen*, Moore attempts first to re-conceive of physical conception, then also of the ideas which formulate women's identities and embodiment and how women respond to them, and, finally, she attempts to re-conceive of the way this story is told or formulated with words. Thus, as I argued in my introduction about the Corporeum, I suggest first that the conceptions of the physical body, specifically the female body, are linked to conceptions of land and nation as each are complicated through feminized imagery. The body of the text, finally, incorporates these feminized identities into a textual hybrid that retains the shape of a fleshy feminine textual embodiment fused with male modernist ideology and literary tradition. For Ruth and Moore, re-conceiving of the female body includes re-imagining maternity as well as extending this project of imagining alternatives to the ways in which lands and nations (or people of other nations) have been imperialistically imagined as feminized bodies and, as I will show, subsequently subjugated through other kinds of production in support of imperial ideology.

I begin by first exploring how, in each of the physical, geographical and national bodies, Moore both exposes and critiques essentialized notions of the feminine and also proposes alternate identities through hybrid embodiments and identities. I argue that each of these attempts at hybridity ultimately fail to offer satisfactory alternatives to the identities already inscribed upon the feminine by patriarchy. The textual body, I argue in the final section of this chapter, through its experimentations, ultimately succeeds in creating the hybridized body that flounders in the other bodies' attempted incarnations of hybridity.

## FEMALE EMBODIMENT: BEYOND THE HEADLESS CO/INSCRIPTIONS OF THE FEMININE

> Women occupy a discursive and social space not of their own making, whose logic is structured to reflect and sustain a subject position directly opposed to their own.
>
> Kathleen Kirby (100)

As if in anticipation of Kirby's statement above, *Spleen* concerns itself with women's subject position as it is determined by their bodies and by the cultural demarcations upon them. Moore explores the issues of female embodiment and feminine inscription through maternity, turning Pound's edict of "make it new" into Ruth's maternal mission, and suggesting, too, modernism's anxieties about the feminine.[9] David Trotter summarizes this anxiety when he states that:

> Of the "Men of 1914," Eliot, Pound and Lewis all evolved doctrines whose main function was to convert difference-within into difference-between. Their insistence on impersonality, and on the primacy of the "world of objects," in Eliot's phrase, was an effort to control the unsettling drift of desire, and to preempt the messy sexual and political coalitions into which its compulsive mimeticism, its insatiable "herd instinct," might lead it: the autonomy of art would ensure the autonomy of the self. (86)

If, as Trotter argues, the aesthetics of these high modernists were tied implicitly with issues of control and control of gender, or "sexual and political coalitions," then Moore's exploration of female embodiment and identity become even more salient.[10] But, Moore's revaluations and re-conceptions of the feminine do not necessarily operate in contradiction to male modernist paradigms, or at least, not completely, as she seeks to both criticize the entrapments male modernism placed upon women and their bodies and explore new modernisms which find a way out of them.[11]

Moore's textual developments extend directly from her concern with women's identity and performance, and how this identity is contained and determined by their physical identification as women which forces them, as Kirby suggests earlier and as I will argue later, to "occupy a discursive and social space not of their own making" and "sustain a subject position directly opposed to their own" (100).[12] Thus, I look at how Moore reveals and criticizes these physical embodiments in the novel and then how she proposes alternatives to these embodiments through experiments in physical and identity hybridity.

First, Moore's criticism encompasses several different spheres such as the ideas of the feminine that Kirby defines earlier, which require women to occupy a space and subject position opposed to their own as well as women's complicity with this occupation. Another, connected sphere includes Mariana Torgovnick's association of the feminine with the primitive that I discussed Chapter 2 on *The Waves*, and which places women in a subjective position that is subordinate to man's civilized position: "the primitive was coded metaphorically as feminine, collective, and ecstatic, and civilization was coded as masculine, individualistic, and devoted to the quotidian business of the family, city, or state" (14).[13] Torgovnick, in her discussion of Gide and Jung in Africa, also situates the primitive as "a tendency to think about the primitive, the female, and the oceanic as almost interchangeable" (24). Torgovnick's arguments about the primitive helps us to see the ways Moore exposes women's subordinate subjective position and the ways in which the female body is then harnessed into maternity. Through the character of Ruth, her reaction to her maternity, and her interactions with lands and nations, Moore criticizes both the scaffolding that creates and supports this association with the primitive upon which women's physical and ideological identities are based and women's participation and complicity within the structures of maternity and patriarchy. This discussion of the primitive serves as point of entry into the structure of female identification by patriarchy that Moore seeks to expose and rewrite in *Spleen*.[14]

Ruth's struggle to understand her child's conception, development, and her lack of participation and control of it, foregrounds issues of female embodiment and societal constraints, which is also the basis of Moore's criticism. Her critique begins with Ruth's maternity, as Moore draws attention to the physical and ideological entrapments of female embodiment, specifically how the feminine is both lauded and imprisoned in its maternal state, unable to escape it and its association with both the sacred and the savage. Through Ruth's experience in maternity and her responses to it, Moore criticizes the maternal by exposing it as a physical and cultural condition which contributes to the lifelong subjugation of women. In other words, she depicts through fiction Linda McDowell's contention that

> [w]omen are seen as closer to nature, as irrational, as polluters, as sacred but as inferior because they menstruate and because of their ability to bear children. Men, on the other hand, are seen as civilized, rational and superior, mind to women's body, even, indeed, unbodied or disembodied. (44)

Women, then, are more primitive in their affiliations with the body and with nature, and this is specifically born out through "their ability to bear children." Moore then seeks to expose the contradictory associations of the primitive with the feminine which, again contradictorily, in its maternity is also seen as pure and redeeming.[15]

The issues of the maternal are raised immediately and metaphorically in the first paragraph, as the novel opens with images of goats' udders and of an Italian mother and child:[16]

> Goats with long purple udders and sly drooping faces passed, trailing a strong smell of goat. She watched the woman take from her skirt a piece of bread, break a corner and give it to the child, a calm socratic child with stony eyes, and return to her business of bringing her stick down sharply across the undulating hindquarters of her goats, undulating slowly over the long Saracen road, their heavy purple udders swinging pendulously to the bleating of their neck-bells. Soon they would be far away, small dark pellets of their own dropping, the woman dwarfed to the size of the child, the child scarcely discernible, passing out under the archway to the town. (112)

This passage introduces the maternal through the goats' udders, associating the bodies of the maternal woman and child with their animals, and associating the feminine with the primitive or animal through their "strong smell of goat" (112), and in their becoming "small dark pellets of their own dropping" (112).[17] The child and the mother devolve until the woman is "dwarfed to the size of the child" (112), and the child is "scarcely discernible" (112). This progression also brings to the fore the status of the feminine as a regressed state in contrast to the absent, but perhaps observing, position of the masculine. In addition, as animalized, the woman and child signal Moore's concern with the ideas of the feminine as maternal body and as primitive/animal rather than as linked with the male sphere of the mind. From this first paragraph, then, the mixture of maternal and primitive herald the concerns of the text regarding the place of women and maternity in society coupled with the primitive and its effect on the devolution of female identity: women and children become almost invisible in this configuration, maternity making women less visible and codifying them as animals.

Ruth's body, figured as constrained within this primitive feminine identity from the beginning of her pregnancy via the invasion of her body by the fetus and the limits placed on her body by social propriety as enacted by Stephen's family, literally incorporates and represents Moore's criticism of the maternal's effect on female embodiment and identity. Initially, Ruth rejects and denies her pregnancy and the subsequent loss of control of her body. Although this reaction surprises her—she was "shocked . . . with the horror that came over her"—she continues by characterizing the pregnancy in terms of demonic possession: "She was a woman possessed; and she was horrified at the possession of herself by this thing she neither understood nor desired . . . as if a part of her were trying to remain aloof and sane in the midst of acting a nightmare" (123). To Ruth, the fetus invades her body, a parasite using her body as its host: "When I breathe, it breathes. When I feed, it feeds also. Against my will . . . it had had nothing to do with her from start to finish" (125). She continually refers to the fetus as an "it" and a "thing," indicating her detachment from the fetus and her conception of the fetus as alien and inhuman. Ruth readily admits that her reactions are aberrant, calling herself "the evil queen of the tales of her childhood returning at midnight to her witchcraft" (125), again associating herself with demonic possession.[18] Moore reveals her criticism of female embodiment and maternity through an unsuspecting Ruth who neither understands nor accepts her maternity. Through Ruth's questioning and denial of her pregnancy, Moore proposes that maternity is not the apex of women's identity; that, instead, it is a key contributor to the ideology of the feminine that entraps women in a primitive condition and, therefore, into subjugation by the "civilized" or patriarchal society.[19] Ruth's horror at her own reaction signals, too, the deviant position of a woman who rejects her proscribed maternity as well as Moore's criticism of Ruth's naiveté about her body, sexuality, and reproduction.

Ruth, tormented by her thoughts of the fetal invader, tries to reconcile herself to her maternity, "[b]ecause a reason had to be found for the sudden and bewildering revulsion which had taken possession of her like some deadly disease, a form of emotional galloping consumption that ravished her physically and mentally" (127). Part of Ruth's horror includes what occurs *to* her and *in spite* of her; she no longer controls what happens to her body, the fetus does, metaphorically performing patriarchy's control of the feminine. Ruth eventually concludes that "[i]t must be that she had no maternal sense. None whatsoever. And they regard me as something unnatural and not sane, and they may be right" (126), locating the rejection of her maternity in her own nature and mind and not in the alien fetus. Ruth's reversal of blame, from the body of the fetus to her own mind, demonstrates the beginning of Ruth's intellectual re-conception of maternity.

Ruth eventually accepts her pregnancy, but only when its physicality becomes undeniable—when the fact of her bulging body can no longer be ignored:

one day in her morning bath she noticed for the first time how large she had become. She couldn't believe it. Impossible! Yet it must be true for the water refused to cover her. . . . Had to admit. That it was not happening in her forehead at all, but was happening very much where it was meant to happen. That while she had been angry and despairing it was growing. It was becoming. It was happening. . . . And all her anger and despair had meant less than nothing to it. All her revulsion had had no effect. For answer a heavy white bubble of a tightly stretched stomach and water below lap-lapping round its sides. (131)

Her mind questioned, "despair[ed]," and was "angry," but her body "answer[ed]:" she is, inevitably, stuck in her maternity; she cannot escape her feminine, maternal body. Moore here situates the body—the "heavy white bubble of a tightly stretched stomach" is the "answer"—as the locus of truth, the undeniable reality in which Ruth is situated. For Moore, the body does not perform or represent some ideology of maternity that can therefore be manipulated or re-conceived through thoughts and words; it *is* pregnant in a very unalterable and material sense. At the same time, Moore criticizes the male position as intellect in relation to the female body in Ruth's inability to remake her body by imagining it differently, undermining the place of the (read male) intellect and sublimating it to the power of the (female and maternal) body's unavoidable presence.

Moore continues her critique by criticizing not only the entrapment of women in maternity but also women's inability to escape maternity or what could also be called women's complicity with maternity: "One thing she would not, she could not accept: that women went through it all without question; were creatures possessed and content to have no say in the matter" (129). Ruth cannot "accept" that all women agree to the constraints of their maternity "content to have no say in the matter." She then realizes the possibility of questioning and refusing maternity:

They won't bake buns? Let them bake cakes. And should they not want to bake even cakes? And not only not want, but refuse? If something outside one refuses: something one cannot control because one cannot fathom? Darkness. But nothing physical. Nor pain nor even death. Futility, perhaps. (129)

In this passage, Ruth reveals not only her anger with and depression about her pregnancy, but also about the years of complicity by women with their maternity which she "cannot fathom" and describes as "darkness" and "futility." Moore plays with the maternity metaphor of having "a bun in the oven," merging it with an allusion to Rousseau/Marie Antoinette's famous "let them eat cake," and positioning maternity as both bourgeois and domestic and the resistance to it as socially and politically revolutionary.[20]

Her angry questioning culminates in a conversation with her sister-in-law, Dora. When Dora states that "this is what woman is made for," Ruth replies: "[w]as made for, corrected Ruth. Was made for" (130).[21]

With this statement, Ruth heralds a moment of change for women from one kind of identity through maternity, something acting upon and through them, to another kind of identity through creation, something that they enact (with/in) themselves.[22] Ruth realizes that:

> she was not the only woman to feel about her child as she felt . . . that it is not only a few unnatural and unbalanced women who feel as I feel. . . . There had always been . . . many such perplexed uneasy creatures, unsure, hesitating. . . . Only their opinion was never asked or heeded. (130)

With this realization, Ruth comes to accept her condition—both her pregnancy and her rejection of it—and to challenge the notion that her rejection is "unnatural and unbalanced" (130), rejecting, too, the social positioning of women in maternity as primitive in their hysteria. It is not just that women have always been invaded by pregnancy, or that "many perplexed uneasy creatures" exist, but also that "their opinion was never asked or heeded" (130). Ruth rejects not just maternity but the social subjugation that it requires of women, placing them as primitive, animalistic, and therefore as "creatures" rather than people. For Ruth, maternity seems not to be something that she, like the etymology of "conceive" suggests, "took into herself." Rather, it is, as Kathleen Kirby suggests, a physical "space not of [her] own making" (100). Women's response to maternity is as illogical to her as her physical condition itself, and when this kind occupation occurs, women are forced to live in a conflicted subject position. Moore criticizes the double alien status of women in maternity: first, the alien occupation of their physical bodies, and, second, the alien status in which they must continue to live if they refuse patriarchy's constraints.

Beyond the trap of female embodiment in maternity that Moore criticizes, she also exposes patriarchy's conception of women as purely body throughout the discussions of Ruth's maternity. Ruth explains to Dora:

> Some there are . . . whose souls are more pregnant than their bodies. No. Socrates. And no one has ever thought of applying it to women. Why? Because the soul Dora is man's prerogative and woman is but the eternal oven in which to bake the eternal bun. (128)

Part of the conscription to maternity for Ruth, and that which she rebels against, develops from the inscription of her female identity that she is body, not mind—that she is of nature, not intellect. In this configuration, female embodiment is headless, or according to Ruth:

*Modernist Con(Tra)Ceptions* 83

> Woman from the neck downward. Man from the neck downward and upward, as he chose. But for woman no choice. I think, Stephen. I think. I think I carry my womb in my forehead. And she did. And still did. And always would. Because some there are whose souls are more pregnant than their bodies. No, Socrates. And no one has ever thought of applying that to women, because women, Dora. From the neck down, breasts and thighs and pelvic bone. And for head an enlarged heart. A fatty noble heart swollen with appropriate emotions. (161)

Woman is a patchwork of corporeal and psychic identities, and an unfinished body compared to man's finished one. Within this passage, Ruth repeats, "I think" three times, asserting and enacting the use of her mind in the process of her argument. But woman's sphere, according to Ruth's cultural criticism, is, in the absence of a cerebral sphere, the heart, the emotion, and, from the ways in which Ruth has responded to her pregnancy and maternity, she is without those "appropriate emotions" (161) as well. She, then, is culturally seen without a head, and psychically seen without a heart, making her incomplete as either man or woman. In addition, her use of "I think" (161) relegates Ruth to a subjective position which no one recognizes, as that of male mind and female body, further removing her from either male or female identification and disrupting the entrenched identities of each. In addition, as I will discuss in detail later in this chapter, the formal strategies deployed in this passage of fragmentation, repetition and stream-of-consciousness contribute to the disruption and instability of the way subjectivity is staged and formally illuminate Ruth's complicated and precarious positioning.

The critique of woman's incomplete embodiment continues in the novel through a discussion of Greek statuary, specifically the Victory of Samothrace figure (see Figure 3.1), between Ruth and her companion and perhaps lover, the artist Uller. The following passage begins with Uller's adamantly patriarchal and condescending comments to Ruth which lead to Ruth's analysis of her body and mind:

> I never see a greek statue, he once said, without being grateful to Time for knocking off its head and arms. That was it. A statue without a head. Or was she not rather a head without a statue? A head, she decided, going back many years and remembering, a head without its statue.
>
> Brave and serious her head; a little severe perhaps, judged by certain standards, but with a definite calm speechlessness of stone about it. A head, as he looked up suddenly at her unseeing upheld profile against the sky, that would sit well on the Victory of Samothrace. . . . She remained: the headless woman. And later how right it seemed: there to accept man not to question him and complicate a simple and necessary

## 84  Female Embodiment and Subjectivity in the Modernist Novel

act. Off, off with their heads! That was what men felt in their bones; the perfect, the headless woman. And there worshipped. Like that should she come to meet one on brave wings outspread: but headless, headless. He was amazed at how well her head (at this moment, at this angle, angles and moments having much to do with the conduct of emotions) would fit: so brave and sightless it looked upheld on its neck-column. (207)

Ruth moves back and forth in describing her embodiment in this passage: she is a statue without a head, then a head without a statue, and then a headless woman. The final embodiment is repeated "headless, headless" (207) re-inscribing it again and again.[23] In the first paragraph, it is Ruth who sees herself as the head without a statue and, in the second paragraph, it is Uller—and, by extension, all men—who see her, and all women, as statues without heads. Throughout the passage, her head is described, not her body or the body of the statue, making it more present in the text than in Ruth's conceptions of herself. Her head is "brave," "serious," "with a definite calm speechlessness of stone about it" and "sightless" (207). Sightless and mute,

*Figure 3.1* Winged Victory of Samothrace, Randy Plett/Effinity Stock Photograpy[24]

it is a head that only looks good on a preconceived and mythologized body (according to Uller). In this configuration, women's embodiment is roughly sutured together, a head of flesh onto a body of stone. Significantly, this configuration does not grant Ruth any kind of agency in her body or head; she is still a cultural construction of patriarchy and still without agency of speech or sight. In this portrayal, female embodiment reveals itself as just and only that: body.

Moore's criticism, though, extends beyond the female body and its production of maternity to the cultural inscriptions of female embodiment as demonstrated through this description of the statue and the cultural ideologies that produced and understood it as ideal. Through Ruth's reactions, Moore criticizes patriarchy's misogyny: Ruth is to "[remain] the headless woman" (207) because this is what "men felt in their bones" (207) she should be. The violence with which Ruth grants men's edict, "off with their heads!" (207), reflects not only Ruth's anger toward patriarchy's control and beheading of women but also Moore's criticism of patriarchy's fear of a woman with a head and, therefore, mind.[25]

To be clear, Moore does not advocate the complete abandonment of the female body and it's (re)production. Instead she argues for a merging of male and female identities so that women can be both body *and* mind. The beginning of Ruth's re-conception of her maternity begins with an intellectual transformation, extending the disconnection from her body and developing an alternate maternal sense: that of willfully creating through her intellectual powers. Here Moore complicates but does not abandon the mind/body dualism. Ruth's act of creation becomes an act of the mind as if in defiance and as if to control the act of creation that is already at work in her body. The mind and body still appear pitted against one another, but this time, Ruth attempts to control the actions of the body through the actions of her mind. As Ruth begins to *come to terms* with her pregnancy, she tells Stephen, "I carry my womb in my forehead.—I quite definitely feel it here, pursued Ruth, drawing her brows sharply together and staring across at her husband perplexedly. Whereas I do not feel it here at all (and her hand touched her body)" (128). Ruth's relationship to her pregnant body demonstrates a kind of trauma, a schism between her body and mind—she does not feel pregnant in her body but in her head—significantly placing her pregnancy in her mind, which has rejected it, and registering Ruth's maternity as an intellectual conception.

Ruth's revelation also situates her in a mythic state in which she associates herself with Zeus, who birthed Athena from his head.[26] She sees herself as both godlike and male, and this sets the stage for the conclusion of her query about the possibility of creating something new through her maternity. Initially, though, she tells Dora: "I think I carry my womb in my forehead. And I think that that, perhaps, is my curse" (128), as if her divinity is another kind of deviance. In addition, through the association with Zeus, Ruth becomes, at least conceptually, a kind of male/female god/

human hybrid. Here, Ruth conceives of her pregnancy as an intellectual activity, enacting again her (male) intellect and moving not only her pregnancy but also her subjective position from her body to her mind.[27]

Ruth also attempts to re-conceive of the way the body conceives physically beyond how she intellectualizes conception. In the bath, as Ruth realizes that she can no longer ignore the bubble of her belly, she also realizes the potential of her pregnancy to create something new: "[a]n answer had been found to her questioning. Something different, said the message. Something worth having. Something beyond and above it all, said the message. Something new" (132). The answer, then, is not to escape maternity, but to re-conceive it, to use the body and its ability to create, to use her corporeal servitude to maternity, in order to escape it. If Ruth can create "something new" with her body rather than be at her body's mercy, she might somehow be able to escape the entrapments if not of physical maternity itself than the product of it. But, again she gains access by positioning herself as male: "she found herself believing that had it been left to men centuries of creation would have produced some thing more vital, more exciting. But then men were the active and not the passive instruments of nature. Men questioned" (129). Ruth again identifies herself as male in her "active" participation in her reproduction.[28]

Rather than situating herself fully as male, though, she envisions a hybridized position of male intellectual power fused with female physical power, a hybrid more powerful than either position alone. She sees herself and the maternal woman in contrast to man:

> a witch filled with a great and terrible power over mankind. The power of life, of creation, of death. How puny then the thunder of man! Jove's toy squibbs. Vulcan's toy swords. Woman's thunderbolt. . . . But she was going to use her power. If I am to create, she told the eager creature in her mirror, I will create. Only of course something new. Something different. Something beyond and above it all. Something worth having. (132–33)

Situating herself as powerful in her maternity requires a new identification, here as "witch," and a new critique, here of "Jove" and "Vulcan," in an overthrow of symbolic paternal figures who now shrink before woman's creative maternity.[29] Ruth continues, "[d]runk with the terrible knowledge of her terrible power" (133), deciding that "she intended no replica of herself or Stephen. That would indeed be a shocking waste of her new-found and terrible power. . . . Something free that would defy the dreary inevitable round of years" (134). Ruth attempts to re-conceive maternity from servitude to patriarchy, family, female embodiment and "the dreary inevitable round of years" into a hybridized power that as both masculine and feminine allows her to create a new kind of embodiment and identity.

Beyond the abstract musings earlier, however, Ruth does not specify how this new hybridity is configured physically or ideologically. This vagueness may be the cause of Richard's resulting deformity, and it may also reveal the inability of women to create when they lack the means to envision and articulate their potential creation. It also reveals, as I develop later in this chapter, Moore's position on ideas of the new. Despite her own developments of textual experimentation, Moore seems insistently skeptical of modernism's emphasis on the new, where the "it" of "make it new" is also vague and leaves open the option for monstrosity.

Unfortunately, Ruth's mission fails. Richard's deformed corporeality offers evidence to Ruth that her thunderbolt destroyed rather than created. He is born "beautifully whole and finished; except for his feet. They hung loose and shapeless from the ankle, soft loose pads of waxen flesh" (153).[30] Like Ruth's feet, bound in constricting fashion upon arrival at Foria, his unfinished feet feminize him, remove him from possible connection to the earth and the stability of standing stature, and represent an unfinished and disabled existence:

> such a newly created being gathers itself together in its feet, grasps with them, beats at the air with them, eagerly draws them in in small soft folds. . . . Knowing this she raised her eyes from the loose formless pads of waxen flesh that were his feet to his impassive infant face in which two light eyes widely spaced and set stared at her and stared; and this time she understood the vacant fixity of his infant stare and his utter soundlessness and immobility. (153)

Richard's feet are an indication of his mental condition; in his feet his body performs—or fails to perform—his cognitive and cultural potential. In his "useless" body, for her, lays the reality of her experiment's consequences:

> Faced with the useless feet and staring silence she had known at once that she was wrong. . . . She knew very well how far from grace she had fallen. But what if she had succeeded? She could still wonder about that at the back of her willful half-repentant heart. Half-repentant: repenting the consequences and not the cause, which is hardly a repentance at all. (161–62)

Despite the consequences of Richard's deformed body and inaccessible mind, Ruth continues to defend her experiment of creating something new through her mind and body in maternity. This does not, though, transfer to a connection with or defense of Richard himself. Before leaving for England, Ruth comments that "he was rootless, null, unproductive: therefore not a living being at all" (213). For Ruth, Richard's useless body makes him not only incapable but inhuman. Without being grounded in an able body, specifically in able feet, "rootless," he cannot fully develop in body or mind. The creation of something new, then, requires both an able body and an able mind, a hybridization of male and female identifications into a new kind of modern subject. Neither Ruth nor Moore recuperates Richard from his deformity and muteness. Even in Ruth's transformation of Sharvells into a home for needy children, she specifically excludes children like Richard. Not completely abandoned, Richard is set aside, removed from the action of the novel and from the machinations of modernity. At the same time, Richard is the pivot around which Ruth and the novel operate: she exiles herself to Italy because of and with him. If he does figure as a product of modernism, he is a failed one, physically monstrous and mute, and in him, modernism—at least in this incarnation—may not continue. The "new" of modernity is thus revealed as an ineffective and monstrous waste.

Moore presents another attempt at a new kind of modern subject through the character of Joan Agnew, the novel's sole representative of the young and new modern woman that Ruth meets upon her return to England. Through Joan, we see that in Ruth's absence British women have begun to create their own new identities and take control of their own bodies. One could hope that after the twenty-two years between Ruth's escape to Foria and her return to London, female identity would have progressed beyond its inscriptions. But, at the end of the novel, when Ruth meets Joan, Ruth finds these developments to fall quite short and finds Joan to be an unsatisfactory female incarnation. At first:

> Ruth liked her. She was shocked and impressed and amazed. This, then, was the modern girl the newspapers spoke so much about. Keen-eyed, fleshless, arrogant. She liked it. It was new to her. It had promise. Everywhere there was fear, a sense of danger, a sense of despair, a smell of decay: but the young women had a certain hard fleshless courage. They had promise. It was new to her and interesting. (227)

The modern woman's embodiment is "hard" and "fleshless;" her body is refashioned as more boylike or absent, a denial of woman's fleshiness or of the feminine of the female body. Her life is a "version of herself" in which "[e]verybody works these days. . . . One must do *something* or life would be too damned dull" (227), disavowing a secure identity or story beneath the versioning she lives out. There is "promise" but it comes embodied differently, concerned differently, as an imitation of man, his embodiment and his story rather than as a creation of a new kind of female embodiment and identity.

Although initially Ruth says that she likes Joan's newness and promise, she criticizes Joan for failing to fulfill her new potential. After seeing a play together, Ruth's response reveals the difference between her and the modern woman as represented by Joan. Ruth begins:

—To me you all seem to be prying into other people's bedrooms. You have all an eye at the bedroom keyholes of the world. I don't like your idea of what you call sex. There is too much of it. It is an obsession or a disease. You turn love either into a wasting disease or a perpetual Chopin nocturne.

—Um, said the girl throwing a match out of the window. There's something in what you say. It is rather a dirty business. Tonight's papers say the Luff divorce cost over £50,000. Nasty, isn't it? As though it matters in whose bed one sleeps. . . . (228)

The difference between Ruth and Joan concerns love and sex for Ruth, and money and contracts for Joan. And, for Ruth, love and sex contribute to or parallel the changes in women's embodiment. It is "a wasting disease," similar to the boy-like or fleshless physical embodiment of the modern woman. Two pages later, Ruth comments:

There was a novelty and a certain glamour about the new young woman: but was she altogether satisfying? Had she attained anything not previously attained? A certain independence and what she called self-expression. A following less efficiently and more loudly professions which men had followed for years as a matter of course. There was about her a look of impermanence difficult to classify. A look of today. Something momentary. She would grow old and leave the world exactly as she found it. (229)

In a word, Ruth is disappointed in the modern woman's selfishness and superficial developments which, in the end, leave her just as trapped as her previous embodiments. Instead of creating something new, the modern woman has replicated man—her "fleshless" body revealing her imitation of man as well as the lack of substance and promise that this new identity creates. In response, Ruth "was shocked. She could not understand. Now, it seemed, the emancipated woman wanted no children. Women kept their figures and their jobs. . . . How monstrous! she thought, understanding not at all. How mean" (230).[31] Different, for the modern woman, is a fashion. She has refashioned herself differently, but to no permanent effect. Ruth's response is that she is "monstrous!" and "mean." Rather than "taking into oneself" or "taking into one's mind" in order to re-conceive female embodiment and identity, the new, modern woman has reshaped the body and redressed it, changing only the shell of her identity when, according to Ruth, she could have created a new identity entirely.[32] Joan then operates as another failed hybrid that attempts to identify with the male mind by eliminating the female body. Moore complicates her critique even further by disallowing the modern woman's attempts at legitimate subjectivity through physical and lifestyle changes which Ruth finds superficial and "monstrous." Although Ruth continually identifies with the masculine, she does not support the abandonment of the feminine and its maternity or the false hybrid that the modern woman portrays.

Through Ruth and Joan, Moore proposes two alternatives for the creation of new embodiment and identity, but finds neither satisfactory. Throughout Moore's writings, she is ruthless in her criticism of women, and here, in *Spleen*, seems to agree with Uller's perspective that women mostly operate as "the receptacles for man's thought and children" (194–95). Although Moore does not privilege the abandoning of the female body to the boyish body of the new modern woman, she does, in fact, continue to identify with the masculine mind. She criticizes the new modern woman for discarding the body instead of making something new with or from it as Ruth, at least, attempted. In Ruth and Joan's experiments with the creation of new subjectivity, both means, maternity and physical-social modification, prove insufficient and incapable of creating the kind of (albeit vague) change that Ruth and Moore desire. In this criticism, Ruth implies that she still finds promise in a hybridized identity of male mind and female embodiment. Joan has tried to imitate the male body without achieving the male mind; Ruth, instead, wants to place a thinking head on the Victory of Samothrace and by doing so re-conceive of the entirety of female embodiment and identity.

## GEOGRAPHICAL (DIS)EMBODIMENT, OR: THE FEMININE UNGROUNDED

> [S]pace helps us to recognize that "subjects" are determined by their anchoring within particular bodies or countries.
>
> Kathleen Kirby (7)

In addition to criticizing the ways women's subjective positions are anchored in their femininely marked bodies and maternity, Moore also criticizes the conception of the land as feminized. The countryside figures as feminine in the novel, continuing the extension of the feminine onto the land seen in *Mrs. Dalloway* and *The Waves*, and extending the feminizing of women's bodies to the geographical body. The geographical body extends, too, the ways in which the feminine has been conceived, or "taken into the mind" and reproduced as representative feminine bodies that are also inscripted.[33] I repeat here Anne McClintock's suggestion that, "[l]inked symbolically to the land, women are relegated to a realm beyond history and thus bear a particularly vexed relation to narratives of historical change and political effect" (31), suggesting again how both women and the feminized land are relegated to a discursive place that is out of reach. Coupled with Kirby's argument, earlier, "that 'subjects' are determined by their anchoring within particular bodies or countries," the discovery of women's identity and subjectivity is inherently linked to their location in place or space, making both identities untethered and ungrounded despite the affiliation of women to the land.[34] Ruth's "anchoring" within her body is already troubled by her maternity and by the incongruity she finds between her body and her mind. In addition, Ruth's deep connection to the land, specifically to the English soil, places her in relationship to another femininely marked body. Moore emphasizes the importance of being rooted in the land just as she prefers female identity to remain rooted in the body, and Ruth's ultimate status as geographically ungrounded in her expatriation reinforces her ambiguous status in the culture as well. Ruth's physical and metaphorical connections with the English landscape conflict with her choice to live in Italy and extend the criticism of British female identity to its countryside, that hallmark of Englishness.[35]

Moore's critique of the feminizing of the geographical body begins with a description of Ruth's physical body when she arrives at Foria as one constrained in fashion and fear. Here, Ruth's accommodation to fashion signals her accommodation to English female identity, which Moore describes as "tight shoes and propriety . . . bodily movement in the female was restricted and rendered painful by whalebone and yards of heavy unwieldy cloth" (140–41). This fashion not only restricts her body as a whole; it specifically restricts her feet, her ability to move, keeping her (and by extension women) literally in their place:[36]

> her small patent leather feet, so correct, so refinedly helpless, looking out from under the heavy folds of the blue serge skirt of her travelling costume, ample, braided, the cape coming to her elbows covered with the very latest ornamentation in shining silk, heavy, solid, expensive; the hat a masterpiece of discretion, four brims of fine straw, laced and interlaced, escaping, recaptured, poised well forward on the brow and held there by coils of hair, an elegant misshapen mass of curls and puffs leaping forward and outward from behind the ears. (112)

Ruth's body, specifically her feet which are reminiscent of Chinese women's bound feet (as well as Richard's waxen feet), signals a kind of beauty that makes her body useless and tragic. Her feet are "refinedly helpless" and her hair is "an elegant misshapen mass," denoting the unfortunate construction of each as well as her accommodation to fashion, and figuring her body as a prop for ornamentation, a moveable statue of English culture's conception of female identity.

Prior to Ruth's move to Italy, the English countryside, via her ex-husband's estate, Sharvells, represents feminine ornamentation and constraint, and Moore figures the landscape as too highly cultivated and, therefore, inaccessible. Uller's comment that "[t]o the english a pictorial flower of civilisation is a hunting-field or a garden party" (198), captures at once Moore's criticism of the highly cultivated English landscape in its emphasis on the pastoral and social characteristics of the English manor life. For

Moore, the over-cultivated English land, like the female body as represented in Ruth's portrayal upon her arrival in Foria, creates an unnatural and hideous landscape. For example, as Ruth looks at Sharvells, Ruth describes it as "this cumbersome imposing mansion, grey, lichened, terraced, beautiful in so many ways, pretentious and uncomfortable in so many more . . . and set on a stretch of land which after two years upon it she was still ignorant as to where it began or ended" (142), and its grounds as "tulip beds arranged with stiff and formidable precision and colour-graded with monotonous regard for formal landscape harmony, and none whatever for Spring itself" (127). She even tells her child in utero:

> You will not like it, said Ruth to the edge of flinty stone which could be seen in the distance half-hidden by labyrinths of yew-hedge, spacious towering single trees, old walls enclosing separate and tidy gardens, littering the ground which separated her from the house. (144)

For Moore, through Ruth's perceptions of Sharvells, the constrictive botanic shaping of Sharvells extends and represents the control of women's bodies exerted by English culture evidenced in Ruth's restrictive fashion on traveling to Italy. Rather than exalting this landscape and the pastoral, Moore sees the English landscape as cultivation and civilization gone too far. These attempts by English patriarchy to control and contain the feminized English landscape echo the constraints placed on women's bodies and echo also the double movement of this effort: the English land, as I will show, is at once both sacred and savage in its cultivation and its wilderness. The attempts to cultivate the land, then, can be seen as attempts to constrain the unwieldy feminine as represented by the land.

Moore criticizes not only this contradictory representation of the land as both constraining and unwieldy, but also Ruth's contradictory relationship with the land: she is at once critical of the constrained and cultivated feminine landscape and deeply connected to it. Ruth's connection with the English soil, though, is a connection with its wilderness and thus an even more femininely marked or primitive form of landscape, one that has not been as controlled by the cultivating forces of English civilization. This connection begins as a young child and facilitated by her father: Ruth's father instructs Ruth to walk barefoot in the grass not just for pleasure but also to cure "the ills of the body" (141). Rather than a casual stroll, this is described by Ruth as an "experiment" conducted by her father "every morning" to put "herself . . . in direct contact with the earth" (140–41) which has the power to heal, create, and evolve in dramatic ways—emphasizing again the impossibility for recuperation for Richard whose feet are unable to provide the conduit for the earth's healing.[45] The "potency" (133) of the earth's drug can, perhaps, be too strong as is shown when Ruth embraces the earth during pregnancy:

She took to avoiding the house a good deal and to wandering secretly in the isolated and unsought woods bordering a part of the grounds. Here she would lie for hours on the earth as though embracing it. She had not done such a thing since she was a child and it brought her immense comfort and a spiritual content, in which, as in a trance, the life around her vanished and was forgotten, leaving her alone on her patch of mossy grass among the trees. (133)

The earth provides "comfort" and "spiritual content" significantly in the "woods bordering" the grounds of Sharvells. Ruth takes herself to the geographical border of the English wilderness even before she removes herself to Italy, a place described as even more wild and primitive, and yet which also summons Moore's classical agrarian ideal of an older and more "natural" civilization.

Ruth's connection to nature continues after she moves to Italy. It is as if, on Foria, she attempts to get back to a purer nature, less altered by human hands, or more primitive and, therefore, feminine. This connection to the land is essential to her rediscovery of her self. Her descriptions and observations of the Forians, as well as her reporting of her encounters and life with them, often read like exploration literature such as Joseph Conrad's *Heart of Darkness*, albeit in a historically and culturally considered more civilized or westernized region than Conrad's Belgian Congo. Simon Gikandi explains that:

> the trope of travel generates narratives that are acutely concerned with self-realization in the spaces of the other, that the European excursion (and incursion) into the colonial space is one of the most important vehicles by which . . . Europe and its others are re-created. (8)

Like Conrad's Marlow, who must travel to the "the very end of the world" to recognize that "this [England] also . . . has been one of the dark places of the earth," (5) Ruth travels to Foria in search of escape, explanation, and "self-realization." Moore then creates a text which requires the Forians to be "othered" in order for Ruth to come to her "self-realization." Ruth's self-realization that "[s]he no longer reproached herself" (232) does not occur to her until she returns home to England. Mary Louise Pratt suggests that this is partly due to the fact that in "the imperial act of discovery," "the discovery has no existence on its own: It only gets "made" for real after the traveler (or other survivor) returns home and brings it into being through texts" (qtd. in McClintock 29–30). Ruth's contradictory position of the feminine, here on the feminine land, and her participation within it begin to be revealed. She at once both rails against society's constraints on female embodiment and identity and, as I discuss in the next section of this chapter on the national body, participates in a feminizing of another land and culture through her language of the travel narrative.[37]

Ruth continues to transform throughout her years on Foria, further associating with the Italian landscape which, paradoxically, considering the patriarchal structure of the Forian society, she sees as placing her further out of patriarchy's reach. After Uller leaves Foria, Ruth comments that:

> Now once again she could walk on the earth alone. . . . It made her feel light and unreal and transparent, this belonging again to herself; of being one with the orchestration of scent and sound: blend of incense and manure: heaven and earth. . . . What happened to the earth, she felt, must happen to her seeing that there she would sit will-less and wait for it to happen. (203)

Ruth's connection with nature, and her solace with/in it, grants or returns her, as seen previously in England, to an idyllic identity in which she feels "light," "unreal," "transparent," and as "belonging again to herself." Belonging to herself follows immediately with her statement of "being one with" nature. For Ruth, connecting to or being one with nature does not make her beholden to nature, but frees her from the bounds of society, culture, and community, a freedom she cannot find until she is removed from the bonds of patriarchy through a representative such as Stephen or Uller. Her communion with nature provides such a connection that she feels that "[w]hat happened to the earth . . . must happen to her" (203).

The island of Foria, then, offers an alternative interaction with nature and an alternative feminine identification for Ruth. Although Foria is cultivated through the growing of grapes and raising of goats, it is still "wild and disorderly" and "for ever drawing breath between one rage and another" (214). Foria's status as "island space" contributes to its identity as a different kind of place, a liminal space. As Linda McDowell explains, "in that liminal space between the land and the sea—literally a place on the edge—the sets of binary associations that structure Western social relations are made visible, and in some cases transgressed" (166). This kind of island space, off the coast of Italy, is never associated with the kind of island space that is England; Foria's free-floating status sharply contrasts with England's constraint. Ruth recounts her sensation of living in Foria's island space when she describes the early hours of the afternoon: a place of "suspension" where Ruth is "detached," "mindless," and "lost" in an "unreality" (185). Despite all of this inaction and lack of agency on the part of Ruth, the island itself is active. It may "at any moment thrust down again to the floor of the sea" (185), situating Foria as a land that is literally uncontrollable and unpredictable. It is a place of willing loss of control. If Foria is an attempt to find another kind of land, or island, in which to re-conceive female identity, it is especially troubling to see Ruth's passivity, inaction, and loss of agency within such an active space. In characterizing Ruth and Foria in these ways, Moore suggests the difficulties inherent in locating a space which allows for the development of new and independent subjectivities.

If, too, as Kathleen Kirby suggests, "'subjects' are determined by their anchoring within particular bodies or countries," Ruth is, again, an unfinished, unanchored subject in her geographical body because, as an expatriate, she no longer has a land to claim as her own. Like her description of herself as flesh and stone, a human head sutured to a stone statue, her geographical subjective position is also a patchwork—an Englishwoman stitched into the Italian countryside. Again, she does not suggest the abandoning of the feminine, here read land, but the discovery of a land in which the feminine can be unconstrained. It is not the land, like the body, that needs to be reconstructed, but the ideas which govern one's "anchoring" to and within it that need to be re-conceived or "take[n] into the mind" differently. Ruth does not abandon the English soil because it is feminized, or not feminine enough, but because it is not feminine in the way in which she is: it is controlled and sculpted, like the body of the Victory of Samothrace, not wild and freefloating like the island of Foria, a place where Ruth attempts to rediscover the land and herself. Unfortunately, despite these attempts, Ruth remains ungrounded or unanchored in both land and body as seen in her physical identity as a broken statue absent of head and arms, and in her geographical identity as broken between two locales and belonging to neither.

Just as Moore proposes (failed) hybridized physical embodiments through Richard and Joan, she proposes another kind of hybrid embodiment through Ruth's attempts to re-conceive of the English manor house and landscape. Although Ruth abandons England for Foria, Moore does not propose the abandonment of the English landscape but attempts to recuperate the feminine land through the conversion of Sharvells, the manor home which Ruth inherits. Through reclamation of Sharvells, Moore offers the most possibility for successful hybridity.

Ruth attempts a reclamation of the English land with the transformation of Sharvells into a children's charity home. She describes the re-conception of Sharvells as:

> the permanent home of a charitable institute which provided holidays for London's slum children. . . . It was to be a permanent all-the-year round home for poor children who were weak or had been ill, and especially for ill-treated children; at certain times of the year (they were hoping to arrange) slum mothers could take their holidays with their children. It had nothing to do with mentally defective children . . . who were in no sense, she believed, worth saving. (220)

Ruth does not sell Sharvells as the solicitor suggests to become a golf course for the empire; she remakes it into something new, something worth having.[38] She explains to the solicitor that:

> [I]t would not be expensive to run as the children would do practically all the work (under a new training scheme) their own gardening,

producing their own food. The great thing was that the Society should have a home and headquarters and an income of its own, so as not to be entirely dependent on a precarious and reluctant charity. (221)

Ruth reclaims and recreates Sharvells into a sociological and ecological experiment, providing underprivileged children with access to the land that she and her father so valued. Her action encourages access and appreciation of the feminine landscape, not in its pastoral beauty or recreation but in its production potential. Her action also removes Sharvells from the hands of empire and from the hands of "precarious and reluctant" charitable givers. Ruth, in a sense, makes Sharvells the geographical equivalent of a room of one's own by providing space and means for the feminine (land) to be productive and independent. Sharvells, therefore, becomes a hybrid of the feminine land and masculine financial freedom. In addition, the hybridity of the Sharvells project operates outside of gender in its focus on children.[39] Here, Moore proposes that re-conceiving the land provides equality to the next generation as they have equal rights to work the land and are considered equally. In addition, Moore continues to advocate the re-conceiving of the feminine rather than the abandonment of it. Rather than having Ruth sell Sharvells to the dominantly male, golfing empire, Moore writes a novel in which Ruth uses her financial position to create an English landscape that embodies a hybridized position of the masculine and feminine and overthrows the manipulations of patriarchy and the feminine as in service to it (here as recreation).

Yet, even this apparently effective proposal for hybridity through the conversion of Sharvells, is accompanied by the irony of Ruth's previous positions on reproduction and her rejection of her own child, Richard. Ruth specifically does not want Sharvells to be used to help "mentally defective" children (220), a category in which Richard could surely qualify. The body again figures as central to Ruth's social ideology: not only does it determine gender and reproductive roles; it also determines one's engagement with society and its development. In Ruth's configuration of the use of Sharvells, Moore inserts the complication of physical purity through production rather than sexual or social standing. Ruth, therefore, does not attempt to reclaim her previous experiments with physical hybridity but rather seeks to offer opportunity to those able-bodied children who are disabled by class. Ruth's rejection of her own pregnancy and child is not remedied or absolved either. In addition, Ruth's use of Sharvells insists on the production of the feminine, on teaching people to make the feminine productive, and on creating a link between children and the feminine that situates the land as a kind of proxy maternal figure. Rather than resolving this paradox, Moore leaves Ruth in this ironic and complicated position that both critiques the practices of human reproduction and advocates botanical production, demonstrating through this complication the split subjectivity of the modern female subject who, like

Ruth, must walk with one foot in both worlds of corporeal reproductivity and corporate productivity.

## NATIONAL (RE)EMBODIMENTS: RE-ENACTING VERSUS RE-CONCEIVING THE NATIONAL BODY

> Controlling women's sexuality, exalting maternity and breeding a virile race of empire-builders were widely perceived as the paramount means for controlling the health and wealth of the male imperial body politic, so that, by the turn of the century, sexual purity emerged as a controlling metaphor for racial, economic and political power.
>
> Anne McClintock (47)

Controlling women's bodies and the feminized land, according to this passage by Anne McClintock, is another way of controlling and building the empire. Women's bodies become not only a synecdoche for empire, but metonymous as well—it is not just that women are a part of the imperial body, they are *the* attribute selected to represent the empire both as a troubling fissure of uncontained femininity that must be suppressed, and as a maternal purity that must be protected. In controlling the representation of the empire, specifically the thing that represents the empire's "purity," the imperial project situates women's bodies as the molding clay out of which imperial identity is formed and maintained. As McClintock points out, it is not merely their bodies, but specifically women's "sexuality" and "maternity" that must be controlled, maintained, and protected.

Women's role in nationalism, then, includes operating as figure(without) heads and as producers of citizens. In this divided position, Ruth again becomes a contradictory figure. When Ruth returns to England she discusses the difference between English and Italian women which leads to a discussion of Englishwomen's professions and utility: "—No, said Ruth replying to a direct question. I hardly agree. A million shorthand-typists remain a million shorthand-typists, but a million mothers can found a nation" (227). We do not hear the direct question to which Ruth responds, but implied within this half of the dialogue is Ruth's reaction to the new opportunities for women. It is not progressive enough, for Ruth, that women be working women if all they do is become shorthand-typists. Ruth remains convinced that women can contribute more by producing citizens than by typing. In fact, instead of contributing to an already established male-dominated empire, they can create their own. Despite the failure of the creation of her own child, Ruth advocates for the creation of something new in the founding of a nation through reproduction. Mothers, it seems without any supporting examples in England or Italy, are still powerful, creative and independent figures for Ruth. Moore implies through Ruth's admonition that empires are not actually built by men but by women, by mothers. Ruth's argument here suggests that women can somehow reclaim this process, but it also suggests Ruth's conflicted position on women's bodies and nationalism and reveals her lack of knowledge of childrearing: if a million mothers are producing a nation, who among them will have time to govern that nation?[40] Will it not still be a nation governed by men? Empires then become feminized, but feminized in such a way that they still place women in a complicit position with maternity. Therefore, another conscription is added to the inscription of maternity that of creating and supporting empire.

Ruth's contradictory position continues when she moves to Italy. Through Ruth's expatriate status, Moore reveals Ruth to be both a participant in stereotypical attitudes towards other cultures, as seen in male imperial ideologies, and as valorizing that same culture. Moore also criticizes both Ruth's fears of the Forians and the history of colonization that underlies the Forian culture. In so doing, Moore also criticizes the history of English colonization, exemplifying through Ruth the uneasy position of both male and female citizens of the British Empire in their complicity with the imperial project and inability to escape imperial ideologies.

In choosing to live on Foria, outside of the British Empire, Ruth chooses to align herself with a more rural/primitive/feminine land and culture. But, at the same time that she selects the Forians as her new companions and valorizes their peasant culture, she also distances herself from the Forians through her criticism of them, as if to say, "I may be primitive/feminine but I'm not *that* primitive." Torgovnick argues that "[d]ifferentiation from the Other is a response to the disruptive effects of identification with the Other" (8). Or, because Ruth fears her identification with the Forians, she must distance herself from them even in her retrospections. She describes the Forians as "garlic-reeking unclean foreigners" (112) and repeatedly as "savage" (113, 180), and the island as "strange" and "dark-hearted" (114).[41] When Ruth first arrives, she must take a boat in which she sits between wine barrels, melons and a melon-merchant "with the naked bristling chest" (112), a description that, when repeated twice in two paragraphs, depicts a kind of raw primitive quality of the people. She remembers her initial contact with them, "beyond her first and physical fear of them," as "silent indifferent dark-hearted people," with "complete absence or understanding of respect or deference" (118). Simply, they are not, in her sense, "civilized," and eventually she comes to embrace their impropriety or primitivism. They are "fierce" and "hostile," and she is "very much in their power" (118). Ruth's responses to the Forians bring to the fore Ruth's contradictions. Here, Ruth becomes equivalent to the racist male modernist mind that Torgovinick discusses, only able to save herself from "their power" by seeing them as inferior.[42]

Ruth's superiority is demonstrated clearly in her reaction against their "power" and in her attempts to align herself with the Forians by asking: "Why was she always going out of her way like this to propitiate these childish dark-hearted people to whom she was less than nothing, and must go on for ever being less than nothing no matter what she did, because the only tie they understood, the blood-tie, was not there?" (119–20). Here, she sees all of them as childish.[42] Their only understanding of society appears based on "the blood-tie," reaffirming their status as other, pure, and primitive: other in blood from Ruth and more primitively concerned with blood. The connection between the primitive and blood is made through descriptions of them as bloodthirsty in their primitivism or savagery as well. On the boat to Foria for the first time, she wonders "What would become of her she had wondered foolishly if she disobeyed?" (113). As she lands, she sees,

> rows of brown faces and foaming teeth gathering on the jetty and hemming her in, leagued against her with this savage to whose arms she was hanging. . . . She must stay where she was for fear of treading on a grinning mouth with a voice shrieking out of it like an evil flame. (113)

Later, she refers to a young Forian woman, Graziella, as having "that Madonna-monkey look that creeps slyly into such eyes in unguarded moments" (120) asserting both Graziella's piety (and with it both high culture representations of the Madonna and pagan folklore) and Graziella's status as savage other. Through these descriptions of their savage appearances, that is with animalized, rabid, "foaming teeth;" with racialized "brown faces" and "Madonna-monkey look[s];" and demonized with "an evil flame" of a shrieking voice, Ruth reveals her underlying racism and feelings of cultural supremacy, utilizing the language of colonizer as she describes them. Ruth both valorizes their culture and appears to condescend in accepting them. She eventually grows accustomed to their ways, rather than embracing or acknowledging them and their culture immediately.

Moore also reminds us of the Forians' history as conquerors and empire builders and the blindness of the colonizer to his/her own position within imperialism. Despite Ruth designating them as primitive or as the conquered, they, too, have been conquerors and, in fact, are at once both conquered and conquerors. Daily they walk the "Saracen road" (112), reenacting their own history of conquering during the Crusades both as Saracen descendents and Saracen conquerors.[44] As Ruth watches from her verandah, she sees,

> a sudden kindling of movement on the goat road; road which, legacy of Saracen conquerors twelve hundred years since, the Forian traitors to this early blood ridiculously called Via dei Angeli. Absurd as the crosses and campanili attached to the humped and tiled mosques and remnant walls of pagan temples scattered in profusion over the island. (115–16)

According to this passage, and to Ruth, the Forians betrayed their Saracen ancestors and assimilated into the Italian culture. Both histories, Italian and Muslim, remain marked on the landscape and culture through the mosques, temples, and crosses. This road, the Saracen road, also "the goat road" (115), is the main road through the village and from the docks to the village, its names accruing into an association of the Saracens with the animals. It is on this road that Ruth watches the men reenact their conquering through their beating of the goats and vociferous shouting as well as the disappearance of the woman and child in the first paragraph.[45] Ruth acknowledges that the Forians, who she at most times valorizes, contain within their national history betrayal and the "ridiculous" and "absurd" (115) palimpsests of cultures and national identities. Although firmly rooted in their Roman Catholicism, the peasants also engage with and utilize their Saracen, pagan, and conquering past. These cultural and national symbols betray the confusion of the Forians' history and identity as conquerors and also their need for valor and might to elevate them above their daily labor with goats, grapes, and fish. It also betrays their commitment to the "blood-tie" by indicating through their history of conquest that the blood on which these ties are built must not be pure. With this comes a critique of British history that also includes a miscellany of colonial domination and bastardized subjects, as well as a leveling of Ruth's imposed hierarchies of the supposed civilized English culture and the agrarian and "savage" Forian culture. Moore criticizes Ruth's perspective of cultural superiority, presenting an opposite vision of imperial savagery through the subtext of the Forians' history and, by doing so reveals Ruth's limited vision of her own relation to imperialism.

Moore's criticism of empire building includes the conscription of women and women's bodies. The Forians, too, contribute to the subjugation of women through their history of conquering and through their patriarchal social structure.[46] Ruth's escape from the patriarchal constraints of maternity and British empire building in England result not only in living surrounded by reminders of the savageness of the actions of empire building: her expatriate and financial status and her cultural critique of the Forians remove her from direct participation in their culture and the consequences of it. This position keeps Ruth's national attachments nebulous and untethered as well, less affected by empire but not free from participation within it; neither British nor Italian, she is just foreign, and, in that, continues to be marked as other, primitive, and feminine despite her gestures toward masculine colonial ideologies in her positioning as culturally superior and her blindness toward her own complicity with them. Ruth becomes a hybrid, but a hybrid of what she criticizes as both primitive/feminine and colonizing/masculine. Identifying her with the Forian wilderness, then, Moore can situate Ruth as escaping her constrained subjective position, but it then also results in her repulsion from the primitive and her desire to constrain it.

Unfortunately, Ruth does not adapt her attempts at hybridity in the land to allow her to rethink relations between cultures, namely between her English self and the Forians, which could then lead to some sort of national or international transformation. She remains entrenched in a male colonizer position which continues the subjugation of primitive peoples through ideology and attitudes of superiority and, subsequently, of the feminine which is inherently associated with them. Through Ruth's variously ambiguous and contradictory positions on nationalism and empire, Moore inserts a criticism of imperialism and its participants, and asserts, too, that neither position of all male mind nor all female body is the answer to patriarchy and imperialism. Moore fails to reverse the power of patriarchy and empire or to assert a new model of national or global hybridity, presenting Ruth instead as an ambiguous interloper who seems more to take advantage of her class and visitor status than to contribute to either nation or culture.

## THE HYBRIDIZED TEXT: CHANGING EVERYTHING

> When you change the metaphor, said George Eliot most cannily in *The Mill on the Floss*, . . . you change everything. And so it is with fictional form: change the frame, change the form, the formal model, and everything changes.
>
> Valentine Cunningham (150-1)

Moore's criticism of women's entrenched identities is juxtaposed with her proposal for a merging of the masculine with the feminine to create a hybridized identity in the textual body that no longer entraps women. In this, the text poses a reversal to the embodiment of the feminine from those embodiments seen in the physical, geographical, and national manifestations of the feminine. Consider an alternative reading of the first paragraph of the novel in which the woman, child, and goats disappear from view, cited in full on page 79. Rather than an annihilation of female identity, Moore can be seen to instead propose the removal of woman's association with the primitive and codification as animals. As these figures and their associations disappear, they make way for new or re-conceptions of women, embodiment, and identity. At the same time, *Spleen* suggests that experiments in hybridity can produce deformities. Ruth's son, Richard, operates as a failed attempt at hybridity, complete neither in body nor mind, and dramatizes another possible direction in contrast to a progressive, forward-moving hybrid that both Moore and Ruth seek to create.

Moore attempts to re-conceive the modernist text, so that it is still rooted in its own kind of fleshy embodiment, by changing "the formal model" through textual experimentation. Like the portrayal of women's bodies as demonstrated in the Victory of Samothrace, Moore creates a text that is both broken and connected, that both stands on its own and continually references and incorporates other texts through allusion and reference. It is as if it is impossible to imagine a text (or a female body) without also referencing something else, impossible to create something completely new. Moore's version of Pound's modernist edict, "make it new," puts an emphasis on the "it": make *it* new, whatever *it* may be.⁴⁷ This shift of emphasis places less importance on the newness of the creation and its subsequent difficulties and complications, focusing instead on the thing, the "it," that is being created. The vagueness of the term coincides and corroborates Moore's ambiguous terminology throughout *Spleen*, especially her description of Ruth's maternal experimentations of making "something" new (133). Within Moore's experimentations with the text, the "something" becomes more concrete and actually becomes embodied as the novel itself. The text then can be seen as a body in that it is a container, here for Moore's ideologies, and enacts or performs these ideologies through Moore's textual experimentation. Within her experimentation with narrative construction and form, Moore does not abandon the scaffolding provided by literary history just as she does not abandon the body or the land. Instead, through the use of references and allusion to mythological and poetical texts, Moore creates a densely textured novel that accumulates images and impressions of literary history through modernist experimentation. *Spleen*, then, operates as a textual hybrid whose intertextuality between male modernist ideals of literary tradition, specifically the role of myth, and female modernist forms of both excess and fragmentation provides some success in its equality.

The novel is constructed through a series of inconsecutive flashbacks, embodying the untethered female subjectivity in its unhindered movements from dialogue to description. The novel begins in Italy, in the almost present day of the novel, recaps Ruth's history in England, her arrival in Italy, her relationship with Uller, and her relationship with Richard, in haphazard and slippery chunks, and then moves with Ruth to England upon her return. In doing so, Moore utilizes a stream-of-consciousness form which also slips from third to first person and from interior to exterior monologue. When Ruth is traveling to Foria, she wonders about Stephen's family: "What would they say to her sitting among the wine barrels and the melons and the garlic-reeking unclean foreigners" (112). The next paragraph responds:

> She has gone back, back to where she belongs. For the best. As I said at the beginning of this painful. I know. I know I should not say so, but I did say. And it is always a mistake to raise people from. The crimson satin walls of the dining-room and the vast curved window admitting one to the finest view in the county. (112)

In this passage, the narration moves from third to first person in a form which continues the truncated sentences seen above. The last sentence of the paragraph is full and complete, and removes the narration from the dialogue to a description of the room in Sharvells in which the dialogue would occur. The use of stream-of-consciousness form, as I have argued in the first chapter on *Mrs. Dalloway*, grants access to the interiority of the female mind and, here, to memory as well.

The text's internal structure enacts the concerns of the narrative through its inclusion of both fragmentation and fluidity. The novel begins with long, chunky, dense, and broken paragraphs and sentences, the paragraphs and sentences interrupted by the use of dashes instead of quotation marks and by frequent insertions of other thoughts and other characters. For example, Ruth reflects how: "Plaintively and helplessly impatient her voice came to her again over the years. *But you see I do not care for men, Dora. . . .*" (122). Unfinished sentences, like this one, like the unfinished body of Richard, or like the headless statue, "The Victory of Samothrace," are instead linguistic bodies lacking tails rather than heads, reversing the images of headless female embodiments purported by patriarchs like Uller throughout the novel. Revisiting a passage discussed earlier, several pieces from conversations are patched together, replicating Ruth's concern about women's patched embodiments in the texture of the sentences:

> Woman from the neck downward. Man from the neck downward and upward, as he chose. But for woman no choice. I think, Stephen. I think. I think I carry my womb in my forehead. And she did. And still did. And always would. Because some there are whose souls are more pregnant than their bodies. No, Socrates. And no one has ever thought of applying that to women, because women, Dora. From the neck down, breasts and thighs and pelvic bone. And for head an enlarged heart. A fatty noble heart swollen with appropriate emotions. (161)

Many of the sentences are unfinished, especially "I think," and "because women." This paragraph creates a textual microcosm of hybrid embodiment: broken bits fused together in unfinished sentences and ideas. To conceive of a new narrative, "to formulate with words," then, is a complicated task.[48] If conception is inherently an embodied activity, conceiving ideas and words requires a body with which to conceive. If that body is broken, as is the case of the female body as metaphorically represented by "The Victory of Samothrace," so, too, are its words.

At the same time, the text also presents a fluid form of dense paragraphs and the absence of breaks and commas in long, extended sentences. The fluidity develops through the use of repetition and the accumulation of these repetitive pieces collaged together. For example, in the following passage Moore repeats the phrase "she did not want" several times before bringing the idea and sentence to completion. In this passage, Ruth suddenly decides not to meet Uller alone in Naples for the weekend:

> She walked quickly away from the bench towards the street. She did not want. She just did not want. Suddenly, she had no desire. She walked out of the gardens and hailed a carrozzella. . . . She did not want. Again it had been mental, as sensation came over her. And even had

she missed passion in her life, which she had, now that it was offered her she did not want it. (201)

The repetition of "she did not want" accumulates over the course of the paragraph into her rejection of Uller's passion. Although Ruth supposedly suddenly arrived at this conclusion, the repetition of "she did not want" (201) gives the impression that Ruth must build up to her conclusion like a train building up steam, that she requires repeated attempts at conclusion. Moore, though, is able to arrive at the conclusion for Ruth; the sentence is able to be finished. Words, sentences, and thoughts can be finished if not by the conflicted characters then by the experimental author.

Underlying Moore's textual experimentation lays her concerns about and commitment to elements of male modernist form. Moore criticizes but does not abandon male modernist ideals, incorporating their use of mythology and tradition but not utilizing their form. Part of the difficulty with male modernist form, as I discussed earlier in Chapter 1 on *Mrs. Dalloway* and as explicated by Leslie Heywood, is that the literary modernism practiced and preached by such influential male modernists as Franz Kafka, Ezra Pound, T. S. Eliot, and William Carlos Williams, carries out what Heywood describes as "anorexic" behavior in its quest for differentiation and superiority and in its denial of fleshy and feminine elements:

> the individualism of the modernist artist . . . sets a paradigm for the anorexic, who wants beyond all things to be different, to stand out as superior. The claim to superiority and truth within modernism most often involves the renunciation of the feminine, just as the anorexic excises the outward sign of her femininity in her quest for distinction. (61–62)

For Heywood, this "quest for distinction" is accomplished through the "renunciation of the feminine," or "the male creative principle defined in opposition to feminine flesh, a creativity made possible by an expurgation of the flesh as female" (63).[49] She sees that "the negation of the body in literary modernism seems, quite explicitly, a negation of the feminine, a reinscription and privileging of masculine prerogative in a realm of human activity that in the nineteenth century had become progressively 'feminized', that of literary production" (63). In order to masculinize this feminized arena of literary production,

> the female body is consumed in order to give birth to the male body as text. This is specifically modernist because the privileged term here is not the *spirit* but the *male body* as *created through words*—the "hard body" of the imagist poem, the "extinction of personality," the insistence on purification, dissection, cutting to arrive at the work of art. (69)

Here, Heywood connects the ideas of the anorexic body to the production of the modernist text as specifically located in "the 'hard body' of the imagist poem" and "the insistence on purification, dissection, cutting to arrive at the work of art."[50] For Pound and Eliot, this was a movement toward neo-classicism as expressed by T. E. Hulme: "'a desire for austerity and bareness, a striving toward structure and away from the messiness and confusion of nature and natural things'" (Nicholls 179), implying within this statement a movement away from the "messiness" of the feminine.[70] Although the examples earlier reflect Heywood's emphasis on the modern poetry of Pound and Eliot, she consistently addresses these "anorexic" techniques and the repudiation of the feminine as found in "male modernism" in general and the "modernist artist" and "the male creative principle" in particular, placing the female modernist in a contradictory position of denying her own subjective position in order to conform to (another) patriarchal ideal.[51]

In *Spleen*, as Ruth tries to "be different" through her maternity, she enacts through her body "the individualism of the modernist artist" (61) that Heywood discusses. Maternity here then is used similarly and conversely to the anorexic textual behaviors Heywood describes. Similarly, through the character of Ruth, Moore uses the female body's maternity rather than the "male," "'hard body'" (69) of words, and tries to create something new, to be different. But, conversely, through the feminine rather than the masculine, Moore tries to create a new identity for women that is still feminine and a new identity for the text that is fleshy and full.

To continue to develop the associations between the gendered body and writing and their consequences for women modernists, I incorporate Vicki Kirby's theories on hysteria and language. Kirby corroborates Heywood in citing woman's subject position as absence. She states that "[a]s woman is ceaselessly refigured as an absence such that man can be rendered present in every account, the very repetition of this mode of reckoning is itself differentiating and transformational: it is never identical with itself" (79). From this, I add that this continual repetition of differentiating stems from the anxiety to separate from the feminine, as I will explain further later in my discussion on Julia Kristeva's theories of abjection. Kirby develops her theories by analyzing Charcot's studies of hysterical women at the Satpâtière hospital in Paris in the 1870s. Specifically, Kirby is concerned with the ways the hysteric would imitate bodily behaviors such as small pox and even "perform their symptomatology" (57) on demand. The hysterics' use of imitation: "is so entirely persuasive that the difference between reality and theater, disease and its imitation, is difficult to determine" (57). For Kirby, "[i]t is as if the hysteric is a mirror of her surroundings, incorporating the signs from an other's body as the reflection of her own" (57). Kirby's suggestions, laid alongside Heywood's, indicate the problems for the modernist woman writer who, in practicing male modernist form, subsequently takes on the position of the hysteric.⁵² Both Heywood and Kirby help to diagnose the problematic positioning of the modernist woman writer.

As I discussed in my introduction, Julia Kristeva's theories on "abjection" help to further investigate the characterizations of woman/the feminine and their consequences for female modernists. Specifically, Kristeva's theories help us to understand the use of a textual form of excess and the feminine figure in *Spleen*, and how these activities of the text respond to the male modernist's concern with excising the fleshy feminine from literary production. Based in psychoanalysis, Kristeva's theories delineate the metaphorical and symbolic suturing of the feminine to excess and, therefore, the apparent need to excise it or separate from it. The abject is one who or that which "disturbs identity, system, order" (*Powers* 4) when it, as excess, becomes a "stray" (*Powers* 8) by wandering outside of the symbolic system.⁵³ There is, therefore, a profound connection between ideas of the abject and the feminine, especially the maternal, as through childbirth a part of the self transgresses the boundary of the self to become the other. Through maternity, then, woman is both abject and abjecting. Because the abject is a *"confrontation with the feminine"* around which "societies code themselves in order to accompany as far as possible the speaking subject on that journey" away from it (58), it places women "in the position of passive objects" who "are none the less felt to be wily powers, 'baleful schemers' from whom rightful beneficiaries must protect themselves" (70). Thus, for Kristeva, "the feminine becomes synonymous with a radical evil that is to be suppressed" (70). The rejection of the feminine asserts the abject status of the feminine as physical excess, societal contamination, threat of death, and a straying from the body and society. In sum, the feminine is inherently abject in its excess and, as abject, is necessarily rejected.⁵⁴

Kristeva extends her theorizing of the abject into the arena of literature as she sees that "[i]t is the Word that discloses the abject" (*Powers* 23). Specifically, Kristeva argues that "[i]f language, like culture, sets up a separation and, starting with discrete elements, concatenates an order, it does so precisely by repressing maternal authority and the corporeal mapping that abuts against them" (*Powers* 72). Language, therefore, both enacts and attempts to control the abject, and when these acts are conducted by patriarchy, women are inherently excluded from a language which does not o/abjectify them.⁵⁵ Like the male modernist's technique described by Heywood, Kristeva's understanding of the abject reveals the role of language in erasing (or containing) the fleshy feminine abject and, thus, the difficulties for women modernists to find and use language to express issues of female subjectivity.⁵⁶

With Kristeva's ideas of how language contributes to the objectification and abjectification of the feminine in mind, we can better understand how Moore's use of textual experimentation attempts to reverse the exorcism of the feminine from the modernist text. Moore criticizes this male modernist or "anorexic" form through her criticism of Joan Agnew and the new modern woman whose boyish form of embodiment Ruth describes as "hard" and "fleshless." Ruth sees this new corporeation (creation of the body) as "monstrous" (230), and in that, I argue, reflects Moore's understanding of the fleshless modern text as also monstrous. Moore reveals her criticism of the male modernist form through such metaphorical analysis in the narrative, but also carries out her criticism by not deploying male modernist form in her fiction. When Moore tries to conceive or "formulate in words," she does not use a fleshless form of fiction equivalent to the imagist poem which, among other things, "attempt[s] to recover a stylistic purity" (Nicholls 170). *Spleen* is instead a loose, "fleshy" text with abundant words, images and unedited fragments and unfinished sentences. As the first paragraph of the novel demonstrates through the goats' udders, the female body, specifically in its maternity, is present, vivid and overflowing in the text. Yet, even in this passage (112), Moore flanks expressions of feminine excess with self-conscious moments of restraint and control. The slow-motion dilatory descriptions of the goats are abruptly interrupted as the woman "bring[s] her stick down sharply" (112) and by the "wild and shrill salute" (112) of the bells. Moore creates a stylistic tension between the abject feminine excess—the long sentences which accumute and repeat imagery of "udders," "undulating hindquarters," "undulating slowly," "heavy purple udders swinging pendulously" (112) and in which we see the excessive seeping of the inside into the outside—and these moments of intervening control. Through the additional layering of the images of the goats' udders with the imagery of the mother and child, Moore specifically connects this excessive imagery to the feminine and maternal, fusing excess form specifically to the excesses of the feminine's physical body. As if to underscore the presence of the abject and its subsequent erasure, in this maternal imagery the figures shrink: the goat becomes its feces, the woman becomes a child and the child becomes invisible. Moore produces a text that, instead of continuing this diffusion of the feminine, foregrounds the mother and child through the characters of Ruth and Richard and asserts the impossibility of excising the feminine excess, its maternity and, as in the first passage of the novel, its metaphorical excrement both in imagery and form.

Although Moore is critical of the kind of literary modernist form practiced and espoused by Eliot and Pound as an excising of the feminine form, she does incorporate their modernist ideals of tradition and myth into her text. Her use of references, specifically to Greek mythology, agrees with their emphasis on building a new tradition on the old.[57] Throughout the novel, she refers to the Forian women as human caryatids (116), Pomona (119), Artemis (119), and Ceres (121) and her son, Richard, as Bacchus (169) and Vesuvius (177), and compares women to Leda (282) and Greek statuary (207), and herself with Zeus (128). Through the use of Ancient Greek mythology and culture as a site of reference and as valorized as a kind of true or higher civilization, Moore continues the male modernist support of tradition in their attempts to "correct the apparently amnesiac tendencies of modernity by reconnecting it to a valued cultural tradition" and to build a "strong and reverent sense of literary tradition" (Nicholls 167).[58] Although women modernists used myth as well, the male modernists use of myth was specifically situated in "a renovated culture [which] often carried a paternal sanction, with resulting forms of 'filial' emulation actually providing the condition of an authentic modernism" (Nicholls 167). Moore, then, appears to operate within the sanctions of the male modernist tradition as seen in her reliance upon mythical narratives and allusion, again creating a contradictory position in which her form and content engage in perpetual reversals.

In addition, Moore self-consciously intersperses the text with literary references to male authors such as Donne (118), Blake (147, 185), Browning (215), and Shakespeare (160). For instance, as she recounts her silent life on Foria of being her own "sole companion," Ruth states, "I am, she quoted Donne, the self-consumer of my woes" (118), highlighting the use of the reference and her building upon it.[59] These outside texts are brought in to the novel and not criticized but seen as necessary. Experimental modernism, according to Moore's experiments here, should not abandon the body of literature, including the works of male authors that has gone before, but use, modify, and build on it just as Ruth has used her body to create something new. The experiments of the text, though, do not produce the monstrous hybrids as seen in the corporeal manifestations of Richard and Joan. Instead, by fusing the fleshy, female form of textual experimentation to the traditions of male modernist ideals, Moore creates a hybridized text that works to embody female subjectivity as both body and mind, both flesh and intellect. If, as Valentine Cunningham cites from George Eliot, "change the form . . . and everything changes" (150–51) then Moore successfully changes the possibilities for female subjectivity through changing the form of the text.

## CONCLUDING CONSEQUENCES FOR THE BODY AND THE TEXT

Moore reveals several dangers of hybridity, complicating the proposal of a male mind/female body hybrid with the "monstrous" (230) creations of Richard, Joan, and the continuation of Ruth's colonialist position on the Forians. Moore also criticizes the dangers of the modernist project, specifically of Pound's decree to "make it new." Newness, Moore asserts, possibly creates as many problems as possibilities. Specifically, Moore (ex)poses Ruth's contradictory position in Foria as one of both complicity with the language of colonization and, therefore, with patriarchal imperialism, and of the primitive feminine on which the impulse of patriarchal imperialism acts. Ruth's criticism of the Forians, as well as of Joan, reveals her blindness to her own subjective position which so longs to access the male mind that it also takes on the male role of subjugation, not specifically of women but of the inherently feminine Other of the primitive or "savage" Forians. Moore, too, may be implicated in this blindness, although her inclusion of characters and ideologies such as those of Ruth's father make her less culpable. It is not Ruth, then, that acts out the successful male/female hybrid in her reproduction of Richard or in her conceiving of cultural change.

Instead, Moore as author re-conceives of female embodiment and identity through the experimental modernist text. At the beginning of the novel, Ruth comments on the prescribed litany of life and specifically on how this litany limits the lives of women:

> And you know before hand every possibility of its life, and like a litany the answer is unalterable and as assured. Birth. Adolescence. Marriage. Birth Old Age. Death.
>
> She paused as though to make sure that it was she who had formed the words: then in the silence she repeated them. Birth Adolescence. Marriage. Birth. Old Age. Death. That then was their wonderful thing! (126)

This litany is repeated at various moments in the novel (134) and fused with other "litanies" that Ruth remembers and repeats such as: "Wash child, wash corpse" (161, 163). Moore, too, does not want to simply repeat what has gone before, does not want to tell the same story. Instead, Moore, too, wants to create something new with these pieces of body, land, nation, and text. In re-conceiving the text, Moore seeks to reshape this litany—"Birth. Adolescence. Marriage. Birth Old Age. Death" (126)—that, especially for women, results in the repetition of women's corporeal and cultural entrapments such as the conscriptions to maternity, landscape and empire. Or, as Kathleen Kirby argues, "[b]y softening the fixity of the discursive landscape, they attempt to ventriloquize change in the social realm" (120). Despite the failed attempts at hybridity in the novel—Richard, Joan, Ruth's colonialist position—Moore's textual experimentation and hybridity continue to assert the possibility for "change in the social realm" as signaled by her changes in "the discursive landscape," of the body, and in the text.

# 4 Flight of the Feminine and Textual Orientation in Olive Moore's *Fugue*[1]

In *Spleen*, Olive Moore's textual experimentation and hybridity offer the possibility for "change in the social realm" for women through changes in "the discursive landscape" of the body and of the text. In *Fugue*, Moore abandons the possibility of changing feminine corporeal inscriptions of body, land, and nation, and, with them, nearly abandons a new conception of female subjectivity at all. Instead of creating new possibilities for women, she reiterates the sites of entrapment for the feminine as delineated in the previous chapters on *Mrs. Dalloway*, *The Waves*, and *Spleen*. Although much of the female character's physical circumstances have not changed from *Spleen* to *Fugue*—another young woman struggling with her maternity—the attitude towards her has: Lavinia is portrayed by Moore as silly, ignorant, and desperate. As if in response, *Fugue* is concerned with issues of escape, and escape attempts litter the text of *Fugue*: characters attempt to escape from relationships, from England, from the feminine abject, and, for the novel's protagonist, Lavinia, from pre-inscribed female embodiments such as both mother and sexualized object. These escapes underscore Moore's figurative attempts to escape patriarchal linearity and conclusion through modernist experimentations of narrative and form.[2] Thus, Moore continues to attempt change in the "discursive landscape" in *Fugue* despite narrative's apparent ineffectiveness in the "social realm" and the inability to escape the various female embodiments inscribed within society as seen in *Spleen*.

Olive Moore's third novel, *Fugue* (1932), tells the twin stories of Lavinia Reade and her former lover, Harrion. The novel begins with an attempted escape—from the Wynstub Inn in the Alsace—as Harrion repeatedly tries to flee the newly pregnant Lavinia. The narrative shifts between the Alsace present and the London past, and between the stories of Lavinia, Harrion, and their tumultuous love affair, significantly placing the bulk of the novel in the confused national state of the Alsace. After enduring a series of mostly abusive lovers (one of the affairs resulted in an illegitimate child being sent to a farm in Cornwall) Lavinia meets Harrion at a party.[3] Harrion hires Lavinia to work for him at a weekly book review only to dismiss her once they begin their affair. Ultimately,

Harrion leaves the Alsace alone, traveling to Paris where he daily observes the smoke and, occasionally, the burning bodies of the crematorium. Lavinia, accepting the end of her relationship with Harrion, transfers her affections to another expatriate and writer, Sebastian. The novel stops its twin narratives of Lavinia and Harrion abruptly and doubly, leaving Harrion watching the rising smoke and Lavinia and Sebastian in a moment of postcoital and Alsatian pastoral bliss.

Although the narrative of *Fugue* revisits territory similar to that traversed in *Spleen*—maternity and sexuality, female embodiment and subjectivity, connection with and expatriation from England, textual experimentation of disintegration and in-conclusion—*Fugue*'s narrative abandons Lavinia, landscape, and nation to the pre-inscribed female embodiments that *Spleen* attempts to discredit and discard. The female body as sexual, reproductive, and abject, the landscape as feminine and with similar reproductive expectations, England as both pure and despicable—all are painted in a wash of the feminine abject, thus justifying the characters' need to escape them. Just as the entrapments of Lavinia's sexuality and maternity reveal her inability to extricate herself from abusive relationships and protect herself from subsequent pregnancies; almost all possibilities for escape from the entrapments of female embodiment reveal essentialized notions of the feminine as abject in her body and maternity. The essentialized feminine continues from the physical body into feminized notions of the land and nation as already observed in *Mrs. Dalloway, The Waves,* and *Spleen. Fugue*'s position on female embodiment and subjectivity, therefore, is roughly situated between Moore's self-aware criticism of the status of the modern woman and her portrayal of that woman as abandoned within her split subjectivity as both the abject feminine and as the modern woman trying to both escape and rewrite the inscription of the feminine.

The split subjectivities of the characters in the novel, and the subsequent split of the narrative as it follows Lavinia and Harrion separately, are heralded in the title of the novel, *Fugue*. In fact, the layered definition of "fugue" points to the multiple mechanisms at work in the text, and signals, too, Moore's play with formal technique. "Fugue," meaning "to flee" or "flight," denotes both a musical form and a psychological condition.[4] I argue that, through her experimentations with narrative and form, Moore explores all these meanings in her text, thus illustrating the necessary and multiple flights of the modern, and especially female, subject.

In its utilization of the first definition of "fugue," *Fugue* explores the issues of psychological dissociation through its characters and narrative construction. As a psychological condition, "fugue" refers to a mental state of dissociation or "dissociative amnesia plus travel" which "is accompanied by either confusion about personal identity or the assumption of a new identity, either partial or complete."[5] Here, fugue's root meaning "to flee" manifests itself as the subject dissociating from a geographical location in order to escape a psychological condition.

In Moore's *Fugue*, Harrion and Lavinia both "travel" to the Alsace (and Paris for Harrion) and experience "confusion about personal identity."[6] For Harrion, this dissociation is much more complete and profound.[7] In both cases, the fugue state of the characters contributes to their sense of being lost through their physical and psychical disorientation. Therefore, I will argue that the narrative of *Fugue* enacts the psychological definition of "fugue" as it portrays the various flights of the characters and of the text through the dissociation between mind and body of both Harrion and Lavinia, the division between the mother and the modern woman, the geographical split between London and the Alsace, the inter/national splitting of countries and national consciousness between the wars, and the opposing drives of the narrative and the form.

Utilizing the second definition, *Fugue* explores the musical form of "fugue" through its contrapuntal narrative techniques. Here, "fugue" refers to a composition whose musical "flight" is portrayed "when a succession of notes in one part is taken over in another part, with due regard for the mode, and especially for the position of whole- and half-tone steps" (80).[8] The fugue uses imitative counterpoint where the musical theme is developed through reversal, inversion, augmentation, or diminution. More than a round, a fugue expands or plays with the theme in each voice, typically returning to a restatement of the theme. In a "double fugue," two subjects simultaneously develop throughout the piece either concurrently or consecutively, again elaborating each subject until the conclusion. In other words, "simple fugues are based on a single theme; multiple fugues are as a rule summarily called double fugues" (Mann 157).

In borrowing the structure of the musical fugue for its narrative(s), *Fugue* presents the two subjects of Lavinia and Harrion as they overlap and move in opposite directions throughout the novel, eventually developing beyond a point–counterpoint representation. For example, Harrion is not simply the counterpoint or inversion of Lavinia. Instead, his narrative strives to develop and move independently from Lavinia's, often working through counterpoint, but ultimately ending up in a very different place. *Fugue*, then, works as a double fugue which develops two subjects simultaneously, keeping them separate throughout. Significantly, though, the two themes are never reconciled by returning to a unified restatement of the theme. The form of *Fugue*, then, with its doubled narratives that overlap throughout the novel, reworks modernist tropes and techniques, utilizes fugue forms to its own, incomplete, ends, and, as I will show, exposes the psychological dissociation of the modern woman's split subjectivities.

In sum, while the narrative of *Fugue*, develops a psychological fugueing or splitting of dissociation in the separation of mind and body by the characters, in the separation of geographical bodies, and in the separation of national ideologies, the form of *Fugue,* through its dissolving contrapuntal techniques, reverses the narrative's portrayal of the fugue states of the modern woman by presenting new possibilities for female subjectivity.

*Flight of the Feminine and Textual Orientation* 113

Through its textual experimentation and resistance to conclusion, the form of *Fugue* provides a textual orientation to the schizophrenic splits of modern female subjectivity, the text operating as the place in which the feminine can be re- or ungrounded and also find articulation and presence. These formal experimentations of *Fugue* open the way to new kinds of proceedings (rather than conclusions) for the modern woman in particular. In the first section of this chapter, I delineate the narrative's portrayal of the psychological dissociation inherent in the position of the feminine as seen in the character of Lavinia, the land, and the nation. In the second section, I continue by analyzing the reversals of this portrayal accomplished through the formal experimentations of the text.

## THE FLIGHTY FEMININE: FLEEING THE FEMININE ABJECT AND THE NARRATIVE OF DISSOCIATION

> How then regret mistakes, when one could but repeat and repeat them?
>
> Lavinia Reade, *Fugue* (315)

Lavinia's musings earlier indicate both Moore's use of the fugue form, in its emphasis on repetition, and reveal Moore's disdainful attitude toward her protagonist: even when Lavinia recognizes her "mistakes," she dismisses them as unavoidable and circuitous. Through Moore's characterization of Lavinia, Lavinia's relationship to her body, and Lavinia's relationship to Harrion, the dissociations of the characters and the text are inherently connected to the feminine and to the female body. In *Fugue*, the feminine becomes uncontainable and contaminating in its representations as body, land, and nation. In this characterization of the feminine, Moore develops the idea of the feminine as abject, fleshy corporeality that constantly threatens to cross its borders and contaminate the masculine and its world as both the female characters who literally embody the feminine, and the male characters, who interact with them, display their repulsion and need to flee the feminine abject.[9] The abject, then, precipitates the flights the characters take in their attempts to escape the feminine and, ultimately, the text's splits as well.

### The Feminine Flesh: The Body is too Much with Us

The character of Lavinia, particularly the portrayal of Lavinia's body, reveals how Moore's concerns with the feminine abject and the subsequent need to flee the feminine begin with feminine corporeality. In considering the portrayal of the feminine abject in *Fugue*, I first look at how Lavinia's body is described as abject, second, how it contributes to the characters' desire for flight, and, third, how these portrayals of the feminine abject contribute to the psychological dissociations of the modern female subject. For example, while Harrion can act out his desire to flee the feminine abject through his flight to the Alsace and later Paris, the problem for Lavinia, and women in general, is that she cannot flee herself. Thus, the attempt to separate from the abject creates the split subjectivity of the modern female subject: she acknowledges her own abject status but is unable to remove herself from its lodgment in her corporeality.

In Lavinia, the feminine body is continuously re-inscribed as abject in its status as a sexual object and the subsequent merging with the feminine that sex requires. Moore introduces Lavinia as vibrant and bold, a "tall undaunted creature" (240) that lights "the darkened room like a torch: like a long static flame burning from the floor" (240), connoting sex, life and danger:

> One felt visibly her abundant life and the bold rhythm of her blood. In her movements, in her words, in that long independent neck, in her silence, one felt the bold rhythm of her heart-beats. . . . For on a word, on a silence, she could seem all at once immeasurably old and versed in sorrow, and seeming to have wept through many lives as deeply as she laughed through this one. But unaware of it herself she gave an instant impression of courage, even of foolhardiness; and the bold rhythm of her blood was infectious. (249–50)

The repetition of "blood" and the description of that blood as "infectious" associates Lavinia with the abject as physically expelling as well as contagious and threatening. This threat stems directly from Lavinia's femaleness, the blood of the passage connoting menses as well as her pulse and courage. Her abject status is also revealed through her sexuality when Lavinia tells Harrion about her son: "with it all she was gay and untouched as a virgin, with a proudly set head and the strong bold rhythm of her heart-beats, which now seemed to him so urgent in their invitation" (250–51). Lavinia's body contradictorily signals sexual desire through its "virgin" like qualities which are also accompanied by the "strong bold rhythm of her heart-beats" and blood. Her powerful physical presence re-inscribes her as sexual in its passion and boldness. The repetition of the "bold rhythm of her heart-beats" (249), previously stated as "blood," affiliates her body's machinations with her abject status, making it an unavoidable essential quality of her biology and her psychology.

The feminine abject, therefore, causes rifts in Lavinia's subjectivity as seen in her contradictory characterizations—she is both "bold" and "silent," full of both "sorrow" and "laughter." Later in the Alsace, Harrion says of her: "[b]y [the stars'] light her face took on a luminous unreal surface-quality of stone" (239).[10] Thus, Lavinia embodies the split subjectivity of the modern woman; she is both "independent" and reliant on her relationships with men. She is both a "torch" and "flame" and having the "unreal surface-quality of stone." Lavinia's evident lack of self-awareness here points to another split: her body acts as an agent separate from her mind.

In addition, Lavinia's mind acts on its own in contradiction to her body, her abject status triggering her psychological need to split from her body. When Harrion first meets Lavinia, it is her un-*self*-conscious separation from her body that attracts him: "Perhaps he liked the wide and eager smile with which she had greeted him; the scarlet frock: a frock a child would choose for best. . . . And not once did she pose for him: neither aware of her legs, nor her nose, nor her hair, nor her wants" (249). Here, Lavinia cannot escape the "wide and eager" performance of her body and what her body does all by itself: how it marks her as sexual and as female although she is not "aware" of it.[11] Her female embodiment not only summons sexual desire, but also inherently grants it, splitting her mind from her body's activity. At this point in the novel she is not consciously fleeing from her abject feminine status, but her mind is already displaying signs of its dissociation from her body through her lack of awareness to her body's performance.

Her mind's awareness of the sexual machinations of her body does not release Lavinia from her abject corporeality; she is still/always trapped within the feminine. Her female body's sexuality and object position operate independently or uncontrollably in the following passage, as Lavinia watches Harrion sneak away from the Wynstub one night at the start of the novel:

> No woman can walk away so completely dead to all things around her. Her hips flutter; her legs look ridiculous and inconclusive; the whole of her is aware of being watched, and irritated by this inescapable awareness of others. Women were scattered in body and scattered in mind; somatic; ever-alert. But the very physical compactness of a man stressed his isolation. So that by chance, looking at a given moment from a window, one surprised this male aura of unapproachableness and indifference. (257–58)

At this point in the chronology of the novel, after Lavinia has pursued Harrion to the Alsace, Lavinia, or "the whole of her," is described in its "inescapable awareness," a shift from the previous passage in which her body seemed to act outside of the awareness of her mind. According to this passage, women are contradictorily both contained and scattered in their female embodiments and intelligence. In *Fugue*, both men and women's specific, gendered embodiments dictate their psychic landscape, their subjectivities determined by their embodiments: women are "scattered in body and scattered in mind" (257), and men are physically compact and isolated, unapproachable and indifferent. Whereas women's bodies are sexualized, men's bodies are "indifferent" (258).

This split between male and female embodiments and identity in *Fugue* reveals the gender differentiation in modernity in general and thus reveals how the novel portrays the modern condition. Rita Felski argues that:

> modernity has become identified with large-scale processes of rationalization, alienation and differentiation that are seen as distinctively

masculine. By contrast, femininity is equated with either a primitive condition of underdevelopment or an edenic state of nonalienated plenitiude. (199)

Felski identifies two possibilities for femininity: as "primitive" or "edenic," and as abject as both "underdevelopment" or absence of civilization and "plenitude" or excess.[12] Significantly, in Felski's analysis, both possibilities leave the feminine outside of the workings of modernity that Felski describes, portraying the feminine as abjected from the developments of society as a whole and masculinity/patriarchy in particular.

The delineation of the feminine as abject and as abjected from masculinity plays out in Harrion and Lavinia's sexual relationship, leading eventually to their relational and psychological dissociation. With Harrion, Lavinia's body is not only sexualized; it is sexed upon by Harrion, revealing not only her status as abject (sex) object but also as sex toy as well:

> It was rather awful the way he came into the room as though expecting her to be ready for him. And hardly an endearment. Afterwards she would lie in that obscene-looking scarlet bed of hers looking at the moon and stars on the absurd blue ceiling, and try not to understand how very different it all was. For it was horrible the way he held her down and consumed her. It was no longer a mutual act, but a thing dark and fearful which he performed despite himself. She thought at first it was because he was a man who had been long denied. But that phase was past and it continued like a war waged against a secret enemy. It seemed a thing he did in fear and secrecy. Some dark forbidden thing, a thing avid, sinful, that he fought to shut out as he held her down, impaled; impaled on the drawn sword between man and woman; enmity eternal. Yet he seemed scarcely conscious of her. He drained her in this dark and secret way. And the result left her lost and impaled, so that she sat and waited for his return; a thing she had never done and could not have conceived herself ever doing. (251–52)

Harrion's dissociation in this passage is clear as sex is something he "perform[s] despite himself . . . that he fought to shut out as he held her down . . . scarcely conscious of her" (251–52). Harrion separates himself from the acts of his body in what is described as an ongoing dissociation observed by Lavinia. Lavinia's dissociation, though, begins to be described in this passage as she is left "lost and impaled" (252). More important, she "waited for his return; a thing she had never done and could not have conceived herself ever doing" (252), indicating her transition from independence to reliance and her dissociation as both "lost" and acting in a way she "could not have conceived." The disassociation from her body signals her entrance into a fugue state through her emphasis on being "lost" and prefaces her own flight to the Alsace and, eventually, into her relationship with Sebastian.

These passages expose further splits in Lavinia's psyche when juxtaposed with Lavinia's own comments about her sexual activity. In conversation with her friend, Evelyn, following Harrion's departure, she responds to Evelyn's accusation about her sexual proclivity:

> Wide and hospitable legs, said Miss [Lavinia] Reade, no whit abashed, are the sign of a god-like and of a generous nature. Beware of all who keep their legs in any other way. Legs held together denote fear and servility. It is the symbol of the waiter, the servant, the Ambassador. Whereas legs apart and firmly planted are a proof of strength and independence. By their sign you may recognize the peasant, the Viking, the grande amoureuse. (280)

This passage paints Lavinia as strong within her positioning on her body and her choices with it in her description of [her] "wide and hospitable legs" as "a proof of strength and independence." Specifically, in it Lavinia is defiant of positions of servitude. Yet these comments split from Lavinia's previous actions as prey to Harrion's predatory sex and from her future actions as she then pursues Harrion to the Alsace. These splits of sexual subjectivity as described above and sexual servitude as seen in Lavinia's relationships to Harrion and Sebastian reaffirm Lavinia's dissociative and "fugue" status.

The effects of dissociation on Lavinia's psyche emerge as despite her conceptions of herself, and despite her description of her sex with Harrion as "awful," "horrible," "dark and fearful" (280), she continues to wait for him. She states that

> [l]ike a fool, like a whore she ached and waited and allowed herself to be ploughed beyond her strength. He burnt her up and she stood it no better than Semelle stood it. And never once had he told her he needed her. Nothing for her. Only this rapt consuming fire of his which slowly and relentlessly extinguished hers. (252)[13]

Lavinia admits that she is a "fool" and that she "allowed herself" to be used by Harrion with "nothing for her."[14] As Lavinia shows that she is now aware of her split subjectivity, half performing with/for Harrion and half recoiling and analyzing her performance, she also shows that she is aware of her own abject status. As abject, the feminine body must be consumed and eliminated (like fire consumes the abject corpse) and/or contained like the now purified but still abject ashes. Confronting her own abject status, therefore, causes Lavinia's dissociation. Moving to the Alsace is then just an extension of or geographical expression of her psychological fugue state.[15]

Lavinia's dissociation from her body includes dissociation from her sex as well, revealing her deeper need to separate from the feminine not just the feminine body:

> Were I a man, Lavinia Reade was thinking, I would love only men. I would not love women with their vacant chatter and soft ornamental bodies. I would not be charmed by womanly tempers when the coveted hat looked cheap and foolish. Nor treat her as a goddess for bearing me a child or two. To be only a woman is not worth very much; and the man who does not know it is a fool and deserves what he gets. (273)

In this passage, Lavinia dissociates herself from women, imagining a male world where women are absent or erased, and situating women as bodies with "vacant" minds as represented by their "chatter," and their interests being in fashion and maternity. Lavinia acknowledges woman's abject status—she is "only a woman" who is "not worth very much."[16]

Lavinia's split subjectivity mirrors that of women as a whole: split between the maternal and the modern woman, the maternal animalizing women and the modern mechanizing women. Lavinia first introduces the connection between human and bovine maternity when she sees a cow in a field: "All this tearing up of grass by these poor patient beasts on whose broad backs the modern woman had shifted her intimate maternal duty" (282), indicating through the use of "intimate" and "duty" that she does not approve of this shift. Yet, in her conversation with Evelyn, two more disturbing and contradictory passages follow. First, Lavinia claims herself as "old-fashioned" and "right":

> Yet I am right, said Miss Reade slowly. And you are wrong. I am old-fashioned. I admit it. I need men. And I need children. I am the human cow. But you are the modern woman. You dislike children. You do not really care for men. Where the fear of Aunt Elizabeth has led you, instinct has led me. Yet one should function correctly, said Lavinia Read with finality. So I am right. (282)[17]

Here Lavinia shifts to a position which places her firmly bound to the services of patriarchy, maternity and within her position as abject. The "modern woman," it seems does not like children or men at all, whereas Lavinia, as the "old-fashioned" woman, embraces them both and submits willingly to her position as another "patient beast" with a "broad back" (282). Moore does not recuperate maternity for the modern female subject; it is still and again that which binds the body and soul of woman to patriarchy.

Moore continues her demonstration of the modern woman's split condition via sex and sexuality as the conversation between Lavinia and Evelyn continues:

> Evelyn would have none of it. She was coldly derisive. She denied that the act of love was for anything as dull and limited as the mere reproduction of self. She called children the compensation of the unloved. That the act of love should be for anything but pleasure (she said) was both immoral and unthinkable. Women who desire only to be mothers should be mechanically fertilized. Let them be placed apart and tended and graded like cattle. Let them admit their cow-like vocation. Let them be contented by the yearly child. Let them leave the passionate act to the passionate. (283)

So, Evelyn, despite her disliking of men, takes sex only as pleasure, leaving maternity to those who should be "mechanically fertilized," "placed apart and tended and graded like cattle" in their "cow-like vocation."[18] Maternity, she argues, is not for the "passionate." In her dismissal of maternity, Evelyn separates herself from one aspect of the feminine's abjection but at the risk of creating a modern woman who is a replication of the masculine.[19] Through these conversations of Lavinia and Evelyn, Moore voices the position of the modern woman as a place of split subjectivity and psychological dissociation.

In addition, through Lavinia's conversations with Sebastian as well as Evelyn, Lavinia scorns the modern woman's "dissatisfaction" that "led nowhere. Women should be pleasant peaceful creatures, generous in youth and wise in age. What more could one ask of them? What more could they ask? Men might be restless, because men could achieve" (309). Later, Sebastian rearticulates Lavinia's opinion when he states that "[t]he modern woman with her militant sterility could quite easily run the world on her own" (307), denying the modern woman the feminine but also the body and the human. Moore, through these conversations between Lavinia and Evelyn and Sebastian, splits woman's body and sex into two distinct and disturbing categories: the "human cow" of Lavinia and the "militant sterility" of Evelyn. As the character of Evelyn is only briefly encountered in the novel and then disappears, and as the novel focuses primarily on Lavinia, Moore appears to privilege the experience of the "human cow" of Lavinia despite her inherent critique of Lavinia throughout the text.

Indeed, Lavinia demonstrates her desire to escape the split subjectivity of the modern woman by ultimately denying her identification with the modern woman. At the end of the novel, as Lavinia considers staying in the Alsace, she comments,

> How pleasant, here among these people. Why could one not live here always? This village was big enough. This was a world. A woman's world: world without end. Why go back? To what? To words? To the hermaphroditism of modern woman in a modern world?.... Must she, too, capitulate? Of all ugly decaying things, a woman dissatisfied. How wearying it was, that modern indecency: the frustrated woman. (309)

Moore presents "the frustrated woman" through both Lavinia and Evelyn, indicating here that Lavinia, too, was part modern woman. The frustration of the modern woman, then, is that the only options for her are mammalia or machinalia. Through them, Moore articulates the split and also the "dissatisf[action]" of these choices as well as of the lives these choices play out.

The only example of alternative female subjectivity offered in *Fugue* is the monstrous fish, the ceratoid. In a long-winded, one-sided dialogue, Sebastian states,

> Only the indispensable is needed and created. That is Nature's demand and supply. In time all that would be required of man was the male semen.
>
> As a living example of how well this worked there were the Ceratiods, most grotesque and efficient of all living creatures, the oceanic angler-fishes, who are all female, the male being dwarfed and parasitic on the females. . . . And how much more pleasant a world with women no longer dissatisfied and masters of the situation, and the harassed male no longer compelled to work for them. (309)

In this configuration, when women are "masters of the situation" (309), it seems, they are "grotesque and efficient" (309), conjuring again the images of the modern machine-like woman. Women's dissatisfaction would be erased and men would no longer be "harassed" and "compelled to work for them" (309). But, this configuration creates another kind of monstrous, abject feminine, reversing the power structure and making matriarchy as monstrous as the current patriarchy. In this, Moore poses a critique of patriarchy through a reversed reflection of a potential matriarchy. Lavinia's response to Sebastian's story is disengagement:

> All of which had been less real than the sight of a field of cabbages so exultantly blue that it had seemed to reflect the sky.
> —Not merely blue blood, had said Lavinia Reade ironically, but the authentic purple. (309)

Lavinia dissociates herself from the conversation, significantly dissociating herself, too, from the dialogue about the monstrous possibilities for women. Lavinia focuses instead on nature as if in its authenticity, it could potentially hold more possibility for women.

## THE FEMININE GROUNDED: THE GEOGRAPHICAL FUGUE AND FURTHER SPLITS OF THE FEMININE

The need to escape the abject feminine not only creates the dissociative fugue state in the modern female subject; it also manifests in geographical wandering or fugue-ing. In this geographical fugue, England is the space that is despised and fled; the Alsace is the shifting, hybridized space to which expatriates wander. The Alsace, having shifted nationalities and lines on the map between France and Germany (and often been at the mercy of either or both), is now, at the time of the novel, French. The Alsace of *Fugue* is made up of Germans, French, and English. It is the place where the dissociation of Harrion and Lavinia and of the expatriates and England fully manifests itself. As I will show, both spaces, even the Alsace on the border of the "fatherland," are also gendered feminine so that, again, the feminine is also split into two (or more) voices.[20] Lavinia, then, may wander from England but she cannot escape the feminine incarnations of her own embodiment and of the landscape through which she travels: she unavoidably associates herself in one way or another with the abject feminine.

The English landscape emerges as feminine first in its association with "hysteria" (283), a condition historically, linguistically, and stereotypically associated with the feminine.[21] Following her discussion with Evelyn regarding "the human cow" (282), and after a hard break in the text, Moore writes: "But soon the earth grew warm, serious, productive. The hysteria of Spring was past" (283). Thus, the English landscape also emerges as feminine in its sexuality. Harrion, again a mouthpiece for a stereotypical patriarchal and misogynistic voice, upon watching a bee in the garden, states, "a large dark bee assaults a dandelion that bends under its weight, grips with amorous knees, opens petals, exposes secret places, and releases it, swaying; flies to the next, deflowers them all, a very Mahomet among the virgins" (295). The "dandelion," assaulted by a "dark bee," also called "Mahomet," demarcates the landscape as feminine and sexualized and links it to the trope of pure English maidens who must be protected from foreign invasion.[22] Later, Harrion even blames the landscape for flirting with him: "As though to distract him a stream crossing the field with the small rustle of a silk petticoat quickened its step" (296). In Harrion's examples, the land's virginal qualities only make way for the deflowering of the "Mahomet" (295), the feminized land shown to be sexual and deviant, "as if to distract him" (296). When Harrion takes Lavinia to Kew Gardens, Lavinia describes the landscape with the same language that Harrion used earlier to describe her vibrancy:

> Willows hung in thin green ropes above the varnished lake. Small yellow ducks threw in their heads and became crocuses. A blackbird put forward his most shining notes. She felt again the beating of the grassy pulse. The beautiful sane green enveloped her. (255)

The English landscape is not only feminine, then, it is Lavinia; it's beating pulse echoing her pulsing blood (249–50 and 268). For Lavinia, though, instead of hysterical, the land is a "sane green" which "envelope[s] her." She becomes subsumed into the land, unidentifiably different. Lavinia and the land, then, are both feminized and both situated as abject in their feminine status as affiliated with blood and as operating on the borders of hysteria.

As the English pastoral landscape is gendered feminine, it represents the "prim" English woman. As Lavinia comments about the dreary English spring, she articulates one version of the feminine English countryside:

> Yet this, too, was May: this discreet reflection of an ardent act; this onlooker at Nature's festival. The sky was long low-lying cloud. The earth cold and desolate. There was a something inhibited and unwilling about it all. Only the birds, twittering like mice in the heavenly wainscoting. And they seemed foreigners. . . . Could it be that in England there must be no display of vitality even on the land and sky? Life's expression must not be extravagant and even Nature's voice may not be raised? All is superior and self-conscious. All things merge. The sun-less tradition of the earth is one with its inhabitants. The people are subdued and the fields are subdued. . . . And over both blows the cold breath of primness and gentility and fear; fear of nakedness, of exuberance, of life. (281)

Unlike Harrion's Mahommadean description of spring above, England is here described in terms of the asexualized feminine: "cold and desolate," "inhibited and unwilling," without "vitality," "superior and self-conscious," "sun-less" and "subdued" in its "primness and gentility" (281). In short, to Lavinia, English spring is a cold, sexless English woman in contrast to the "nakedness" and "exuberance" of "life" (281) that Lavinia and Moore find in Italy and the Alsace.[23]

Furthermore, the English landscape and its climate are associated with English prudery as well as (re)production. First, Lavinia declares that "[e]ven Nature, in England, wears a fig-leaf" (280), asserting England's modesty. She then continues:

> A fig-leaf? Plus-fours! Not Ceres. Not the many-breasted Diana. No goat-footed god. But a well-washed, inhibited, and plus-foured Colonel plodding to the nearest golf-course. And the plus-foured Colonel takes no heed of sodden skies and flowerless hedgerows. He says: this, damme Sir, is England. This is not earth. This is land by the half-acre.
>
> One felt it was. One felt, as one stared, that its sense of decency was being affronted. That being entirely sober, it knew its nakedness and was ashamed. It was eager to be clothed; to be cut in little lots and covered in an excrement of brick; to offer itself up in semi-houses for semi-people. The rounded shoulders of the hills were not for burdens of terraced vine, stiffened maize, or heavy corn. They were for villas back to back, a latched gate, a strip of green, a blue lupin or two. (280–81)

Moore criticizes the "inhibited," "decen[t]," "sober," "ashamed," "rounded" (280–81) landscape of England in its lack of representations of classical Greek and Roman imagery, of gods, goddesses, vines and corn. In England, the land is the product itself as the land participates in a different kind of reproduction of "semi-houses" and "villas back to back" (281), rather than the bounty of the European landscapes. The feminine, in England, has become suburban, reproducing the abject "excrement" (281) rather than life-giving produce as witnessed in the Alsace. The English landscape, then, is not only characterized as abject, but worthy of the characters' desire to flee from it and of their subsequent dissociation from it.

In contrast, the Alsace is feminized in its peasant purity, its maternal (re)productivity and its bounty. Lavinia describes the Alsatians as: "[a] coolness of soul flowed from them effortlessly; a certain serenity of brow. For they did not deal with men but with the earth, which is less treacherous" (272). As cited earlier, Lavinia also sees that the Alsace and the Alsatians make a perfect place for her to stay and raise her child:

> How pleasant, here among these people. Why could one not live here always? This village was big enough. This was a world. A woman's world: world without end. Why go back? To what? To words? To the hermaphroditism of modern woman in a modern world?.... Must she, too, capitulate? Of all ugly decaying things, a woman dissatisfied. How wearying it was, that modern indecency: the frustrated woman. (309)

England, then, is a place of hermaphroditism, of modern monstrosity, as unnatural as its excrement of housing developments, the home of the "modern indecency," the "ugly" and "decaying" "frustrated woman." The Alsace, like the Foria of *Spleen*, is proposed as the feminine ideal, productive, rural and peasant community, yet even these glimmerings of Romantic idealism are confounded by the association of the Alsace with the feminine abject.

Lavinia herself articulates the land's feminine, abject status. When an Alsatian woman claims that "a good year for nuts means that many women are pregnant!" Lavinia replies, "[t]hat, too, was a lovely eternal thing, linking their women so warmly, so unquestioningly, with the earth, sharing the effortless burden of trees and fields" (309). Nature and women are so closely linked that their (re)production rates echo and influence each other. Lavinia asserts the "unquestioning" (309) feminizing of the land, and in its maternity, highlights its status as doubly abject, asserting, too, the novel's emphasis on feminine reproduction as already evidenced in Lavinia herself. As the Alsatian pastoral represents maternity and (re)production, it becomes clear that Lavinia has not escaped from the abject feminine but has associated herself with another (for her, more exalted and enjoyable) version of it.

The characterization of the landscape as feminine is also supported by the form of the novel which utilizes the imagery of the landscape as another voice in its fugue on the feminine. The descriptions of the landscape repeat throughout the novel, a form of repetition which echoes a musical fugue, but one which is stuck in its pattern and cycle and unable to conclude, replicating, too, Lavinia's statement that she is destined to "repeat and repeat" her mistakes (315). Once Harrion has left Lavinia in the Alsace, the narrative makes a hard break and then begins: "The whole earth sang in circles round the sun! Rounded hills, rounded clouds, rounded tree-tops, and wave upon wave of incoming hill. A concourse of meadow-swifts wrote a Gregorian chant on the telegraph wires" (257). While not specifically attributed to Lavinia, this passage, which introduces her abandonment of the relationship with Harrion, repeats the ideas of the fugue in its "circles" and its thrice-repeated "rounded"-ness, as well as the "wave upon wave" of hills. The land, then, repeats or reproduces itself. Rather than a sexual reproduction, the land reproduces the image of itself. Even the birds participate in this repetition through music by creating a chant on the wires, adding another voice to the polyphonic landscape. Lavinia underscores the eternal repetition of the land when she states that "one had no right here. Who had no earth had no right here. Here was the dividing line between the ephemeral and the enduring" (274). The land, then, not only repeats, but repeats "enduring[ly]," implying again the unavoidable and inescapable quality of the feminine. Through these images of repetition and eternity, the images of the land again associate it with the feminine, the maternal, and the entrapments that accompany them.

In addition to the use of repetition, Moore also creates a geographical fugue through imagery of reflection, like a counterpoint with the same theme or subject upside down. Reflection also creates a split or dissociation of the land from its reflection, the landscape. As the landscape in the novel is continually reflected through images of rivers, pools, and mirrors, it reiterates in its reflection the ideal of the feminine as portrayed through the English and Alsatian pastoral. As Lavinia pursues Harrion through the Alsatian village, she describes the houses as "a reflection of themselves in dark water" of the river, which was "like a live thinking mirror" (235). The moon's light works a "distortion" on the face of the river which is "gathered in heavy soundless movement under the cold lunar fingering" (235). Lavinia's own reflections on these images make clear the connections between the feminine—via the domestic "houses" (235), the stereotypically troped feminine "moon" (235)—and the land. The landscape, then, for Lavinia, is a reflection of these feminine spaces. In the reflection of the moon, the image is also sexualized by the moon's "fingering" (235) of the face of the river, further inscribing the feminine body as abject in its sexualized body.

As this imagery repeats, it repeatedly inscribes the affiliation of the feminine with the landscape. As W. J. T. Mitchell suggests, "'Landscape' must represent itself, then, as the antithesis of 'land,' as an 'ideal estate' quite independent of 'real estate,' as a 'poetic' property" (15), as landscape (especially landscape painting which Mitchell analyzes in detail) serves as a reflection of the land itself and also of what it represents. The images of the landscape, then, operate as:

> a trace or icon of nature *in* nature itself, as if nature were imprinting and encoding its essential structures on our perceptual apparatus. Perhaps this is why we place a special value on landscapes with lakes or reflecting pools. The reflection exhibits Nature representing itself to itself, displaying an identity of the Real and the Imaginary that certifies the reality of our own images. (15)

Mitchell's suggestion that the landscape's reflection of the land "certifies the reality of our own images" (15), telescopes out in *Fugue* so that the landscape also reflects the "reality" of the characters' images of the land, such as Lavinia's imparting of the land as feminine. The abject, feminine land continues the abjection of the feminine as a whole and makes the Alsace another embodiment of the feminine abject to which Lavinia flees. Just as Moore shows the split subjectivity of the modern female subject through Lavinia's dissociation with her body and the contrast between the mother and the modern woman, she shows through the feminized land the split between the land and its reflection, emphasizing again the dissociation of the subject from its image and thus from the feminine.

These reflections on and of the landscapes produce a myriad of voices that Moore fugues together. Through their multiple representations, Moore reveals the split consciousness of modern subjectivity on the feminine and also reveals the split identities that the modern woman must then embody and perform: that of (re)production and modernization. The feminized land, then, serves as a reflection of the modern female subject's split subjectivity in its representation here as multiple embodiments and identities.

## NATIONAL DISSOCIATIONS: ALWAYS IN ABJECT TERRITORY

The characters' escape from England is an escape not just from the land but also from the nation of England. Their movement to the Alsace is significant: it is an expatriate state in a region that is constantly shifting in its national affiliation and therefore, filled with multiple nationalisms.[24] By setting the bulk of the novel in the Alsace, Moore places the narrative on a slippery multifarious slope of layered nationalities, loyalties, languages, and histories of violence and inhabitation in which the characters live in an inn inhabited primarily by expatriates and in a region, the Alsace, that has been alternately French and German, the languages and cultures not always so blithely mixing. We see clearly both an abject homeland, marked by hybridity and monstrosity, and an idealized Alsace, each of which are inscribed as feminine and, therefore, as abject. From the excrement of bricks of the English suburbs to the reflection of the feminine in the Alsatian villages, this immersion in abject territories reveals various splits in the characters as displayed in their conversations about nation and international relations, immigration, imperialism, and industrialization, all of which are couched within language of the feminine abject.[25]

Dissociation can be seen in the splits of national consciousness of the expatriates and the Alsatians and in the characters' divided loyalties, both of which extend the trope of the abject feminine into issues of nationalism. As the characters travel from England to the Alsace, they split the narrative into two regions and into many nations. As Lavinia remains in the Alsace, she remains unattached to country and nation, floating in an expatriate state filled with multiple nationalisms. Despite their wandering, fugue-like existence, the characters in *Fugue* display a tremendous amount of concern about their nations of origin.

The conversations between these characters in the Wynstub Inn create a splitting of national consciousness through the multiple voices and their concerns about their various nation states. Moore here inserts the presence of national and international concerns and anxieties into the text, one that, as seen in the two previous sections on women and the land, also concerns anxieties about the feminine abject as well. As the mother country, England is both the pure woman, as seen in the purity of the pastoral landscape, and the abjecting maternal, as seen in her reproductive representative, Lavinia, and in her productive suburban development made up of excremental bricks.[26] The characters respond to the abject feminine of England through their desires to split from, erase, or contain it.

*Fugue* criticizes England with its "plus-foured Colonel" (280) for participating in imperialism and capitalism, reproducing its imperial techniques from abroad in its modern/contemporary inhabitation of the homeland. In the conversations that follow, concerns for the various nations discussed inherently connect to their concerns about women and/or the feminine and are described in terms of the abject: the threat of contamination through the straying or migrating populace.

As the splitting of European national consciousness develops, one of the many voices of nationalistic concern in the text is portrayed in the following monologue by a French doctor Lavinia overhears in the Wynstub. Through him, concerns about the consequences of immigration and hybridity erupt into a politic of exclusion and annihilation:

> Then Russia is off: finished. And so are the hotheads and the two to four million unemployed wandering about in every country and making a cursed nuisance of themselves. So long as they ate up their own savings it was bearable. (The doctor smiled.) But now they would eat up ours. They menace. They dare to threaten. Our answer must be to

## Flight of the Feminine and Textual Orientation 127

get rid of them. So long as they leave us in peace what can it matter how many heads they break: or whose? And what can it matter to us how savagely they annihilate one another so long as they do it thoroughly and in the name of Honour, Liberty, and Truth? (236).

Whereas Harrion has removed himself from the threat of the feminine Lavinia and her maternity, Europe, it seems, has been invaded by it in the form of the refugees from Russia that "threaten" the economies and cultures.[27] They are a "menace" that should be "annihilate[d]" even if it is by each other. The doctor's fears of the invasion, the eruption of the other, are couched in terms of the abject feminine that also strays across borders and threatens the enclosure of the (here, read national) self. In an interesting reversal, this portrays the feminine as both abject in its wandering and contaminating state, and also as invading. This invasion, though, is figured as the invasion of a disease rather than a military or imperialistic occupation, repeating the trope of the feminine abject as contamination.

England and the imperialistic attitudes of the English are also implicated as inevitable victims of this contamination. The French doctor continues by stating: "And do not think that England will escape . . . yes: we know it cannot be. Nothing ever can be, where the English are concerned. The world will continue to be the Englishman's little ball, and he the modern Atlas carrying his golf-clubs on his back" (236). The doctor asserts that England, as Lavinia once was, is not aware of the threat to itself and that its attitudes of enlightened imperialism will not preserve it from this "menace." While everyone else is concerned about the state of the world, the English see the world as its toy and its business with the world as its recreation. England's supposed naiveté about the potential invasion of the abject immigrants points again to its split subjectivity: it cannot recognize the abject or it would have to admit its own abjectness.

The specific threat against England and the English position on its feminine status is revealed through Lorwich, another English expatriate at the Wynstub. While reading the paper, Lorwich, too, advocates exclusion:

> He had now reached the Come to Britain movement. And of all the damned silly nonsense, when the only salvation for England lay in shutting her doors and keeping to herself, instead of inviting inspection. When only the milords came out of England—the others remaining in a dense fog—the world supposed the rest equal to the sample. But, behold, modern communication and the cinema and the radio had dispersed that fog and revealed the ass under the British lion's skin. (261)[28]

Unlike the doctor's concern about the immigrants' threat to economy and culture, Lorwich is concerned that the "ass under the British lion's skin" (261) will be revealed through this travel and immigration, that by "inviting inspection" (261), England will be discovered to not be a country full of "milords" (261). Lorwich's concern is framed in a language which feminizes and sexualizes England as a country which should "shu[t] her doors and kee[p] to herself" (261), who in a sense should, in contrast to Lavinia, keep her legs together. Lorwich reveals that England is not a respectable English prude after all, but somehow common and promiscuous in her willingness to accept immigrants, encouraging possible contamination. England's split subjectivity is then revealed and critiqued as it is both a prude and a whore; both gendered feminine and threatened by the feminine abject.

The abject status of England and the English is also signaled and reinforced through critiques of the Frenchman's and others. For, "evidently it was not for the English, that cursed and misshapen race, whose palate was dulled with swallowing fog and cokketelle, that one hung one's culinary diplomas about the walls.... A barbarous race that should have its food mixed in bowls and served it on the floor!" (267). The English here are embodied as "cursed and misshapen," a configuration that is directly associated to poor British food and, subsequently to British character. The "ass under the British lion's skin," it seems, is a "barbarous" and animalistic ass, not the highly civilized "milord" that used to be its sole representative. Another voice in the Wynstub, a "large man with the beret pulled down so tightly that it seemed to have hit him on the head," complains that:

> you can give them the freshest eggs and still they will make the heaviest omelettes. A matter of climate. No wonder they left their own country and were to be found the world over! What other people had ever been so eager to leave their own part of the earth? When the English boasted themselves world colonizers and victors, they should remember their climate and be more humble. A cold selfish people. (314)

According to this speaker, England is an abject civilization of "cold selfish people" (314). Given the same tools, or "eggs," they cannot create the same culture or "omelette" (314). All of the English expatriates of the Wynstub are explained away—they are "eager to leave" their "climate" (314). It is not about getting to the colonies, it is about leaving the homeland. According to the other patrons of the Wynstub, the flight from England exhibited by the multitude of expatriates in Europe enacts the flight from the feminine abject of not only the English land but the English culture as well. The failings of English culture, specifically culinary, can be further linked to the feminine as a failure of the cold English maidens who cannot cook.[29]

In addition, the split subjectivities of the English echo Moore's criticism of the modern woman who, like Evelyn, sees reproduction as something that should be mechanized. Sebastian also asserts the relationship between the feminized and the mechanical when he claims that:

*Flight of the Feminine and Textual Orientation* 129

> [t]he more mechanical a community, the more feminine: as America, Russia, England. Only in natural (peasant communities, such as Italy, Spain, the Balkans, France) the man still retained his power. To fight it still required a man. To fight with machines, woman sufficed. (308)

Sebastian here splits countries and sexes: England is feminine and "mechanical," France is masculine and "natural." This split again feminizes England, but rather than sexualizing it, places the feminine and England in league with other industrialized nations which, having divorced themselves from the feminized land, have contradictorily become more feminine. Moore here creates another split, that of the feminine maternal (as seen in the Alsace) and the feminine mechanical (as seen in England), both of which are seen as abject in their various relationships to feminine pastoral production or feminine mechanical reproduction. Through her portrayal of the split subjectivities of England and the English, Moore extends her exposure of the feminine into the territory of nationalism, indicating as she does so that Lavinia's flight from England lands her again in abject territory.

## TEXTUAL ORIENTATION: NAVIGATING THE TEXTUAL FUGUE

> No more words (thought Lavinia Reade), no more words. At least not just now. Not on a Sunday afternoon.... Could one not resuscitate or invent some god or hero to whom Sunday afternoon could be sacred in silence?
>
> Lavinia Reade, Fugue (306)

The form of *Fugue*, which undermines patriarchal linear narrative techniques through its broken and inconclusive structure, works in direct opposition to its narrative, which abandons the feminine to its inscriptions as both maternal and sex object. In so doing, the form of *Fugue* reverses the cycle of abjection for women by continuing to search out new female subjectivities through its textual experimentation and its resistance to conclusion. Sites of discrediting and discarding language in the text, like the passage above that indicates instead a longing for silence, are situated in direct conflict with the text's attempts to find release from the entrapments of female embodiment and subjectivity through its language.[30] Although the narrative of *Fugue* might appear to desire the abandonment of language to silence, just as it abandons the feminine to its inscriptions of body, land, and nation, the form of *Fugue* seeks to resuscitate the text for a feminine subjectivity that may exist outside such inscriptions by creating a text that seeks to exist outside of conclusion—modernist, patriarchal, or otherwise—through the use of twinned endings: that of Harrion at the crematorium in Paris and that of Lavinia and Sebastian gazing down upon the "Bacchic frieze" (333) of the people of the Alsace.

This conflict between narrative and form creates a textual fugue, the open form as counterpoint to the closed narrative. Although Moore adopts an archaic mode of the musical fugue, she adapts it into a modernist composition that, despite its position of inescapable embodiments of the feminine, resists conclusion and remains without resolution, indicating opposition to these deeply rooted musical and corporeal inscriptions.

The text of *Fugue* embodies Moore's possibility of a new feminine subjectivity, one that exists in the conflicts and split subjectivities of the modern female subject and that refuses to resolve the split subjectivities of the narrative by using instead a doubled conclusion. In presenting both the point and counterpoint of the form and narrative, Moore does not ignore the context in which female subjectivity must emerge in order to create an edenic place in which to launch it. Instead, *Fugue* insists that not only are all of the voices of the modern polyphonic chaos present; they are all necessary to understand the inherent difficulty of creating alternate feminine subjectivities. This, then, she says, is the real world in which we must live and create a new female subjectivity.

Within the fugue form of *Fugue*, Moore both replicates and criticizes high modernist form. Both Harrion and Lavinia make comments about time and plot that reflect Moore's criticism of high modernist emphases on the new.[31] As a second generation modernist, Moore is already positioned to criticize the tenets of her forebears: Pound, Eliot, Joyce, and even Woolf.[32] As I argue, Moore both continues and critiques the form of other modernists such as Joyce and Woolf as she creates a novel whose form replicates their circadian novels, *Ulysses* and *Mrs. Dalloway*. *Fugue*, in fact, does not occur in just one day, but as its days and hours become obscured, the present-day action of the novel occurs *as if* in just one day, the other events illustrated through flashbacks and flash forwards that become secondary to the day the novel describes. Just as Moore does not propose a new female embodiment but a new female subjectivity that can live out that embodiment differently, Moore proposes new ways to use existing modernist forms such as the circadian novel.

The form of the novel, though, is in conflict with Harrion's language in the narrative, which Moore also uses to self-consciously point to the modernist tropes she is deploying: the expansion of the circadian novel. Early on, Moore comments that "[i]t seemed his [Harrion's] life had been but a magnified day" (294) and, in line with high modernist textual experimentation, Moore makes Harrion's textual life exactly that, one somewhat "magnified day." Harrion's character explicitly critiques the "magnified day," referring to it as a "tyranny of hours," and locating the text of this day in the domestic realm with the bulk of the activities occurring in the home, extending his critique from his daily life to the feminine, domestic life, and (for Moore) to the form of the text itself. In continuing the passage from above, Harrion comments: "Constancy of habit to this tyranny of hours had meant a succession of timed wakings, baths, shaves, breakfasts, work, home-comings, sleep; to wake again to baths, shaves, breakfasts, work, home-comings, sleep" (294). Here, with Harrion's comments, both the circadian plot device and the exploration of the daily routine of the characters are dismissed and criticized. At the same time, Moore employs that somewhat bastardized device in the form of her novel.

Moore situates the narrative against the form, yet she does not complete the cycle of the day that Harrion describes or that Woolf and Joyce explore. Instead, she "break[s] the sequence" and by that "rupture[s] conventional structures of meaning by which the patriarchy reigns in order to give presence and voice to what was denied and repressed" (Friedman & Fuchs 15). Moore not only breaks the sequence of traditional patriarchal narrative through the disruption of linearity, she also disrupts modernist narrative through her lack of completion of that one day, asserting that the first generation or "high" modernists established a new dominant structure which inscribes an additional layer of restriction on the feminine through another closed form. Moore does not abandon modernist experimentation, but unlike her predecessors, neither does she assert its power to, as Peter Nicholls states, "order the flux and chaos of modern phenomenal life" (196). Instead, Moore allows the "flux and chaos" to remain and even to persist by refusing to contain it within linearity or conclusion.

In *Fugue*, Moore does not exalt textual experimentation as a way to, as David Harvey states about high modernists, "establish a new mythology" for women or otherwise as she does in *Spleen*. Harvey explains further that, for the high modernists, "the exploration of aesthetic experience . . . became a powerful means to establish a new mythology as to what the eternal and the immutable might be about in the midst of all the ephemerality, fragmentation, and patent chaos of modern life" (18). *Fugue* does not offer in the text reconciliation of the modernist subject and modern life. Its modernist form does not make sense out of modern life, nor does it suggest that it can. Rather, *Fugue*, embraces the "ephemerality, fragmentation, and . . . chaos of modern life" and sends its characters and narratives reeling in divergent directions. Unlike *Mrs. Dalloway*, which shows how even completely disparate lives of Clarissa and Septimus are ultimately and unavoidably intertwined, *Fugue* shows instead how these seemingly connected of Harrion and Lavinia lives are truly disparate. Any perceived connections completely unravel by the end into haphazard liaisons like that between Lavinia and Sebastian.

Moore disrupts more than a traditional modernist aesthetic; she also exposes its concern with the containment of the feminine. By disrupting the "'true' modernist aesthetic" of the high modernists that is "supported by a mechanism of reference and metaphor, and exhibits a related concern with outlines and borders which protect against the 'chaos' of subjectivity" (Nicholls 196), by refusing to contain the narrative with a single conclusion, *Fugue* seeks to deploy modernist form differently. I argue that despite the use of "reference and metaphor" (Nicholls 196), and especially in the inconclusiveness of the text, the novel seeks to find a new way for the feminine to emerge by removing some of the "outlines and borders which protect against the 'chaos' of subjectivity." Part of this "'chaos'" of modern life is associated directly to the feminine for modernists such as T. S. Eliot. As Nicholls explains, "[f]or Eliot . . . a decadent language is one which has become somehow 'bodily', a condition which prevents 'objectivity' and is quickly marked as 'feminine'" (195). Moore takes up Eliot's "decadent language" in the unavoidable maternal presence of Lavinia who pursues Harrion throughout the novel, in the repetition of the feminine landscape, and in the discussions of migration and nationality; the novel takes up a language which "leav[es] the self immersed in the 'opaque' processes of its own confused desires" (Nicholls 195). Moore not only documents and leaves Lavinia "immersed in the 'opaque' processes of [her] own confused desires, she acknowledges through the novel's 'feminine'" and 'bodily'" form that resists conclusion that this form is the only way to express and expose the struggle high modernists face with the feminine abject.

In addition, with its resistance to conclusion, *Fugue* asserts a version of the feminine through the form of the text. The open-ended antistructure of the text with its doubled in/conclusions place it within what Ellen Friedman and Miriam Fuchs describe as "the radical forms—nonlinear, nonhierarchical, and decentering—[which] are, in themselves, a way of writing the feminine" (3). The close of *Fugue* includes the inconclusions of the two primary subjects or voices in the novel, Harrion and Lavinia. First, Harrion's narrative is halted as he watches the mourners come to the crematorium, realizes that he will not be allowed in to watch the body burn, and instead remains outside to watch the smoke of the burning:

> He leaned against a pillar to steady himself, with nostrils distended like an animal flaring the scent of another; and it came surprisingly quickly after the black burning of the wood, the thin grey column in ascension perpetual with its stench of grease and putrescence. He smiled, and held up his face. (333)

Immediately following Harrion's crematorium moment is a hard break in the text, followed by this last, postcoital scene with Lavinia and Sebastian in the rural Alsatian countryside:

> From a height the sun chose, drowsy fastidious bee, now this village, now that.
> —There is a future for these people, Sebastian was saying.
> And Lavinia Read, shading her eyes from the bright look of the day, and gazing down at the Bacchic frieze of grapes, the tumbling children and burdened, fields, and oxen remote in their unhurried condescension, said: No! There is an eternity. (333)

As the text poses these twin endings, it asserts its resistance to conclusion by asserting the continuance of both narratives. Neither subject/voice/storyline resolves satisfactorily, if at all. Rather, the text suggests that each will continue and continue in its devolution.

Moore, through her resistance to conclusion, can be said to "disrupt" and "explode" what Friedman and Fuchs describe as the "dominant fictional structure" which relies on "plot linearity" (4). They further this argument by asserting that:

> Plot linearity that implies a story's purposeful forward movement; a single, authoritative storyteller; well-motivated characters interacting in recognizable social patterns; the crucial conflict deterring the protagonist from the ultimate goal; the movement to closure—all are parts of dominant fictional structure. Since this fiction is metonymic, reflecting cultural values in its order and progression, its themes and ideals, this fiction represents patriarchal mastery in Western culture. In exploding dominant forms, women experimental writers not only assail the social structure, but also produce an alternate fictional space, a space in which the feminine, marginalized in traditional fiction and patriarchal culture, can be expressed. Thus, the rupturing of traditional forms becomes a political act, and the feminine narrative resulting from such rupture is allied with the feminist project. (4)

For Friedman and Fuchs, the "dominant fictional structure" is not patriarchal solely in its structure but in its metonymy of "cultural values" that "represent patriarchal mastery." Thus, these dominant forms are also enacted through high modernist experimental forms as well as traditional narratives. In *Fugue*, "exploding dominant forms" specifically involves the explosion of the moment of closure, the moment which signals modernism's concern with the ability to "order the flux and chaos of modern phenomenal life" (Nicholls 196).

This inconclusivity, according to Lavinia as well as Friedman and Fuchs, with its disruption of linear (read patriarchal) narratives, is specifically useful in conveying the feminine. Earlier, in her rumination on the Alsace, Lavinia stated, "[t]his village was big enough. This was a world. A woman's world: world without end" (309), indicating in the narrative the link between inconclusion and the feminine. For Lavinia, at least, the unending quality of the world of the Alsace is specifically related to its status as "a woman's world" (309). In this instance, Moore aligns form and narrative, for once asserting her authorial position through her protagonist. Through these experimental modernist forms that break from traditional and modernist (both typically patriarchal) forms, Moore finds a greater opening for the emergence of feminine alterity. Textual orientation, then, is not something arrived at, but something gestured toward. The text points toward a new direction to be discovered in female subjectivity.

## IN/CONCLUSION: FLIGHTS OF FANCY

> [F]requent descriptions of the modern period as a period of deepening despair, paralysis and anxiety fail to address the visions of many female modernists, for whom the idea of the modern was to embody exhilarating possibilities and the potential of new and previously unimaginable sexual and political freedoms.
>
> Rita Felski (194)

Alternatively, it is possible that *Fugue* ultimately resists remediation from inscriptions of the abject feminine completely and tells the story, instead, of the closed, inescapable trap of female embodiment and subjectivity which at once strives for escape and expression and for peace and silence within its bondage, echoed and enhanced by its repetitive and unending form. But, I argue instead that Moore's textual experimentations seek to navigate a way out of the abject status of female subjectivity which she so carefully depicts in each of the bodies of the Corporeum—body, land, nation and (some forms of the) text—and instead of a closed, repetitive textual form that would return the feminine to its inescapable inscriptions as maternal and sexualized, offer an open-ended, inconclusive form that opens the way for new versions of the feminine to be expressed. The hesitancy of the text to conclude itself suggests the expectation or hope of further possibilities.

Ultimately, I argue that there is something inherent about the feminine that requires a splitting of consciousness or of the subject, that there is something inherent about the feminine that requires fugue-ing. The fugue forms of the narrative and text, both psychological and musical, demonstrate the necessity of feminine flight, both of the masculine from the feminine abject and the feminine from the patriarchal reflections of itself. Although *Fugue*, through its primary focus on Lavinia, is mostly concerned with the effects of the fugue state on the modern woman whose split subjectivity is inherent in her position as female, the modern condition, according to *Fugue*, is one in which neither men nor women are at home in the bodies, lands, or nations in which they reside. Rather, *Fugue* poses the split subjectivity of the modern subject through its characterizations of bodies, lands, and nations and through its textual form of doubled (and multiple) narratives. As Rita Felski suggests above, the split offers possibility for the feminine in that it opens a fissure through which the feminine may stray in all its abjectness rather than splitting of parts of itself and ultimately become its own story apart from the limited and binary point/counterpoint form of the musical fugue form and dissociative condition. The flight of the feminine, then, may well become a flight of fancy, a site of imagining where and how the feminine may take wing.

# Epilogue
## Feminine Form and Textual Reform

> *Five hundred a year and a Room of one's Own.* If creative achievement were a matter of a room of one's own, then since the first dawn in which the first woman was pushed to safety in the first cave, she should have been the world's creative artist.
>
> At no time in the world's history has woman been without a room of her own. But it has always been the kitchen. Then write on the kitchen table! Paint on the kitchen walls! Draw on the kitchen floor! Carve into shape the pastry and the butter! And so she would have had it been essential to her nature.
>
> The bitter story of the Arts urges one to ask what man has ever had a room of his own that he did not have to earn with cadging, pandering, humiliation, fill with wives and children and bailiffs, and still produce by the spirit-alchemy of sweat and desire the works he is remembered by?
>
> As though England were not honeycombed with passive aesthetically sterile women of all ages, in rooms of their own ranging from five hundred to five thousand a year! Possibly it produces a local (village) industry. That is as much as five hundred a year will produce anywhere.
>
> To the creative artist 500 is not enough. It must be five millions. Or five pence.
>
>         Olive Moore, *The Apple is Bitten Again* (386)

Olive Moore wrote this long passage in her "Notebook" prior to its publication in 1934 when she was about 29 years old. Virginia Woolf's *A Room of One's Own*, to which Moore responds, was first published in 1929 and based on lectures Woolf gave in 1928 when she was 47 years old. Moore's response to Woolf demonstrates the frustrations of second generation modernists with their predecessors and suggests changes in the perspectives if not the realities of young women on the supposed limits placed on their achievement. Moore refutes Woolf's arguments and, in doing so, places the blame solely on women's shoulders, on their "passive aesthetically sterile" and "essential . . . nature[s]" (386) rather than their environments or the structures of patriarchal society. Although there are many counter arguments to Moore's rebuttal, the turn toward criticism of Woolf's feminism signals a new era in feminism and potentially, in women writers and writing.[1] Clearly, this passage articulates Moore's contradictions between her ideas about women's subjectivity and the enacting of her own: Moore's bold writing (and one suspects her living as well) clearly situates her in a different camp from the women she describes in this passage whose "nature[s]" (386) limit them from achievement in or out of the world of men.

*Female Embodiment and Subjectivity in the Modernist Novel: The Corporeum of Virginia Woolf and Olive Moore* considers these contradictions between the ideology which these authors combat—Victorian patriarchy for Woolf and Edwardian class and propriety for Moore—and the textual strategies they deploy in their novels. These contradictions exemplify the ways in which the female modernist subject and the British modern woman writer live out split subjectivity and navigate the various worlds of bodies, lands, nations, and texts.

Although I do not propose that Woolf and Moore consciously posed these contradictions, my analysis of their novels highlights the juxtaposition of the authors' struggles with feminine embodiment and identity that the narratives depict and the texts themselves embody. These texts reiterate the concerns about the inscriptions of and on the feminine through their connections of the female body to geographical imagery and national ideology, acknowledging the precarious positions for women who either support the institutions of patriarchy and empire or are exiled from them.

Such a broad and integrated approach calls for both separation and synthesis of the issues. To only separate them would be to risk falling prey to the isolated theoretical camps I criticize in my introduction. Instead, this book illustrates each facet of the Corporeum and also unravels the way these four bodies operate together as an integrated web of identifications for women. For example, Clarissa Dalloway is not only a representation of the English pastoral; she and the pastoral are also representatives of the nation and of the imperial ideal that both Peter and Septimus take with them to the colonies and the war, respectively. In addition, Clarissa also serves as the primary medium through which Woolf reveals female interiority, her development of the stream-of-consciousness form permitting not only access to the minds of women but access to the minds of all gender and class participants. Clarissa then becomes a main conduit of a kind of textual reform which utilizes textual form to re-imagine modern subjectivity. Specifically, as this textual reform levels the structures of representation typically unvoiced in male modernist texts, it creates space for the representation of the feminine beyond its corporeal descriptions and inscriptions.

In considering the four bodies of the Corporeum in each of the four novels, this book reveals the complicated interdependence of the ideologies of bodies, lands, and nations on the feminine and the difficulty in extricating the feminine or at least, its inscriptions from them. At the same time, this project reveals the developments of experimental textual form as a mode of countering the inscriptions of and on the feminine in the first three bodies.

Whether depicted as high-brow (Clarissa), reformed wilderness (Sally), a bearer of light (the lady with the lamp), risky experimentalist (Ruth), or passive participant (Lavinia), each of the female incarnations in these novels finds it impossible to escape the entrapments of female subjectivity. This poses a surprising predicament for authors such as Woolf and Moore who articulated progressive politics as well as experimental writings.[2]

In an attempt to understand and rectify this predicament, I have explicated the forms of the texts to show how these authors attempt to free the feminine from its entrapments by carving out a new textual space in which it can come into being. These newly opened spaces for the feminine in the texts, which have often been attributed to spaces of silence and emptiness, are instead filled with possibility.[3] From the undeniable presence of the feminine Clarissa in Mrs. Dalloway, to the encroaching shadow in The Waves, to the textual hybridity in Spleen and the inconclusiveness of Fugue, these authors' textual experimentations fashion concrete textual spaces for the feminine that subvert the paradigms of modernist experimentation posed by the often considered monolithic structure of male high modernism.[4]

Ultimately, this book asks how the developments of textual experimentation elicit new embodiments of female subjectivity through new forms of the text and why women modernists were so inclined toward similar versions of textual experimentation such as the stream-of-consciousness form, repetition, referral, and inconclusivity. These tendencies reveal the concerns, anxieties, and criticism of the feminine within the broader scope of literary modernism. British women modernists' leanings toward the excesses of the text, as well as experiments with form, situate textual experimentation as the only way to refigure the entrapments of the feminine in the other bodies of the Corporeum. For Virginia Woolf and Olive Moore in particular, re-forming the text becomes a way of re-forming female subjectivity. Textual experimentation becomes a way to reshape the feminine if not in one incarnation of the Corporeum, than in another. If women's bodies cannot be reshaped, then perhaps a new form of narrative can re-imagine them within the geographical and national bodies of the Corporeum. Rather than asking for l'écriture féminine, or an only feminine space, these authors seek a literary space which deploys modernist form differently and to their own ends: to release and realize feminine subjectivity from the holds of the patriarchal and/or imperial ideologies of feminized bodies, lands, nations, and texts.

# Appendix

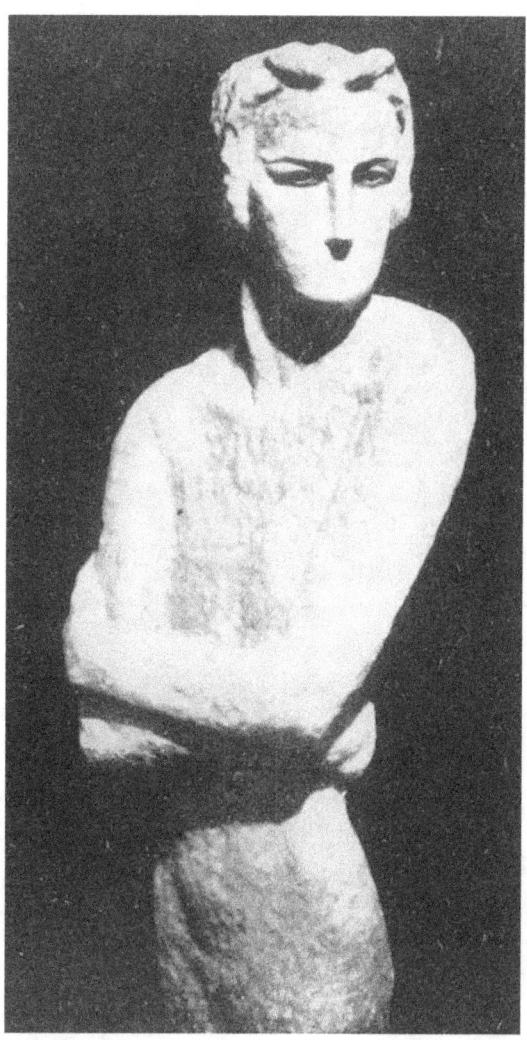

*Figure A.1* Bust of Olive Moore by Sava Botzaris as featured in her collection *The Apple is Bitten Again*.

# Notes

**NOTES TO THE INTRODUCTION**

1. Hynes, Samuel. *A War Imagined: The First World War and English Culture.* New York: Atheneum, 1991: 346.
2. Woolf, Virginia. *Mrs. Dalloway.* New York: Harvest, 1953.
3. For specific analyses of the effects of WWI and literary production, see such journals as *The Space Between: Literature and Culture 1914–1945,* as well as works by Alison Light, Samuel Hynes, Christine Froula, Suzanne Raitt, Catherine O'Brien, Jane Potter, Vincent Sherry, Angela K. Smith, Allyson Booth, Sarah Cole, Andy Crof, Debra Rae Cohen, and Trudi Tate.
4. For more detailed information about Moore's life and work, see the appendix in Olive Moore's *Collected Writings.* Several students and I have been researching Moore's life and have so far discovered that she was in fact married at one time to the sculptor, Sava Botzaris in 1924. Although, per an interview with David Goodway, Charles Lahr did not speak of Moore as being alive after 1970, so far we have not traced her life past 1934, nor found a manuscript of her theatrical endeavor, *Amazon and Hero.* The University of London's Senate House Library does hold a manuscript of *Fugue* as well as a few letters by Moore, and the British Library holds copies of *The Daily Sketch* for which she wrote as a staff writer. I have only begun to plumb these holdings. To date, I have found numerous articles written by Moore for *The Daily Sketch* under her birth name, Constance Vaughan. After advertising in the *Times Literary Supplement*, no response was received.
5. Fowler, H. W., and F. G. Fowler, ed. *The Concise Oxford Dictionary of Current English.* Oxford: Clarendon P, 1995.
6. To be clear, I am looking specifically and often only at women's embodiment, how it is translated and corroborated with geographical and national identities and, finally, how it is embodied in the text. Male embodiment, although offering important counterpoints and alternate corroborations especially in the creation of male identity during and after WWI and how it directly affected female identity, would require more time and space than this project allows and would, indeed, take it in another direction. For resources on male embodiment in British modernist texts and masculine identity, see Klaus Theweleit's *Male Fantasies*, in which he provides, "an analysis of masculine identity as a flight from the feminine, as fear of ego dissolution, and of warfare as the fulfillment of both a longing for fusion (with the military machine) and legitimate explosion in the moment of battle" (xvii), and that "the fear of the feminine is investigated in a seemingly endless series of liquid images in which woman is associated with all that might threaten to deluge or flood the boundaries of the male ego" (xvii).

7. Based in psychoanalysis, Kristeva's theories delineate the suturing of the feminine to the abject and, therefore, the apparent need to excise it or separate from it. According to Kristeva, the abject is one who or that which "disturbs identity, system, order" (*Powers* 4) when it becomes a "stray" (*Powers* 8) by wandering outside of the symbolic system. It contributes to the loss of meaning due to a breakdown between self and other or between subject and object. I am also grateful to Dino Felluga's "Modules on Kristeva: On the Abject."
8. Because for Kristeva the abject is a *"confrontation with the feminine"* around which "societies code themselves in order to accompany as far as possible the speaking subject on that journey" away from it (*Powers* 58), it places women "in the position of passive objects" who "are none the less felt to be wily powers, 'baleful schemers' from whom rightful beneficiaries must protect themselves" (*Powers* 70). Thus, for Kristeva, "the feminine becomes synonymous with a radical evil that is to be suppressed" (*Powers* 70).
9. In contrast, the feminine can also be seen as abject in its absence as Luce Irigaray states, "her sexual organs represents *the horror of nothing to see*" (26).
10. See Alison Light's discussion of interwar Britain in which she suggests that
    > [s]ince war, whatever its horrors, is manly, there is something both lower-class and effeminate about peacetime, [that] Britain is the place where it is no longer possible to be properly male—a country gelded, as Lawrence might have said, and emasculated by the aftermath of war. Domestic life, the emphasis on the world of home and family activity brings down some of the most virulent torrents of abuse: the British Sunday, British cooking, and frequently, British women (foreign maidens are far preferable to awkward English virgins)—these are the outrages which make the British Isles, but especially and usually England, a home unfit for heroes. Indeed Fussell's soldierly imagination is quite right in suggesting that heroes are by definition incapable of domesticity; (7)

    and that

    > the 1920s and '30s saw a move away from formerly heroic and officially masculine public rhetorics of national destiny and from a dynamic and missionary view of the Victorian and Edwardian middle classes in "Great Britain" to an Englishness at once less imperial and more inward-looking, more domestic and more private—and, in terms of pre-war standards, more "feminine." (8)
11. Cixous, Hélène. "The Laugh of the Medusa." *Feminisms: An Anthology of Literary Theory and Criticism.* Eds. Robyn R. Warhol and Diane Price Herndl. New Brunswick: Rutgers UP, 1997.
12. In *A Room of One's Own*, Virginia Woolf writes that "[p]erhaps to think, as I had been thinking these two days, of one sex as distinct from the other is an effort. . . . Coleridge perhaps meant this when he said that a great mind is androgynous. . . . Perhaps a mind that is purely masculine cannot create, any more than a mind that is purely feminine" (97–98). Woolf, Virginia. *A Room of One's Own*. New York: Harvest, 1957.
13. Further claims of Heywood's argument include: "the anorexic logic does not reflect a separation between body and spirit, and a desire to transcend the first; rather, it is a fight between two bodies, male and female, where one remains as the common standard for the body and the other should disappear altogether" (67). "Femaleness is associated with fatness and passivity, (67) "the female body is consumed in order to give birth to the male body as text. This is specifically modernist because the privileged term here is not the *spirit* but the *male body* as *created through words*," (69) and "In male modernist texts an apparently all-encompassing rejection of bodily materiality that cuts across

any designation of gender can be shown to reflect an urge to privilege one kind of sexuality and one kind of body" (70). Rather than follow Heywood in her analysis of the physical body, I instead track the effects of male literary modernism as the standard to which female modernists must conform or not.
14. This argument is complicated by the change in genre from the male modernist poets Heywood discusses here to the female modernist novelists I explore in this project. I propose that even the choice of the novel form is another avenue for female modernists to explore the excesses of the feminine in an extended literary form.
15. Kirby also corroborates Heywood in citing woman's subject position as absence. She states that "[a]s woman is ceaselessly refigured as an absence such that man can be rendered present in every account, the very repetition of this mode of reckoning is itself differentiating and transformational: it is never identical with itself" (79). From this, I add that this continual repetition of differentiating stems from the anxiety to separate from the feminine. Kirby also corroborates Kristeva's theories on the excess and abject of the feminine: "'becoming woman' is written in the spacing of a corporeography from which nothing is exempted" (80). Additional discussion of language and excess from Kirby includes her questions: "What is writing when it is more than writing—when the familiar meaning of the word assumes such monstrous elasticity that it surrounds and invades everything, when it is everything, when there is no getting outside this ubiquitous text? And how is the body itself a scene of writing, subject to a sentence that is never quite legible, because to read it is to write it, again, yet differently?" (56). As with hysteria, where the body acts as an illegible sign of broken psychic and linguistic semiology, Kirby here reaffirms the consequences of a broken sign system which no longer contains language so that it becomes "monstrous," "elastic," and subsequently "bursts the boundaries of its conventional articulation." Again, these terms can be conflated with the feminine as I will argue in the subsequent paragraphs regarding Kristeva's theories on the abject.
16. Kristeva only analyzes male authors in *Powers of Horror*. Regarding *Ulysses*, she states, "[f]ar from preserving us from the abject, Joyce causes it to break out in what he sees as a prototype of literary utterance: Molly's monologue" (22). Significantly her example is of the abject emerging from a female character in a chapter which is indeed excessive in its textual experimentation. One could argue, therefore, that although Joyce does utilize a textual form of excess he deploys it in such a way as to essentialize women as physical and linguistic excess and, therefore, re-abjectifies them.
17. George Bornstein writes in "Ezra Pound and the Making of Modernism," that Pound wrote in "How I Began" (1913): "'Any work of art which is not a beginning, an invention, a discovery, is of little worth.' Indeed, the slogan 'make it new' which he later adopted from the Shang dynasty founder Tching Tang (see Canto LIII) demanded continual renewal rather than ossification yet gestured also toward an 'it' to be remade."
18. A shortened version of this chapter has been accepted for publication as "*Fugue*-ing: Olive Moore, the Feminine and the Multiple Flights of the Modern Subject." *Musical Modernism: Essays on Language and Music in Modernist Literature*. Forthcoming.

## NOTES TO CHAPTER 1

1. *The Tatler*, along with *The Spectator*, was one of the first periodicals and highly influential in creating cultural and national affiliation as it "stated as

its explicit purpose the reformation of manners and morals" (Mackie, Erin, ed. and introduction, *The Commerce of Everyday Life: Selections from* The Tatler *and* The Spectator. Boston: Bedford, 1998: 1).

2. For more on *Mrs. Dalloway* and the city, see Susan Merrill Squier's *Virginia Woolf and London: The Sexual Politics of the City*. For more theoretical background on the body and the city, see Elizabeth Grosz' "Bodies–Cities" in *Sexuality and Space*.
3. In addition, see Anne Fernihough's chapter, "Consciousness as a Stream" in *The Cambridge Companion to the Modernist Novel*.
4. Throughout this chapter, I focus primarily on the character of Clarissa Dalloway. In this focus, I see Clarissa as exemplary rather than archetypal of female embodiment. Although I refer to other female characters for comparison, and one could easily make similar arguments about each of their embodiments in the novel, Clarissa instead serves as the template of the various female embodiments that I discuss as Clarissa is the character most fully developed in the novel.
5. For detailed analyses on performances of the body see Judith Butler's *Gender Trouble* as well as subsequent criticism and commentary such as that by Kathy Dow Magnus.
6. Kathy J. Phillips makes this statement in *Virginia Woolf Against Empire* regarding *To the Lighthouse*, but I suggest that it also rings true for *Mrs. Dalloway*.
7. See Susan Kingsley Kent's *Making Peace*, on British women's purity and resistance as part of the war rhetoric and the national ideal. As I argue, Clarissa's purity figures as essential to her own subjectivity as well as to her role in representing Englishness.
8. This moment contains both male and female sexual imagery, gesturing toward Woolf's argument for androgyny in *A Room of One's Own* and creating an omnisexual moment of sexual expression for Clarissa (97).
9. For a detailed reading on the homoerotic implications and complications in this passage, see Eileen Barrett and Patricia Cramer's *Virginia Woolf: Lesbian Readings* and Kathryn Simpson's "'Queer Fish': Woolf's Writing of Desire Between Women in *The Voyage Out* and *Mrs. Dalloway*."
10. For more on Woolf's disruption of sequence and narrative, see the fourth section of this chapter, "Textual Body: The Shape of Modernism and the Feminine Form," as well as Ellen G. Friedman and Miriam Fuchs' *Breaking the Sequence: Women's Experimental Fiction* and Rachel Blau DuPlessis' *Writing Beyond the Ending: Narrative Strategies of Twentieth-Century Women Writers*.
11. Terry Gifford, in *Pastoral*, delineates three kinds of pastoral: a historical form, specifically of shepherdic poetry, an area of content of "any literature that describes the country with an implicit or explicit contrast to the urban" (2), and an ecocritical, pejorative use "implying that the pastoral vision is too simplified and thus an idealisation of the reality of life in the country" (2). For the purposes of my argument, I will be using the second definition to distinguish between Woolf's conflation of the young Clarissa with the countryside at Bourton in contrast to her adult life in the city. For an analysis of *Mrs. Dalloway* and its relation to the pastoral elegy, see Christine Froula's *Virginia Woolf and the Bloomsbury Avant-Garde: War, Civilization, Modernity*.
12. See Rachel Bowlby's discussion of Elizabeth as the possibility of a new woman in "Thinking Forward through Mrs. Dalloway's Daughter" in *Feminist Destinations and Further Essays on Virginia Woolf*. 69–84.
13. In support of Elizabeth as a new possibility for female identity, she thinks,

> she would like to have a profession. She would become a doctor, a farmer, possibly go into Parliament, if she found it necessary, all because of the Strand. The feet of those people busy about their activities, hands putting stone to stone, minds eternally occupied not with trivial chatterings (comparing women to poplars—which was rather exciting, of course, but very silly), but with thoughts of ships, of business, of law, of administration. (136–37)

> Clearly, Elizabeth considers a broader scope than Clarissa, but, at the moment of this day in the novel, she is still and always compared to the landscape like Clarissa. For further exploration of the character of Elizabeth, see Genevieve Morgan's "Elizabeth Dalloway Talks Back: Students and the Mrs. Dalloway Experience," and Audra Dibert-Himes' "Elizabeth Dalloway: Virginia Woolf's Forward Look at Feminism."

14. This passage from *Between the Acts* is foreshadowed in *Mrs. Dalloway* as Rezia thinks, "I am alone! she cried, by the fountain in Regent's Park (staring at the Indian and his cross), as perhaps at midnight, when all boundaries are lost, the country reverts to its ancient shape, as the Romans saw it, lying cloudy, when they landed, and the hills had no names and rivers wound they knew not where—such was her darkness" (24).
15. See the comparable passage of Mrs. Ramsay's meditations in *To the Lighthouse*, in which she states that she is both

    > something invisible to others [and] it was thus that she felt herself; and this self having shed its attachments was free for the strangest adventures [and] to everybody there was always this sense of unlimited resources. . . . There was freedom, there was peace, there was, most welcome of all, a summoning together, a resting on a platform of stability. Not as oneself did one find rest ever . . . but as a wedge of darkness. Losing personality, one lost the fret, the hurry, the stir; and there rose to her lips always some exclamation of triumph over life. . . . Watching [the strokes of the lighthouse] in this mood always at this hour one could not help attaching oneself to one thing especially of the things one saw. . . . Often she found herself sitting and looking . . . until she became the thing she looked at. (42–43)

16. I refer to imperialism and colonialism according to the definitions I discussed in my introduction. See page 9 of the Introduction.
17. This is similar to Mrs. Ramsay's conflation with the Queen's portrait in *To the Lighthouse*—see Janet Winston's article "'Something Out of Harmony': *To the Lighthouse* and the Subject(s) of Empire."
18. I refer to "nation making" throughout this section to denote Clarissa's activities as an ideal representation of Englishness and of the English woman. This ideal, as I argued, extends into the work of the empire, but Clarissa's activities specifically do not.
19. Racial impurity is also revealed through Woolf's portrayal of Elizabeth's Chinese eyes which are explained through the possibility that "some Mongol had been wrecked on the coast of Norfolk (as Mrs. Hilbery said), had mixed with the Dalloway ladies, a hundred years ago" (123). Here, Woolf directly conflates the feminine and the foreign, removing the feminine even further from a subject position included in patriarchy and empire.
19. As Kathy J. Phillips argues, "For Woolf, such a society molds even the most likable characters to participate in the Empire, in ways that her novels as a whole satirize" (221).
20. Again, as Phillips argues, "One of the most obvious ways women contribute to the imperial civil service and the armed forces is by supplying

them with sons" (226), and so Sally is seen as complicit specifically in her maternity.
21. Significantly, Miss Kilman avoids being associated with the landscape except in two brief instances. First, in her struggle against "the flesh" (128) and with Clarissa's class and position, she states, "How nice it must be, she said, in the country, struggling, as Mr. Whittaker had told her, with that violent grudge against the world which had scorned her" (129). This comment, though, is ungrounded in any conversation with Elizabeth as they walk down Victoria Street. Second, she is described, after Elizabeth leaves her in the stores, she loses her way amongst the commodities and ducks into Westminster to pray: "Miss Kilman at the end of the row, praying, praying, and, being still on the threshold of their underworld, thought of her sympathetically as a soul haunting the same territory; a soul cut out of immaterial substance; not a woman, a soul" (134). This description does little to place Miss Kilman in the geographical body in which the other female characters are situated and, I argue, suggests that her political positions have removed her from the geographical and the national body. She, though, does not find that this allows for certain freedoms of the spirit, but resents and despises her position.
22. See George Robb's discussion of English nationalism after World War I and of German sentiment in *British Culture and the First World War*. "Nationalism attempted to focus conflict outward—against a German foe invariably constructed as a degenerate, barbaric "throwback": the "Hun" of popular propaganda. As successful as such ideas were in garnering support for the war effort, they created problems of their own since "the nation," as defined, clearly could not accommodate the diverse citizenry of Britain itself, let alone its vast, diverse Empire" (5).

   And "Germany and its people were held to embody the worst possible characteristics of a nation; militarism, intolerance, despotism, and slavish obedience to authority; while Britain and the British represented the diametric opposite: peacefulness, broad-mindedness, democracy, and individualism" (6).
23. One could of course see Miss Kilman's alignment with the church as an attempt to access and participate in the (grand) patriarchal system.
24. Lady Bruton's physical body is described only in the abstract, as in the above references to her as a "general of dragoons" (105) or as concretely as "handsome," "erect," "magnificence" (111). Clearly, though, these passages describe her as a formidable woman of power if not of physique.
25. See specifically Modris Eksteins' *Rites of Spring: The Great War and the Birth of the Modern Age*, as well as Paul Fussell's *The Great War and Modern Memory*.
26. Woolf's experimentation, then, can be seen as not only an attempt to change narrative form, but also an attempt to "construct new cultural paradigms" (Garrity 302). Jane Garrity also sees that "Woolf deploys spatial and architectural metaphors to critique masculine literary space as inhospitable and to suggest that women must rebuild the dwelling—despite a 'scarcity and inadequacy of tools' (*ROO*, 77)—by carving a 'home in the symbolic order' through experimentalism" (304).
27. For criticism on fin de siècle fiction, see Sally Ledger and Roger Luckhurst's *The Fin de Siècle: A Reader in Cultural History, c. 1880–1900* and Talia Schaffer's *Literature and Culture at the* Fin de Siècle.
28. See also Ellen Friedman and Miriam Fuchs' argument in *Breaking the Sequence* that "women writers expressed dissatisfaction with or ambivalence toward prevailing ideas of appropriate behavior in fiction and life through

covert means—subtexts, minor characters, patterns of imagery that undermine or question the values that the surface plot and major characters seems to confirm" (3).
29. See also Bonnie Kime Scott on Woolf's experimentation and patriarchal form in *Refiguring Modernism, Volume Two: Postmodern Feminist Readings of Woolf, West, and Barnes*: "Woolf's underground system of tunnels is the figural antithesis of the tower. Its very intricacy almost guarantees a collapse, undermining old systems of support, from the glib phrase to the architecture of Whitehall" (16).

## NOTES TO CHAPTER 2

1. This expression's origins are found in John Wilson's *Noctes Ambrosianae*. 258.
2. A version of this chapter appeared as "Exposure and Development: Reimagining Narrative and Nation in the Interludes of Virginia Woolf's The Waves." *Woolf Studies Annual* 13 (2007): 25–47.
3. I refer to *imperialism* and *colonialism* according to the definitions established in my introduction (see page 9 of the Introduction).
5. See also: Jane Garrity's, *Step-Daughters of England: British Women Modernists and the National Imaginary*.
6. See various critics' positions such as Jed Esty who states in *A Shrinking Island: Modernism and National Culture in England*, that "both modernism and imperialism reached a peak in the period from 1880 to 1945" (6).
7. For the purposes of this book, and in accordance with the focus of the interludes themselves on England, I focus on the effects of the imperial gaze on the homeland, not on the colonies and the colonized. For criticism on *The Waves* analyzing the greater effects of empire in the interludes and elsewhere in the text, see Kathy J. Phillips' *Virginia Woolf Against Empire*, Jane Marcus' "Britannia Rules the Waves," Heidi Stalla's "Empire and Elveden: New Light on *The Waves*," and Patrick McGee's "The Politics of Modernist Form: Or, Who Rules *The Waves*?"
8. See also Cain and Hopkins who claim "elite women acted as influential adjuncts to the masculine empire, whether as missionaries, doctors, managers of emigration societies, founders of the Girl Guides, or as propagandists. The gentlemanly elite was to this extent strengthened by its lady-like complement; both had their roles shaped by the empire they were trying to civilize" (13).
9. See Madeline Moore's proposal that: "[l]ooked at in strictly biographical terms, the cosmological woman-as-sun, who dominates the poetic prologues of *The Waves*, resembles Julia Stephen, who was both nurturing and arbitrary, and was possibly a model of a deified sun goddess for her adoring daughter" (27) in *The Short Season Between Two Silences: The Mystical and the Political in the Novels of Virginia Woolf*, as well as Jane Marcus' argument in "Britannia Rules the Waves" regarding the sun in the interludes comprising an invocation of the sun as in Sanskrit poems, creating "a discourse for an alienated Western woman like Rhoda to have a 'heroic death,' like Indian widows in sati" (137).
10. The narrative of the episodes, while important, useful, and necessary to extend the connections between women, empire, and modernist form that I suggest, have already accrued much critical attention (see footnote 7 of this chapter) and thus are, here, supplemental to the primary focus of this argument on the more neglected developments of narrative and nation in the

interludes. In this reading, then, the episodes become the text *between* the interludes, rather than the typical reading the other way around. To that end, my attention to the episodes is minimal, often footnoted, and discussed in their connection to and in their tension with the interludes.

11. See Susan Kingsley Kent's *Making Peace*, in which she argues that

    metaphors utilized to explain and justify the war drew upon images of women in a variety of ways. Women were depicted variously as the terrain of war in representation that decried the rape of Belgium and France; as the objects of war in propaganda and recruiting posters; as the victims of war in reports of German atrocities; as the parasitic beneficiaries of war in *Punch* cartoons or irate letters to newspaper columns; as the wagers of war in tributes to women's wartime service, particularly that of munitions workers; even as the cause of the war in some accounts of prewar suffrage militancy . . . the two concepts, sex and war, became inextricably intertwined in the mind of contemporaries. . . . War, in other words, found its most pervasive and vivid representations in metaphors of sex and gender. In the postwar period, sexual conflict and polarization between the sexes provided one of the few adequate means by which the political, economic, and social upheaval occasioned by the Great War could be depicted. (9–10)

12. The phrase, "the lady with the lamp," denotes popular depictions of Florence Nightingale which showed Nightingale holding a lamp over the soldiers at Scutari. Woolf would have been familiar with the painting and with Lytton Strachey's critical account of Nightingale's life and work in *Eminent Victorians*. Woolf's depiction of the sun as a lady holding a lamp above the horizon summons these images and their depictions of Nightingale as a ministering angel as well as Strachey's subsequent criticism. See also Lytton Strachey's *Eminent Victorians* as well as Renée Dickinson's "The Lady with the Lamp: Florence Nightingale and *The Waves*."
13. The fans of colors and later of waves further the feminine imagery. The association of this imagery with the feminine is confirmed in the penultimate interlude when the "girls, sitting on verandahs, look up at the snow, shading their faces with their fans" (237).
14. See Jane Garrity's further discussion of women and women's bodies' collaboration in the work of empire, in which she states that "In *The Waves*, perhaps more than in any other of her works, Woolf acknowledges that women's quest for linguistic inclusion is legitimized by and embedded in the doctrine of expansion and rule" (271).
15. See also Eileen B. Sypher's commentary in Ginsberg and Gotlieb's *Virginia Woolf: Centennial Essays* in which she states that "the image of the female sun is tentative. (Often the sun's 'femaleness' is imaged in a simile and after the sun becomes hot, 'uncompromising' (W, p. 148), Woolf drops the metaphor/simile altogether and the sun becomes 'it')" (195).
16. In *A Room of One's Own*, Virginia Woolf writes that "[p]erhaps to think, as I had been thinking these two days, of one sex as distinct from the other is an effort. . . . Coleridge perhaps meant this when he said that a great mind is androgynous. . . . Perhaps a mind that is purely masculine cannot create, any more than a mind that is purely feminine" (97–98).
17. In addition, see Kathy Phillips argument that "[r]eferences to imperialism and militarism often occur together because, once a country accepts the need for colonies, it must rely on force to put down local rebellions and fend off other European nations" (225).
18. At the same time, in the episodes, Percival's work in India represents the work of the empire in the colonies (see pages 116, 123, 126, 136, 137, 145,

147, 151, and 153). The narrative of the episodes adds a double valence to the primitivism of the sun by extending its militaristic violence to the colonies. The primitive, then, as seen in the colonial subject and in the bodies of women, both come under attack by the empire and figures as an image of the attacking empire.

19. See Kathy Phillips argument that "[i]n trying to recreate an unspoiled land in England, Jinny further forgets that she has portrayed the jungle not only as a refuge of beautiful license but also as a place of death" (175). Jinny here actively participates in the creation of nation and imperial identity through her portrayal of the jungle in contrast to England, yet Phillips claims, she does so unwittingly, "forget[ting]" the consequences of her rhetoric.

20. For further discussion of military violence in the episodes, see Philips' discussion of Percival, Louis, and British education where she argues that "Percival epitomizes . . . two of the most dangerous qualities inculcated by the schools—regimentation and militarism" (155), culminating in Woolf "expos[ing] the totalizing impulse of Empire as totalitarian, and, in fact, Louis resembles the fascists coming to power in Europe in the decade before *The Waves*" (161).

21. This progression of increased violence demonstrates the anxiety of the feminine in the homeland during peacetime. To review a specific example, Alison Light argues that "[s]ince war, whatever its horrors, is manly, there is something both lower-class and effeminate about peacetime" (7).

22. For further discussion of the implications of Woolf's use of light and shadow see Patrick McGee's argument that in the episodes,"[t]he collective identity of all these individualized characters depends on the ethnocentric mapping of the world into areas of light and areas of darkness" (645). In addition, though, he claims that "[Marcus'] reading still would have Woolf dividing the world along ethnocentric lines into a zone of light associated with culture (the West) and a zone of darkness associated with nature (the East)" (646). Thus, McGee asks us to consider the ways in which we read light and darkness and suggests, too, that Woolf attempts to question and undermine these associations with culture and nature.

23. See again Kathy Phillips' argument that "[r]eferences to imperialism and militarism often occur together because, once a country accepts the need for colonies, it must rely on force to put down local rebellions and fend off other European nations" (225).

24. This combination of violence, military, and machine imagery also arguably signals a critique of vorticism such as that practiced by Wyndham Lewis—and the accompanying slide into fascism. See Rebeccca Beasley's "Wyndham Lewis and modernist satire."

25. Specifically, this imagery is reminiscent of the reports of the German soldiers in World War I coming in waves into the Belgian countryside and their bodies stacking up on each other at the foot of the fortifications. For one example, see Barbara W. Tuchman's vivid descriptions in *Guns of August*. The *Oxford English Dictionary* cites one definition of "fall" as the "shedding, effusion (of blood)" (I.1.f) as well as "the downward stroke (of a sword)" (I.1.h) and "a falling to the ground . . . of persons" (III.12.a) and "the fact of being struck down by calamity or disease, in battle, etc.; death, destruction, overthrow" (III.18.a).

26. From the first episode, Louis speaks of a stamping beast: "'*The beast stamps; the elephant with its food chained; the great brute on the beach stamps*'" (10), and this figure repeats throughout the episodes and interludes.

27. See footnote 25 of this chapter.

28. See W. J. T. Mitchell's theories on English landscape and landscape painting in which he suggests that "the representation of landscape is not only a matter of internal politics and national or class ideology but also an international, global phenomenon, intimately bound up with the discourses of imperialism" (9), suggesting the ways in which the landscape and "the discourses of imperialism" are interconnected. As well, he argues that

> the discourse of imperialism . . . conceives itself precisely (and simultaneously) as an expansion of landscape understood as an inevitable, progressive development in history, an expansion of 'culture' and 'civilization' into a 'natural' space in a progress that is itself narrated as 'natural.' Empires move outward in space as a way of moving forward in time . . . in the re-presentation of the home landscape, the 'nature' of the imperial center. (17)

suggesting that the landscape and empire are not only interconnected but inter-reliant.
29. Simon Gikandi argues that "the reason the Norman conquest of England was to function as the inaugural moment in colonial histories was that, in quite insidious ways, it alienated the colonized from their immanent history by performing a palatable narrative of imperial conquest" (26). In addition, see Pat Thane's suggestion that "[i]n practice, the Dominions did not, as Britain expected, simply adopt the British legislation, but rather enacted their own similar, but not identical, statutes" (42).
30. In the last episode, Bernard asks, "*Should this be the end of the story? a kind of sigh? a last ripple of the wave? a trickle of the water to some gutter where, burbling, it dies away?. . . . But if there are no stories, what end can there be, or what beginning? . . . our waters can only just surround feebly that spike of sea-holly; we cannot reach that further pebble so as to wet it. It is over, we are ended*" (267), fusing both anxieties about narrative, imperial activities, and closure in his concerns about the processes of narrative through the metaphor of accessing other lands.
31. See Marlow's confession in Joseph Conrad's *Heart of Darkness* as an example:

> "Now when I was a little chap I had a passion for maps. I would look for hours at South America, or Africa, or Australia and lose myself in all the glories of exploration. At that time there were many blank spaces on the earth and when I saw one that looked particularly inviting on a map (but they all look that) I would put my finger on it and say: When I grow up I will go there. . . . But there was one yet—the biggest—the most blank, so to speak—that I had a hankering after" (7–8).

32. Jane Marcus argues that not only are "[t]he fragmented selves of the 'civilized' characters in *The Waves* . . . directly related to the politics of British imperialism" (144), Bernard's character specifically enacts these imperial politics as his "is an act of literary hegemony; he absorbs the voices of his marginalized peers into his own voice" (142). Bernard's "literary hegemony" then narratizes the visual production of the text in its own encroachment on the margins.
33. Homi Bhabha, as I described in my Introduction, explains *hybridity* as

> the sign of the productivity of colonial power, it's shifting forces and fixities; it is the name for the strategic reversal of the process of domination through disavowal . . . the revaluation of the assumption of colonial identity through the repetition of discriminatory identity effects. It displays the necessary deformation and displacement of all sites of discrimination and domination. It unsettles the mimetic or narcissistic demands of colonial power but reimplicates its identifica-

tions in strategies of subversion that turn the gaze of the discriminated back upon the eye of power" (*Post-Colonial* 34–5).

As well as:

"The paranoid threat from the hybrid is finally uncontainable because it breaks down the symmetry and the duality of self/other, inside/outside. In the productivity of power, the boundaries of authority—its reality effects—are always besieged by 'the other scene' of fixations and phantoms" (*Location* 116).

34. An alternative reading here, by looking at the episodes, would consider the following (fourth) episode's dinner with Percival as a moment of unification. Rather than creating monstrous, hybridized identities that merge one character into another, this moment creates a unifying identity around Percival in which the characters relish. Jinny, in fact, says: "Let us hold it for one moment, . . . love, hatred, by whatever name we call it, this globe whose walls are made of Percival, of youth and beauty, and something so deep sunk within us that we shall perhaps never make this moment out of one man again" (145).

35. The violent entry of the sun in the domestic sphere of the house precedes the characters' remembrance of the colonist, Percival, during their everyday living of the sixth episode. Louis considers his death as one of many ("all deaths are one death" 170) and then exhorts himself to "out of the many men in me make one" (170), echoing the unifying effect of Percival. Susan imagines Percival "com[ing] home, bringing me trophies to be laid at my feet. He will increase my possessions" (172), echoing the booty of imperialism in this interlude. Jinny briefly alludes to Percival as "[i]n one way or another we make this day. . . . Some take the train for France; other ship for India. Some will never come into this room again. One may die tonight" (176), but, like Louis, couches this in a discussion of unification as "[t]he common fund of experience is very deep" (175). Neville compares himself to Percival and finds that he "could not ride about India in a sun-helmet and return to a bungalow," and compares his lover to Percival who consoles Louis "for the lack of many things—I am ugly, I am weak—and the depravity of the world, and the flight of youth and Percival's death, and bitterness and rancour and envies innumerable" (181). In all, the characters of the episodes recall the unity brought by the imperialist, Percival, a unity that the imperial sun here, in the preceding interlude, disfigures and destroys. In this comparison, then, the ideals of imperialism as represented by Percival in the episodes, are shown to be false compared to the realities of its consequences as shown by the activities of the sun in the interludes.

36. Miriam Wallace also argues that "Even the interstices of italicized text are contiguous: to each other visually, to the voices sequentially, and through shared images" (299).

37. See also Gillian Beer's discussion of "Virginia Woolf and Prehistory" in *Virginia Woolf: The Common Ground* in which she writes that "prehistory is seen not simply as part of a remote past, but as contiguous, continuous, a part of ordinary present-day life" (9) and that "in Woolf" there is an "emphasis upon lost and unreclaimable origins" as well as "a counter-insistence on perpetuity and on the survival of what precedes consciousness, precedes history" (11). Both movements, of a lost origin and of a survival of prehistory are at work here in the interludes of *The Waves* as we see Woolf both yearning for an imagined and attempting to locate an actual reality of the feminine outside of patriarchal and imperial history.

38. The narrative device of stage setting is witnessed even more clearly in the conclusion of *Between the Acts* which poses the main characters Isa and Giles as if on a dark stage and about to perform: "Isa let her sewing drop. The great hooded chairs had become enormous. And Giles too. And Isa too against the window. The window was all sky without colour. The house had lost its shelter. It was night before roads were made, or houses. It was the night that dwellers in caves had watched from some high place among rocks. Then the curtain rose. They spoke" (219).

39. See also characters' comments throughout the episodes in which Woolf claims spaces of darkness and shadow as places of possibility for new identity formation. At Percival's dinner, Bernard comments: "I have been traversing the sunless territory of non-identity. A strange land. I have heard in my moment of appeasement, in my moment of obliterating satisfaction, the sigh, as it goes in, comes out, of the tide that draws beyond this circle of bright light, this drumming of insensate fury" (116). Rhoda, at the same dinner, states: "and look—the outermost parts of the earth—pale shadows on the utmost horizon, India for instance, rise into our purview. The world that had been shriveled, rounds itself; remote provinces are fetched up out of darkness; we see muddy roads, twisted jungle, swarms of men, and the vulture that feeds on some bloated carcass as within our scope, part of our proud and splendid province, since Percival, riding alone on a flea-bitten mare, advances down a solitary path, has his camp pitched among desolate trees, and sits alone, looking at the enormous mountains" (137). In both musings, these territories of opportunity are described in terms of imperialism and sites of the other which are both inherently feminine and colonial. In this way, identity formation is linked again to the feminine, nationalism and imperial activity. Bernard's comment on the "sunless territory of non-identity" confirms the places of darkness and shadow as outside of preconceived identity demarcations, again making it a place filled with possibility for the feminine.

## NOTES TO CHAPTER 3

1. Whereas Homi Bhabha identifies the term *hybrid* as that which is "produced through . . . a process of splitting as the condition of subjection: a discrimination between the mother culture and its bastards, the self and its doubles, where the trace of what is disavowed is not repressed but repeated as something *different*—a mutation, a hybrid" (*Culture* 111), in this case "hybrid" is utilized in its botanical or zoological context as that which is a compound or cross between two different elements or species, although the complications of hybridity that Bhabha and others have highlighted are also at play.
2. See her description cited in the appendix of Moore's *Collected Writings*.
3. This is per David Goodway's comment in the appendix of *Collected Writings*, and my subsequent interview with him. Personal Interview. 18 May 2007.
4. The manuscript of *Fugue* is available at the University of London's Senate House Library. Also, see the appendix in Olive Moore, *Collected Writings*, for information on previous publications of her novels.
5. Although Moore's first novel, *Celestial Seraglio*, concerns itself with issues of female gender, sexual, and spiritual identity, as it is situated in the lives of young girls at a Belgian boarding school, it does not include

the development of maternity in these identity developments. *Spleen* and *Fugue*, therefore, are the most characteristic representation of Moore's exploration of the possibilities of new identity configurations that maternity and textual experimentation could provide for modern women.
6. Foria does not exist although a town, Forio, does appear on the map of the island of Ischia. As many of the names in the novel correspond with names on the island and in the town of Forio, it is safe to assume that this is the setting of the novel.
7. The title of the novel, *Spleen*, can be seen to allude directly to the definition of *spleen* as anger, melancholy, and crankiness. In addition, the appendix to the Dalkey Archive Press edition of Moore's *Collected Writings* states that Moore based the title of this novel after her reading of Baudelaire's "Spleen et Idéal" (423). Significantly, Peter Nicholls in his discourse on the evolution and many incarnations of modernism, *Modernisms: A Literary Guide*, begins with a reading of Baudelaire's poem, "To a Red-haired Beggar Girl," and sees this as a moment of an emerging modernist literary production or, at least, of containing "traces of modernism" (1). In his reading of this poem, Nicholls comments on the role of the female figure: "Baudelaire's way of making a representation of the feminine the means by which to construct an ironically anti-social position for the writer contains in germ many of the problems of the later modernisms" (3) and "the cruelty of seduction collapses ethical values into aesthetic ones, making the 'elimination' of the feminine the very mark of that triumph of form over 'bodily' content on which one major strand of modernism will depend" (4). Thus, Nicholls establishes that even at the early beginnings of modernism lay the twinned concerns of form and the feminine and the necessary repudiation of the one for the development of the other.
8. *The Oxford Dictionary of English Etymology*. Ed. C. T. Onions. New York: Oxford UP, 1966.
9. See George Bornstein's "Pound and the making of modernism."
10. In addition, James Longenbach argues that "Pound and Eliot decided that the imagist movement had gone too far and that a 'counter-current' to free verse needed to be established. This decision was provoked in part by aesthetic concerns, but it was also determined by Pound's inability to remain content with Imagism's implicitly feminized aesthetic–especially after Amy Lowell took a more active role in the movement" (119). In the final section of this chapter, I further explore and explicate the role of gender in literary modernism and its effects on modern women writers in general and Olive Moore's writing of *Spleen* in particular.
11. Here, I borrow from Peter Nicholls' term *modernisms*.
12. Whereas *primitive* connotes prehistoric, precolonial, or non-Western, *savage* connotes barbarism and violence. It is the first definition upon which I rely. Torgovnick, on the other hand, utilizes "primitive" to conjure both non-Western and violent connotations.
13. One of the many contradictions in the text, and one that I will discuss later in this chapter, reveals that Moore rejects the primitive status of women unless it suits her purpose as a British woman. Ruth repeatedly primitivizes the Forian women in contrast to her (parodied) self, and Moore often positions the Forian society as a kind of agrarian ideal which, although still seen as primitive in its rural state, is for Moore more authentic and natural (where natural means both closer to and essential in nature). In this way, the novel trades the male/female binary for a Northern European (or British)/Southern European one.

14. Susan Kent writes on the role of maternity and motherhood for the "new" feminists after World War I:

    Britons sought a return to the "traditional" order of the prewar world, an order based on natural biological categories of which imagined sexual differences were a familiar and readily available expression.... A gender system of separate spheres for men and women based upon scientific theories of sexual difference, a new emphasis upon motherhood, and an urgent insistence upon mutual sexual pleasure within marriage provided parameters within which "normal" activity was to be carried out and a return to normalcy effected.... As Riley has argued, "women's" thorough implication in "the social"—especially as it became, in the interwar years, obsessively focused on maternity and motherhood—limited feminism's ability to exist and operate effectively. (140–41)

    See also Denise Riley's *War in the Nursery: Theories of the Child and Mother* and Jane Lewis's *The Politics of Motherhood: Child and Maternal Welfare in England, 1900–1939.*
15. Throughout the novel, images of mother and child, rather than figured as the holy and "civilized" Madonna and Christ, recall instead more mythic, pagan, and rural representations of maternity and family (and Christian iconography), emphasizing Moore's concern with the mythic ideals of stereotypically male high modernism.
16. Although there is evidence of Saracen attacks on the town of Forio and the island of Ischia, I can find no evidence for a "Saracen Road" (Moore 112). I will discuss this use of Saracen later in this chapter.
17. See Sylvia Townsend Warner's *Lolly Willowes: or The Loving Huntsman* as another text which develops the relationship between women's rejection of societal constraints and demon possession.
18. Susan Kent documents how Maude Royden, one of the "new" feminist supporters "believed that the 'best' and most absorbing work women could do was the bearing and rearing of children" (117). Also, Kent states that "[a] more insistent ideology of motherhood demanded that women leave their wartime jobs, give up their independence, and return to home and family, where their primary occupation—their obligation, in fact—would be the bearing and rearing of children" (108), and the rhetoric of the "new" feminists such as Eleanor Rathbone "drew upon and furthered those discourses which insisted upon motherhood as women's primary and even exclusive function in life" (120).
19. For the numerous possible sources for "let them eat cake," see William Saffire's "The Way We Live Now: 6-25-00: On Language; Never Said It." In addition, Antonia Fraser writes: "This story was first told about the Spanish Princess who married Louis XIV a hundred years before the arrival of Marie Antoinette in France; it continued to be repeated about a series of other Princesses throughout the eighteenth century. As a handy journalistic cliché, it may never die. Yet, not only was the story wrongly ascribed to Marie Antoinette in the first place, but such ignorant behaviour would have been quite out of character. The unfashionably philanthropic Marie Antoinette would have been far more likely to bestow her own cake (or *brioche*) impulsively upon the starving people before her" (xix–xx).
20. Although Marie Stopes established the first birth control clinic in London in 1921, birth control was not widely available or reliable in the 1920s and 1930s. Ruth's later comments about Joan Agnew and the modern woman who "wanted no children. Women kept their figures and their jobs" (230) situate the specifics of birth control uncertainly. Hall, Lesley. Message to

author. 3 Feb. 2006. E-mail, and Hall, Lesley. "Questions of Control and Choice: Women and Reproduction in Britain since 1900" in Birth and Breeding: The Politics of Reproduction in Modern Britain. Catalogue of an exhibition at the Wellcome Institute for the History of Medicine, Oct 1993–Feb 1994.
21. Susan Kent documents the developments in the ideology of maternity and motherhood:
> In the first six months of the war, the idea of women as mothers, as givers of life, emerged from rhetoric that focused on women's roles in wartime and from arguments about the relationship between feminism and pacifism. It was accompanied, indeed, it depended upon, the notion of men as warriors, life-destroyers, and—in the context of the Belgian atrocity stories—as bloodthirsty and rapacious. After 1915, as women flocked to munitions factories and auxiliary organizations, the predominant image of women as mothers gave way to that of women as warriors; in some representations, women could be seen as destroyers of men. . . . . The postwar backlash against women extended beyond the question of women's employment; a *Kinder, Küche, Kirche* ideology stressing traditional femininity and motherhood permeated British culture. (115)
22. Moore's repetition of the description of Ruth operates similarly to Woolf's repetition of Clarissa Dalloway's appearance with "there she was" (see p. 50), the difference being that Clarissa is being seen suddenly by other people and in that sight granted presence, and Ruth is seeing herself as absent at least in head/mind.
23. The "Winged Victory of Samothrace" serves as a strikingly appropriate metaphor for female embodiment and identity as "The original *Winged Victory (Nike) of Samothrace* was created by the Greeks in the period between 190–180 BC. . . . *Winged Victory* (eight feet tall) portrays the Greek goddess of victory standing on the prow of a ship with her wings spread and her clinging garments rippling in the wind as she descends from the sky to celebrate the naval triumph of the fleet." Goldstein, Joseph L. "60 Years of Winged Victory for Biomedical Research." 1023. The statue, then, embodies the confluence of female imagery and identity with imperialism and war as well as the subsequent destruction of the feminine through the dismemberment of the statue. It is also important to note that Marinetti in his "The Founding and Manifesto of Futurism" wrote that "We affirm that the worlds magnificence has been enriched by a new beauty: the beauty of speed. A racing car whose hood is adorned with great pipes, like serpents of explosive breath—a roaring car that seems to ride on grapeshot is more beautiful than the Victory of Samothrace."
24. See the Appendix for a picture of Sava Botsaris' bust of Olive Moore.
25. See Edith Hamilton's *Mythology* for a full accounting of the birth of Athena.
26. This movement or location of Ruth's pregnancy signals toward stories of the traveling uterus in early theories on hysteria. See footnote 21 in Chapter 4 on the history of hysteria.
27. In Moore's fourth book, *The Apple Is Bitten Again*, which is a series of journal entries, Moore continues her vitriolic critique of women and alignment with men. An intertextual reading, then, would situate Moore as sympathetic with Ruth and as using her as a mouthpiece of her complicated and contradictory philosophies. See footnote 16, of Chapter 4, for specific examples of Moore's critique.
28. Not until the end of the novel, when Ruth meets Joan Agnew, does Moore introduce a female character who is not a mother—all of the female characters

in Italy are mothers or mothers in the making and even her sister-in-law, Dora, is figured as mother-like to Ruth although unmarried. Joan, as I discuss later in this chapter, also falls under Ruth/Moore's critical eye. Simply not having children at all is not an acceptable solution either.
29. Richard's feet also allude to Oedipus' swollen feet which were caused by the deliberate mutilation by his father prior to his abandonment. In this allusion, Richard becomes the product of Ruth's defiance against nature (maternal rather than marital). But Richard is not developed as a central character or given much agency throughout the novel, and the allusion, then, is not sustained.
30. Ruth's "shocked" reaction reveals her ironic position as both rejecting her own maternity and child but also advocating for maternity here and later (see pages 96–7).
31. See page 76 and footnote 8 on the etymology of "conceive."
32. See page 76 and footnote 8 on the etymology of "conceive."
33. McClintock, Anne. *Imperial Leather: Race, Gender and Sexuality in the Colonial Contest*. New York: Routledge, 1995.
34. See Virginia Woolf's comment in *Three Guineas* that "in fact, as a woman, I have no country" (109).
35. Ruth's restriction by fashion which marks her gender, class, and nationality contradicts her geographical mobility in moving from England to Italy, traveling virtually alone. Significantly, after just a week on the island Ruth adapts to the island dress: "the dark, sprigged apron, the dark tucked blouse, the long dark petticoat . . . no stockings even in winter . . . she disliked zoccoli for their dreadful clap-clapping on the stone floors, and wore instead light low-heeled shoes sent especially from Naples. She cut off her elegant mountain of hair to the neck. . . . Not until her early thirties did Ruth let her hair grow again and make a twist of it in the nape of her neck as the other women" (118–19). Ruth willingly and quickly abandons most of the hindrances of fashion and appearance making as if relieved to live out her body in function rather than fashion through her "rigid rejection of all clothes and elegances associated with her former life" (119).
36. Ruth's father plays a significant role in her upbringing, her mother having tried to abort her and abandoning her after her birth. Although Ruth is lost after her father's death, she does not prove to continue in his footsteps, loving the earth but not necessarily its people equally (see my subsequent discussion of her colonialist position). Moore's brief discussions of Ruth's father situate him as highly formative in her development, but his subsequent absence vacates the place of a guide to her young adult development and disrupts the legacy of his ideologies. Again, Moore seems to comment on the position of the modern woman as unable to proceed successfully in any direction.
37. I repeat Torgovnick's contribution to this argument that: "Both European women and colonized peoples were, relative to European men, associated with the childlike, the irrational, and the dependent—and so linked. . . . Immediate precedents for gendering the land female and symbolizing Africa in female terms were available in popular writers like Rider Haggard and Joseph Conrad. In addition, the popularity and renown of historical figures like La Malinche in Mexico and Pocahontas in Virginia tended to make females into symbols of access to indigenous peoples and their land" (37).
38. Kirby, Kathleen M. *Indifferent Boundaries: Spatial Concepts of Human Subjectivity*. New York: Guilford P, 1996: 7.

39. When the solicitor first hears Ruth's plan for Sharvells, he "hesitat[ed] whether to treat her as a lady or a lunatic for wishing to deprive the empire of a golf-course within easy reach" (223) for "[i]t seemed that the country had great need of golf-courses easy of access at week-ends" (221).
40. Gil Kirkwood, Chairman of the Women's Golfers Museum in Britain, states that "By the time it got to the 1920s and 30s, women had no problem with length and could play on any course. Their tees were forward, but apart from that, it was the same course. Of course some golf clubs only accepted male members, and if this was the case, women were often not allowed as guests. This is still prevalent today." Message with the Chairman, 5 Feb. 2006. E-mail. It is not entirely clear, then, if the golf club and course the solicitor proposes would be open to women or not.
41. See also the discussion of maternity and work by Virginia Woolf in *A Room of One's Own*. 22, 50–51.
42. Here, again, we see Ruth's language as comparable to exploration literature, revealing her imperialist mindset and cultural supremacy in an archetypal example of western attitudes toward non-Western cultures.
43. Significantly, Ruth's father provides an example of male mind that was not imperialist, and Ruth has rejected his model. See such passages as: "The distinction her father had made as between races, peoples, classes, differed in many ways from the distinctions common to his day . . . which was a pleasant one of smug imperialism, good queens and good will; and particularly did they differ in their not being calculated on a monetary or patriotic basis. . . . it is as unwise as it is impossible to define where races begin, end and merge, as it is to define where art and the noises of races such as music and speech begin, end, and merge' (140). Moore's representation of Ruth's father presents another contradictory voice in Ruth's repertoire of criticism and ideologies. At best, Moore offers Ruth's father as the voice of enlightened reason that Ruth seemingly ignorantly rejects. To complicate this further, though, if Ruth's father is Moore's voice of enlightened reason, Moore reaffirms the dichotomy of male intellect to female blank/empty body.
44. Again, Ruth situates herself as colonizer and missionary, reiterating the language of the colonizer in seeing the Forians as childish in their primitivism. Ruth's colonizer/missionary status plays out further as she tries to teach the Forian children to groom themselves and to learn English manners and language (179–80).
45. I include here a brief history of the island of Ischia which hosts the town Forio that Moore appears to be adapting here. To summarize, Ischia has been home to Greeks, Romans, Napolitans, Germans, Saracens, Normans, Spaniards, Turks, Corsairs, Austrians, Bourbons, and the English (not to mention earthquakes, volcanic eruptions, typhus, cholera, and the plague). It is uncertain, then, why the Saracen influence would specifically be so strong upon the island (as in the naming of the road) and upon the novel. Surely, the emphasis on the Saracens allows for Moore to further contrast the civilized/savage dichotomy on the island through the association of the Saracens as Arab opponents to the Crusades and, broadly, to nomadic cultures that emphasizing the Norman or English influence would not. This history does demonstrate that by the twentieth century, the inhabitants of the island would necessarily be the physical and metaphorical products of all of this genealogic and genetic history and thus embody both the colonizer and the colonized. See Girolamo Arnaldi's *Italy and Its Invaders* which states that in the ninth century "from Sicily, Africa, and Spain the Saracens—this is what medieval chroniclers called the Arab Muslims, using the name of an

ancient tribe of robbers from the southern Sinai—staged numerous raids on the coasts of central and southern Italy" (66).

46. Initially, Ruth recoils from their apparent savagery: "She could not bear the shrill curses and crackling whips and heavy buttock-blows as the beasts tore by, panic in their hoofs. . . . holding her hands over her eyes, aghast at the pleasure it would have given her to rush out in the road, wrest the sticks from the men and bring them down on their own backs, thrashing them down on to the ground, striking them heavily about the eyes and face as in their slyer moments they struck their beasts" (154). But when Lisetta responds, "Macche, macche, who is cruel? Do you not see how hard they work themselves? Five times as hard as they can ever get their beasts to work. Pity the men, said Lisetta dismissing it impatiently; it is sadder to be the tamer than the lion," Ruth comments,

    In time she came also to see it in its truer light and to justify the blows by the prodigious display of sustained energy the men put up daily, year in year out. But even now at times she could still feel the blows on her own back, and could still dread their muted approach as acutely as on hearing it for the first time. The logic of the thing she understood. Crude nature against crude nature was their affair, with a turn of the quick head and a spit true-aimed over the shoulder. It was not easy to regard one's beast in heroic light with one's own feet thick with blisters, and one's own back aching under a load almost as heavy and a march every bit as long. Then why should the sight of a man sweating under a load too large for him arouse in her less pity than the sight of a beast overladen and the sound of blows and galloping hoofs? (154)

47. Specific examples of patriarchal Forian culture are seen in the making of the wine, as Andrea tells Ruth: "You couldn't let a woman tread the grapes or the wine would be sour and unsaleable. Why? Because it always had been so: who would drink wine that a woman trod? Andrea spat. It was a man's job and a man's drink" (187–88). As well, women must drink after the men: "taking a jug . . . Andrea . . . took it in his hands, drank some himself first, and then handed the jug to Uller, who offered it first to Ruth, who saw the amazement in Andrea's round eye, knew what it meant and wouldn't have hurt his phallic pride for the world; and made Uller drink first and drank after him, though properly he should have passed it on to Domenicos, Andrea's son-in-law who stood by and the two men workers and then to the several male children: after which she came and the female children" (187–88).
48. See page 76 and footnote 8 on the etymology of *conceive*.
49. In addressing the issues of gender and anorexia, Heywood asserts that "anorexics and figures of anorexia in canonical male modernist texts are almost exclusively male, while contemporary cases of anorexia involve women" (63).
50. Nicholls encapsulates Pound's directives of the imagiste as follows: "he defined the image as the presentation of 'an intellectual and emotional complex in an instant of time.' Three other 'rules' by poet and translator F. S. Flint complemented Pound's essay: 1. Direct treatment of the 'thing,' whether subjective and objective. 2. To use absolutely no word that did not contribute to the presentation. 3. As regarding rhythm: to compose in sequence of the musical phrase, not in sequence of a metronome" (Nicholls 169). Lawrence Rainey cites the foundation of Imagism as "purely a matter of writerly technique: 'Their watchword was Precision,' and they opposed only 'interminable effusions'" (39).
51. Heywood's analysis poses a direct contrast with other male modernists, specifically Joyce, who also develop fleshy and excessive texts. See footnote 54

for other possible analyses of Joyce and his place within these theories of the feminine and literary production.
52. Kirby also indicates the excess of the feminine: "'becoming woman' is written in the spacing of a corporeography from which nothing is exempted" (80), and from this, I add that this excessiveness of woman is exactly what contributes to the anxiety of and desire for separation from the feminine. Additional discussion of language and excess from Kirby includes the following post-structural argumentations: "with no 'outside the sign' there can be no 'outside the system' that gives it value. Consequently, language bursts the boundaries of its conventional articulation, engendering a reality whose inscriptive production implicates the ideological with/in the physical" (52), "the nature of signification's dynamic flux is identified against the mute reality of stable objects. But if the critique of the sign is to be taken seriously, if materiality is a type of 'writing' wherein difference is permeable to what we describe as culture, and that the transformational plasticity that identifies the latter must also inhabit the former" (56), and "What is writing when it is more than writing—when the familiar meaning of the word assumes such monstrous elasticity that it surrounds and invades everything, when it is everything, when there is no getting outside this ubiquitous text? And how is the body itself a scene of writing, subject to a sentence that is never quite legible, because to read it is to write it, again, yet differently?" (56). As with hysteria, where the body acts as an illegible sign of broken psychic and linguistic semiology, Kirby here reaffirms the consequences of a broken sign system which no longer contains language so that it becomes "monstrous," "elastic," and subsequently "bursts the boundaries of its conventional articulation." Again, these terms can be conflated with the feminine as I will argue in the subsequent paragraphs regarding Kristeva's theories on the abject.
53. In contrast, the feminine can also be seen as abject in its absence as when Luce Irigaray states: "her sexual organs represents *the horror of nothing to see*" (26).
54. Again, Kristeva only analyzes male authors in *Powers of Horror*. Regarding *Ulysses*, she states: "[f]ar from preserving us from the abject, Joyce causes it to break out in what he sees as prototype of literary utterance: Molly's monologue" (22). Her example, of the abject emerging from a female character in a chapter which is indeed excessive in its textual experimentation reveals that although Joyce does utilize a textual form of excess he deploys it in such a way as to essentialize women as physical and linguistic excess and, therefore, re-abjectifies them. Peter Nicholls also includes Joyce in the list of those that Eliot and Pound saw as declining "in terms of loss of clarity" into a "decadent language . . . which has become somehow 'bodily,' a condition which prevents 'objectivity' and which is quickly marked as 'feminine'" such as Pound's description of the "the descent into the 'brown meat' of Rembrandt, the 'thickening line,' and the increasing opacity of the word," and Lewis' description "the 'heavy, sticky, opaque mass' of Gertrude Stein's writing and the 'stupednous outpouring of *matter*, or *stuff*' which is Joyce's *Ulysses*" (195–96).
55. Kristeva also claims that "all literature is probably a version of the apocalypse that seems to her rooted, no matter what its socio-historical conditions might be, on the fragile border (borderline cases) where identities (subject/object, etc.) do not exist or only barely so—double, fuzzy, heterogeneous, animal, metamorphosed, altered, abject" (*Powers* 207). As such, language is not necessarily gendered but is seen to be that which hovers and attempts to operate in and around this "fuzzy," "fragile" border of both literary production and subjectivity identification.

56. In his essay, "Tradition and the Individual Talent" T. S. Eliot writes, "No poet, no artist of any art, has his complete meaning alone. His significance, his appreciation is the appreciation of his relation to the dead poets and artists" (4), asserting his belief in the importance of literary tradition for the modern artist. In addition, in "*Ulysses*, Order and Myth," Eliot writes of Joyce: "In using the myth, in manipulating a continuous parallel between contemporaneity and antiquity, Mr. Joyce is pursuing a method which others must pursue after him. They will not be imitators, any more than the scientist who uses the discoveries of an Einstein in pursuing his own, independent, further investigations. It is simply a way of controlling, of ordering, of giving a shape and a significance to the immense panorama of futility and anarchy which is contemporary history. . . . Instead of narrative method, we may now use the mythical method. It is, I seriously believe, a step toward making the modern world possible in art" (372–73). Here, Eliot asserts the use of myth to order the "anarchy" of the modern world. As well, he understands the adoption of the "mythical method" not as imitation (he, then, does not see himself as encouraging the kind of hysteria that Kirby theorizes) but as a continuing development of Joyce's theories and experimentation. This, then, is further evidence of Joyce as residing in the camp of the male high modernists, at least according to Eliot, and as aligned with their position on the annihilation of the feminine.
57. Nicholls also points out the contradictions in the high modernists' ideas of tradition: "Here the 'new' was a highly equivocal category, since the cultural renovation was frequently projected as a *return* to the values of a previous age. . . . The modernism presided over by Pound and Eliot (one among several, but arguably still the hegemonic one) thus issued a call to order in the name of values which were explicitly anti-modern, though it did so by developing literary forms which were overtly modernist" (166–67). In addition, Michael Bell argues that "Like Pound and other Modernists, Eliot thought closely about the paradoxes of tradition in relation to creativity; the most original is not only bound within a tradition but is most likely to reaffirm it; in this connection, 'renewing' is a bottomlessly ambiguous term" (16).
58. Moore is actually citing "I Am" by John Clare.
59. See Bornstein, George. "Ezra Pound and the Making of Modernism."

## NOTES TO CHAPTER 4

1. A shortened version of this chapter has been accepted for publication as "*Fugue*-ing: Olive Moore, the Feminine and the Multiple Flights of the Modern Subject." *Musical Modernism: Essays on Language and Music in Modernist Literature*. Forthcoming.
2. For further discussion of the connection between patriarchy and linear and conclusive narratives, see Chapter 1 on *Mrs. Dalloway* and textual experimentation.
3. Harrion's marriage to his wife, Frances, resulted in two children. The oldest, a daughter (Selina), was closest to Harrion but was hit by a truck and killed at a very young age. Harrion spends much of the novel pursuing Selina, seeing her in Lavinia, the landscape, and in the smoke at the crematorium.
4. "The term fugue, which Matteson properly explains as a piece in which the voices answer each other, has been derived by some musical scholars from *fugare*, to chase—since one part chases the other, so to speak—and by others, from *fugere*, to flee—since one part flees another" (154). Mann, Alfred.

*The Study of Fugue. The Oxford English Dictionary* assigns the following definition: "A flight from one's own identity, often involving travel to some unconsciously desired locality. It is a dissociative reaction to shock or emotional stress in a neurotic, during which all awareness of personal identity is lost though the person's outward behaviour may appear rational" (2).
5. Coons, Philip M. "THE DISSOCIATIVE DISORDERS Rarely Considered and Underdiagnosed." In addition, "[t]he fugue usually comes into being owing to the fact that some unpleasant experience has become unconscious by the unwitting process of suppression or is tending to pass into the unconscious through the agency of the witting process of repression. In such a fugue the dissociation is complete. On return to the normal state there is no memory of the behaviour during the fugue or of any conscious processes which accompanied this behaviour." Rivers, William H. R. "Instinct and the Unconscious: A Contribution to a Biological Theory of the Psycho-Neuroses. Chapter X: Dissociation" (1920).
6. Coons, Philip M. "THE DISSOCIATIVE DISORDERS Rarely Considered and Underdiagnosed."
7. Due to my focus on female embodiments and subjectivities, I will not be pursuing the various flights of Harrion except as they contribute to the analysis of the feminine and, specifically, of Lavinia. The analysis of Harrion, albeit rife with possibility, will be largely relegated to a footnoted supporting role.
8. Mann elaborates thus: "When one part flees, pursued by another, this is actually nothing but what has been explained as imitation. . . . A fugue arises when a succession of notes in one part is taken over in another part, with due regard for the mode, and especially for the position of whole- and half-tone steps" (80).
9. Julia Kristeva's theories in *Powers* on the abject again prove useful here, specifically in locating the psychological underpinnings of the rejection of the feminine and delineating the various incarnations that the abject may take. To review, the abject is that which "disturbs identity, system, order" (4) or who becomes a "stray" (8) by wandering outside of the symbolic system, that is, anything which transgresses the boundary of the self: blood, pus, semen, and so forth. The connection between ideas of the abject and the feminine becomes most evident through maternity: in childbirth a part of the self transgresses the boundary of the self to become other, making woman both abject and abjecting. Because of its abject status, the feminine is rejected by the keepers of the symbolic system (i.e., patriarchy), and this rejection reflects the abject status of the feminine's physical excess, societal contamination, threat of death, and straying from the body and society.
10. In an interesting biographical aside, of the two images available of Olive Moore, one is a photograph of a bust of Moore sculpted by her husband, Sava Botzaris. See the appendix for a photograph of the sculpture.
11. Harrion's viewpoint of Lavinia is overtly misogynistic in its sexualizing of her body. At the same time, and even in this way, Harrion serves as a mouthpiece for the "symbolic system" (*Powers* 65) that inscribes the feminine body as both abject and sexual.
12. In addition, as I have cited previously, Mariana Torgovnick states, in her discussion on the primitive, that there was "a tendency to think about the primitive, the female, and the oceanic as almost interchangeable" (24).
13. The story of Semele's being burnt by Zeus' fire from Hamilton's Greek mythology is as follows:
> Zeus was madly in love with her and told her that anything she asked of him he would do; he swore it by the river Styx, the oath which not even he himself could break. She told him that what she wanted above

all else was to see him in his full splendor as King of Heaven and Lord of the Thunderbolt. It was Hera who had put that wish into her heart. Zeus knew that no mortal could behold him thus and live, but he could do nothing. He had sworn by the Styx. He came as she asked, and before that awful glory of burning light she died. But Zeus snatched from her her child that was near birth, and hid it in his own side away from Hera until the time had come for it [Dionysus] to be born. (65)

14. Lavinia's description of Harrion's approach to sex parallels his description of his visits to the crematorium, extending the connection between Lavinia and the abject through the abjection of the corpse: "Here once more desire returned to him. Once again life held an interest; an interest that now could never fail and which he shared alone. For here and at last one could love without fear or rebuff. Indeed, could be so filled with a love for all mankind as to burn in a glowing heat of ecstasy that made one's footsteps light and suspect" (329).

15. According to Kristeva and Felluga, the rejection of the feminine and the entrapment of the feminine in its embodiment both reflect on the abject status of the feminine as physical excess, societal contamination, threat of death, and a straying from the body and society. Issues of containment also infuse the issues of the abject and especially surround issues of the feminine. Abject as the feminine body is more abject in its expulsion not only of the fetus but also of blood. Through maternity, then, woman is both abject and abjecting.

16. Moore here inserts her own vitriolic critique of women that often borders on misogyny. In her notebooks which form *The Apple is Bitten Again*, Moore's vitriol continues: "Yet is there more a woman can be, but unfaithful? Is not unfaithfulness her ultimate achievement? By the act of unfaithfulness and all its emotional-nervous excitements woman is crowned queen of her restricted kingdom. Her dominion the eruptive, useless, emotions: jealousy, uncertainty, despair" (340). "Woman is the vacuum which Nature abhors and must see filled. Consequently woman is always slightly ridiculous unless stretched on a bed or with a child in her arms" (343). And "*Girl Guides in Passing hold-up a Tram.* No wonder men rape children! They seem the only female things that have softness, gentleness, curiosity, sex-appeal, and no moral consciousness. From fourteen onward they harden to granite. Frigid, and with strident hygienic voices" (346–47). Moore's misogynistic comments further include lesbians and extend into her critique of men as well: "*Man.* A person, how like a cloud. It shapes itself as the wind blows. Like a cloud it is a dragon and becomes a lamb" (349). Everyone, it seems, is filleted by her pen. These "notes" are complicated further by our (albeit limited) understandings of Moore herself as "intimidating" and who "made her presence felt in any company" through her "carrying voice and penetrating laugh" (424) as described by Alec Bristow in the appendix to Dalkey Archives' *Collected Works*.

17. This is the only reference to Aunt Elizabeth in the text; it is not clear then if Aunt Elizabeth perhaps was a spinster, and therefore Evelyn feared a life alone, or, alternatively, if Aunt Elizabeth was an unwed mother, and therefore Evelyn feared being outcast (other possibilities are numerous).

18. The relationship between Evelyn and Lavinia is roughly sketched and included almost in its entirety in these conversations above. From these brief interactions, then, there is possibility for a queer reading of their relationship or, at least, of Evelyn's sexuality in the mere absence and/or avoidance of explicit information.

19. Luce Irigaray's summation of this problem: "In other words, the issue is not one of elaborating a new theory of which woman would be the *subject* or

the *object*, but of jamming the theoretical machinery itself, of suspending its pretension to the production of a truth and of a meaning that are excessively univocal" (78).
20. "Fatherland" is a term, according to *The Oxford English Dictionary*, with specific ties to Germany: "used to translate the Dutch or German *vaderland, vaterland*. the Fatherland: now usually = Germany."
21. For a brief history on hysteria and its relationship to women and the feminine see "Defining Hysteria" in Showalter, Elaine. *Hystories: Hysterical Epidemics and Modern Media*.
22. See Susan Kingsley Kent's *Making Peace: The Reconstruction of Gender in Interwar Britain*, on British women's purity and resistance as part of the war rhetoric and the national ideal as well as Kathy J. Phillips' *Virginia Woolf Against Empire*, in which she states "if chastity in women is not a value, and if women are not under threat from supposedly lustful colonized men, then what excuse do the Europeans have to keep those would-be rapists in the preventive detention of Empire?" (12–13).
23. Throughout *Fugue*, Moore alludes to Italy but does not directly describe or discuss it. Such understandings, then, are intertextual based on readings of *Spleen* as well which is located in Italy and in which Moore valorizes the rural Italian landscape over dreary, grey London as she does of the Alsatian landscape in *Fugue*.
24. I am here reminded of Woolf's discussion of "the Outsider" in *Three Guineas* when she states: "as a woman, I have no country. As a woman my country is the whole world" (109). In *Fugue*, Moore creates characters whose nationalism is so split they, too, seem to have no country.
25. In hindsight, Moore's prescience about the impulses toward fascism, exclusion, and crematoriums that are horrifyingly realized later in the 1930s and 40s stand out in stark contrast to her insistence on the valorization of Europe—specifically the Alsace and Italy—its people's rootedness in the land, and their sense of the sacredness of life. As if watching a horror movie where one knows the ultimate bloody conclusion, one wants to shout, "No!" as Lavinia proclaims the Alsace the ideal place to settle and raise her child.
26. Margaret R. Higonnet reports that "[Mary Douglas] noted the complex dualisms in symbolic forms of organization, many of them anchored in images of bodily space, that may at once designate women as pure and relegate them to the polluted margins of society" (3).
27. Due to the obscure references in the novel and its setting in time, it is difficult to place the exact moment of Russian immigration to which this passage refers and thus to explicate the characters' (and Moore's) discussion of it. During a discussion of Russian migration in these passages on H-net, I received the following information:
> Most probably . . . the passage is referring to the immigration caused by the October (Socialist) revolution of 1917 and the Civil War of 1918–1921, which followed. The immigrants mostly settled in Germany and France, though every European country (as well as Turkey and Middle East) received some share of them. Socially, these were of either nobility or middle class. Sometimes, very educated people or very high ranking nobility: Russian immigrant fiction is full of referrals to princes and earls becoming taxi drivers, and girls from "decent families" turning out as prostitutes. Normally, these displaced persons were issued what was then called "Nansen passports," i.e. a document stating the name and other personal information, but classifying the holder as not belonging to any country. One can imagine the social vulnerability of the passport holders. Also . . . the doctor, most prob-

ably, discusses creating some kind of "liberation army" (made of immigrants) to send to Russia (the Soviet Union) to fight communists.
Gapova, Elena. "Russian Immigration Question, Part Two."
In addition, I received this comment:
> Elena Gapova is completely right, except for the social structure of the migrants/refugees. In fact, this wave of (mainly) Civil War-refugees comprised also many artisans and Jews, especially from Southern Russia/later Ukraine. Another part was formed by former soldiers and officers from the Wrangel- and Denikin-armies evacuated via Constantinople. Elena's guess is right, too: Already in 1920/21, if I recall it rightly, France organised a troup detachment, consisting of emigrees and parts of the Russian troops sent to France in 1916 and shipped them to the southern front, where many of them preferred to fraternize with the red Army. During the 20s, Russian nobles and high-ranking officers tried to organise either a new big-scale intervention (which failed) or terrorist activities, about which little seems to be known.

Esch, Michael G. "Russian Immigration."
28. The "Come to Britain Movement" was first established in 1926 as an "[i]ndustry grouping promoting tourism in Britain both to potential overseas visitors and to government as an area of trade in which it ought to be involved." Jolley, Tony. "A Chronology of State Involvement in British Tourism." The Come to Britain movement is described as follows: "The Travel Association of Great Britain and Ireland, represented by English traders, tourist agencies, railway and steamship companies, hotel and theatre proprietors, and others, is anxious to increase the number of visitors, chiefly American, who come to England; it wants to keep them here instead of letting them roam about the continent of Europe or further afield. The Government has lent its support to the movement (guaranteeing 5000 pounds towards the funds next year) with Committees and suchlike, which has for its watchword COME TO BRITAIN." From Norman Douglas. *Good-bye to Western Culture*.
29. Again, Alison Light also makes the connections between the feminine, virginity, and bad cooking in her discussion of post-World War I life in Britain: "[d]omestic life, the emphasis on the world of home and family activity brings down some of the most virulent torrents of abuse: the British Sunday, British cooking, and frequently, British women (foreign maidens are far preferable to awkward English virgins" (7).
30. See Laurence, Patricia Ondek. *The Reading of Silence: Virginia Woolf in the English Tradition*, for a discussion of the use of silence in Woolf. She argues that the "'blanks' are not blinders but are infused with the psychic life and historical sense of a woman" (9), "not an 'emptiness' dependent on the notion of lack or absence. It is a presence to be acknowledged" (33–34), so that "Woolf's valuing of the silence of women undermines not only patriarchal but also Western notions of talk and silence" (8).
31. See George Bornstein's "Ezra Pound and the making of modernism."
32. In *The Apple is Bitten Again*, Moore's collection of notebooks or journal entries, she states: "*Five hundred a year and a Room of one's Own*. If creative achievement were a matter of a room of one's own, then since the first dawn in which the first woman was pushed to safety in the first cave, she should have been the world's creative artist. At no time in the world's history has woman been without a room of her own. But it has always been the kitchen. Then write on the kitchen table! Paint on the kitchen walls! Draw on the kitchen floor! Carve into shape the pastry and the butter! And so she would have had it been essential to her nature. . . . To the creative artist £500

is not enough. It must be five millions. Or five pence." For further analysis of this passage see the Epilogue, page 135.

## NOTES TO THE EPILOGUE

1. See Susan Kingsley Kent's *Making Peace* on the developments of feminism during the interwar period.
2. Virginia Woolf's political activity and ideas are well documented by herself, Leonard Woolf, and her literary critics. See Virginia Woolf's *Three Guineas*, Madeline Moores's *The Short Season Between Two Silences*, and Alex Zwerdling's *Virginia Woolf and the Real World*, for a beginning. Some understanding of Olive Moore's political leanings can be gleaned from the appendix to her *Collected Writings*. From this we know that she was "part of Charles Lahr's Red Lion Street Circle, a literary group that gravitated towards a bookstore specializing in radical literature" (422–23). David Goodway's work on Lahr and/as an anarchist can be found in "Charles Lahr: Anarchist, Bookseller, Publisher."
3. For work on the spaces of silence in Woolf's texts, see Patricia Ondek Laurence's *The Reading of Silence: Virginia Woolf in the English Tradition*. Criticism on Moore's texts, regarding silence or otherwise, is as yet unwritten and unavailable.
4. While I have addressed the contradictions and experimentations of these four novels of Woolf and Moore, more work lies ahead in explicating the textual developments of other British women modern novelists. The possible considerations for an extension of this book are endless. Situating this analysis of these texts in comparison with those of male modernists would help to prove or disprove the implications of gender in textual experimentation. In addition, a study of genre—taking into account the work of many male modernists who mostly wrote poetry such as Eliot and Pound—would broaden and deepen these considerations.

# Bibliography

Abel, Elizabeth. *Virginia Woolf and the Fictions of Psychoanalysis.* Chicago: U of Chicago P, 1989.
Arnaldi, Girolamo. *Italy and its Invaders.* Trans. Antony Shugaar. Cambridge: Harvard UP, 2005.
Barrett, Eileen, and Patricia Cramer, ed. *Virginia Woolf: Lesbian Readings.* New York: New York UP, 1997.
Baucom, Ian. *Out of Place: Englishness, Empire, and the Locations of Identity.* Princeton: Princeton UP, 1999.
Beasley, Rebecca. "Wyndham Lewis and Modernist Satire." *The Cambridge Companion to the Modernist Novel.* Ed. Morag Shiach. Cambridge: Cambridge UP, 2007. 126–36.
Beer, Gillian. *Virginia Woolf: The Common Ground.* Ann Arbor: U of Michigan P, 1996.
Bell, Michael. "The Metaphysics of Modernism." *The Cambridge Companion to Modernism.* Ed. Michael Levenson. Cambridge: Cambridge UP, 1999. 9–32.
Bell, Quentin. *Virginia Woolf: A Biography.* New York: Harvest, 1972.
Benstock, Shari. *Textualizing the Feminine: On the Limits of Genre.* Norman: U of Oklahoma P, 1991.
Bhabha, Homi. "Signs Taken for Wonders: Questions of Ambivalence and Authority under a Tree outside Delhi, May 1817." *The Location of Culture.* London: Routledge, 1994, 102–122.
Bhabba, Homi. "Signs Taken for Wonders." *The Post-Colonial Studies Reader.* Bill Ashcroft, Gareth Griffiths & Helen Tiffin, eds. London: Routledge, 1995 29–35.
Boone, Joseph Allen. *Libidinal Currents: Sexuality and the Shaping of Modernism.* Chicago: U of Chicago P, 1998.
Booth, Allyson. *Postcards from the Trenches: Negotiating the Space Between Modernism and the First World War.* New York: Oxford UP, 1996.
Booth, Howard J., and Nigel Rigby, ed. *Modernism and Empire.* Manchester: Manchester UP, 2000.
Bornstein, George. "Ezra Pound and the Making of Modernism." *The Cambridge Companion to Ezra Pound.* Ed. Ira B. Nadel. Cambridge: Cambridge UP, 1999. 22–42.
Bowlby, Rachel. *Feminist Destinations and Further Essays on Virginia Woolf.* Edinburgh: Edinburgh UP, 1997.
Burford, Arianne. "Communities of Silence and Music in Virginia Woolf's *The Waves* and Dorothy Richardson's *Pilgrimage. Virginia Woolf and Communities: Selected Papers from the Eighth Annual Conference on Virginia Woolf.* Ed. Jeanette McVicker and Laura Davis. New York: Pace UP, 1999. 160–181.

Butler, Judith. *Gender Trouble: Feminism and the Subversion of Identity.* New York: Routledge, 1990.
Cain, P. J., and A. G. Hopkins. *British Imperialism, 1688–2000.* 2nd ed. Harlow: Longman, 2002.
Caughie, Pamela L., ed. *Virginia Woolf in the Age of Mechanical Reproduction.* New York: Garland Publishing, 1999.
———. *Virginia Woolf and Postmodernism: Literature in Quest and Question of Itself.* Urbana: U of Illinois P, 1991.
Cixous, Hélène. "The Laugh of the Medusa." *Feminisms: An Anthology of Literary Theory and Criticism.* Ed. Robyn R. Warhol and Diane Price Herndl. New Brunswick: Rutgers UP, 1997. 347–362.
Clare, John. *Selected Poems of John Clare.* Ed. James Reeves. New York: Macmillan, 1957.
Cohen, Debra Rae. *Remapping the Home Front: Locating Citizenship in British Women's Great War Fiction.* Boston: Northeastern UP, 2002.
Cole, Sarah. *Modernism, Male Friendship, and the First World War.* Cambridge: Cambridge UP, 2003.
Conrad, Joseph. *Heart of Darkness.* New York: Authoritative Text, backgrounds and Context, Criticism. Ed. Paul B. Armstrong. New York: Norton, 2006.
Coons, Philip M. "THE DISSOCIATIVE DISORDERS Rarely Considered and Underdiagnosed." *Psychiatric Clinics of North America* 21.3 (1998): 638–39.
Croft, Andy. *Red Letter Days: British Fiction in the 1930s.* London: Lawrence and Wishart, 1990.
Cunningham, Valentine. "Shaping Modern English Fiction." *On Modern British Fiction.* Ed. Zachary Leader. Oxford: Oxford UP, 2002. 150–51.
Dickinson, Renée. "Exposure and Development: Re-Imagining Narrative and Nation in the Interludes of Virginia Woolf's The Waves." *Woolf Studies Annual* 13 (2007): 25–47.
———. "Extinguishing the Lady with the Lamp: Florence Nightingale and the Work of Empire in *The Waves.*" *Woolf and the Art of Exploration: Selected Papers from the Fifteenth Annual International Conference on Virginia Woolf.* Ed. Helen Southworth and Elisa Kay Sparks. Clemson: Clemson U Digital Press, 2006. 186–94.
Dibert-Himes, Audra. "Elizabeth Dalloway: Virginia Woolf's Forward Look at Feminism." *Virginia Woolf Emerging Perspectives: Selected Papers from the Third Annual Conference on Virginia Woolf.* Ed. Mark Hussey and Vara Neverow. New York: Pace UP, 1994. 224–29.
Douglas, Norman. *Good-bye to Western Culture.* 1930. A Project Gutenberg of Australia ebook. March 2003. <http://gutenberg.net.au/ebooks03/0300291.txt>.
Duncan, Nancy, ed. *Bodyspace: Destabilizing Geographies of Gender and Sexuality.* London: Routledge, 1996.
DuPlessis, Rachel Blau. *Writing Beyond the Ending: Narrative Strategies of Twentieth-Century Women Writers.* Bloomington: Indiana UP, 1985.
Easthope, Anthony. *Englishness and National Culture.* London: Routledge, 1999.
Eksteins, Modris. *Rites of Spring: The Great War and the Birth of the Modern Age.* New York: Mariner Books, 2000.
Eliot, T. S. "Tradition and the Individual Talent." *Selected Essays.* New York: Harcourt, 1950. 3–11.
———. "*Ulysses,* Order and Myth." *Modernism: An Anthology of Sources and Documents.* Ed. Jane Goldman, Vassiliki Kolocotroni, and Olga Taxidou. Chicago: U of Chicago P, 1998. 371–373.
Esch, Michael G. "Russian Immigration." Online posting. 8 Nov. 2005 H-net. Migration Discussion Group. <http://h-net.msu.edu/cgi-bin/logbrowse.

pl?trx=vx&list=H-Migration&month=0511&week=b&msg=LlSunXVusRanPtJW9S1QJg&user=&pw=>.
Esty, Jed. *A Shrinking Island: Modernism and National Culture in England*. Princeton: Princeton UP, 2003.
Eysteinsson, Astradur. *The Concept of Modernism*. Ithaca: Cornell UP, 1990.
"Fall." Def. I.1.f. Def. I.1.h. Def. III.12.a. Def. III.18.a. *OED Online*. 2008. Oxford University P. 12 March 2008 <http://dictionary.oed.com/cgi/entry/50081891>.
"Fatherland." *OED Online*. 2008. Oxford University P. 13 March 2008 <http://dictionary.oed.com/cgi/entry/50082669>.
Felluga, Dino. "Modules on Kristeva: On the Abject." *Introductory Guide to Critical Theory*. November 28, 2003. 28 Nov. 2008. Purdue U. <http://www.purdue.edu/guidetotheory/psychoanalysis/kristevaabject.html>.
Felski, Rita. *The Gender of Modernity*. Harvard: Harvard UP, 1995.
———. *Rereading Modernism: New Directions in Feminist Criticism*. Ed. Lisa Rado. New York: Garland, 1994.
Fernihough, Anne. "Consciousness as a Stream." *The Cambridge Companion to the Modernist Novel*. Ed. Morag Shiach. Cambridge: Cambridge UP, 2007. 65–81.
Fowler, H. W., and F. G. Fowler, ed. *The Concise Oxford Dictionary of Current English*. Oxford: Clarendon P, 1995.
Fraser, Antonia. *Marie Antoinette, Queen, Consort of Louis XVI*. New York: Doubleday, 2001.
Friedman, Ellen G., and Miriam Fuchs, ed. *Breaking the Sequence: Women's Experimental Fiction*. Princeton: Princeton UP, 1989.
Friedman, Susan Stanford. "Spatialization, Narrative Theory, and VirginiaWoolf's The Voyage Out," *Ambiguous Discourse: Feminist Narratology andBritish Women Writers*. Ed. Kathy Mezei. Chapel Hill: U of North Carolina P, 1996. 109–136.
Froula, Christine. *Virginia Woolf and the Bloomsbury Avant-Garde: War, Civilization, Modernity*. New York: Columbia UP, 2005.
"Fugue." *OED Online*. 2008. Oxford University P. 20 March 2008 <http://dictionary.oed.com/cgi/entry/50090652>.
Fussell, Paul. *The Great War and Modern Memory*. New York: Oxford UP, 2000.
Gapova, Elena. "Russian Immigration Question, Part Two." Online posting. 14 Feb. 2006. H-net. Migration Discussion Group. < http://h-net.msu.edu/cgi-bin/logbrowse.pl?trx=vx&list=H-Migration&month=0602&week=b&msg=02j8GLbWfFt%2b2pYzoVI5iA&user=&pw=>.
Garrity, Jane. *Step-Daughters of England: British Women Modernists and the National Imaginary*. Manchester: Manchester UP, 2003.
Gifford, Terry. *Pastoral*. London: Routledge, 1999.
Gikandi, Simon. *Maps of Englishness: Writing Identity in the Culture of Colonialism*. New York: Columbia UP, 1996.
Gilbert, Sandra, and Susan Gubar. *No Man's Land: The Place of the Woman Writer in the Twentieth-Century. Volume 1: The War of Words*. New Haven: Yale UP, 1988.
Goldman, Jane. *The Feminist Aesthetics of Virginia Woolf: Modernism,Post-Impressionism, and the Politics of the Visual*. Cambridge: Cambridge UP, 1998.
Goldman, Jane, Vassiliki Kolocotroni, and Olga Taxidou, ed. *Chicago Modernism: An Anthology of Sources and Documents*. U of Chicago P, 1998.
Goldstein, Joseph L. "60 Years of Winged Victory for Biomedical Research." *Nature Medicine* 11.10 (2005): 1023–25.
Goodway, David. "Charles Lahr: Anarchist, Bookseller, Publisher." *London Magazine* June/July (1977): 46–55.

Grosz, Elizabeth. *Sexuality and Space*. New York: Princeton Architectural P, 1992.

———. *Volatile Bodies*. Bloomington: Indiana UP, 1994.

Hall, Lesley. Message to author. 3 Feb. 2006. E-mail. "Questions of Control and Choice: Women and Reproduction in Britain since 1900" in Birth and Breeding: The Politics of Reproduction in Modern Britain. Catalogue of an exhibition at the Wellcome Institute for the History of Medicine, Oct 1993–Feb 1994. <http://homepages.primex.co.uk/~lesleyah/wmhistmy.htm#My%20own%20writings>.

Hamilton, Edith. *Mythology*. Boston: Little, 1942.

Harvey, David. *The Condition of Postmodernity: An Enquiry into the Origins of Cultural Change*. Cambridge: Blackwell, 1990.

Heywood, Leslie. *Dedication to Hunger: The Anorexic Aesthetic in Modern Culture*. Berkeley: U of California P, 1996.

Higonnet, Margaret R., and Joan Templeton, ed. *Reconfigured Space: Feminist Explorations of Literary Space*. Amherst: U of Massachusetts P, 1994.

Hussey, Mark. *Virginia Woolf A–Z: A Comprehensive Reference for Students, Teachers and Common Readers to Her Life, Work and Critical Reception*. Oxford: Oxford UP, 1995.

Hynes, Samuel. *A War Imagined: The First World War and English Culture*. New York: Atheneum, 1991.

Irigaray, Luce. *This Sex Which is Not One*. Trans. Catherine Porter and Carolyn Burke. Ithaca: Cornell UP, 1985.

Joannou, Maroula. *Ladies, Please Don't Smash These Windows: Women's Writing, Feminist Consciousness, and Social Change, 1918–38*. Oxford: Berg, 1995.

Jolley, Tony. "A Chronology of State Involvement in British Tourism." 30 Sept. 1999. <http://apollo4.bournemouth.ac.uk/si/tjolley/teaching_materials/state_involvemt_england/state_tm_int.html>.

Jones, Ellen Carol, ed. *Modern Fiction Studies* 38.1 (1992).

Kaivola, Karen. "Revisiting Woolf's Representation of Androgyny: Gender, Race, Sexuality, and Nation." *Tulsa Studies in Women's Literature* 18.2(1999): 235–61.

Katz, Tamar. "Modernism, Subjectivity, and Narrative Form: Abstraction in *The Waves*." *Narrative* 3.3 (1995). 232–51.

Keane, Melba Cuddy. "Virginia Woolf and the Varieties of Historicist Experience." *Virginia Woolf and the Essay*. Ed. Beth Carole Rosenberg and Jeanne Dubino. New York: St. Martin's P, 1997. 59–77.

Kent, Susan Kingsley. *Making Peace: The Reconstruction of Gender in Interwar Britain*. Princeton: Princeton UP, 1993.

Kirby, Kathleen M. *Indifferent Boundaries: Spatial Concepts of Human Subjectivity*. New York: Guilford P, 1996.

Kirby, Vicki. *Telling Flesh: The Substance of the Corporeal*. New York: Routledge, 1997.

Kirkwood, Gil. Chairman of the Women's Golfers Museum in Britain. Message with the Chairman. 5 Feb. 2006. E-mail.

Kristeva, Julia. *Desire in Language*. New York: Columbia UP, 1980.

———. *Powers of Horror: An Essay on Abjection*. Trans. Leon S. Roudiez. New York: Columbia UP, 1982.

Laurence, Patricia Ondek. *The Reading of Silence: Virginia Woolf in the English Tradition*. Stanford: Stanford UP, 1991.

Ledger, Sally, and Roger Luckhurst, ed. *The Fin de Siècle: A Reader in Cultural History, c. 1880–1900*. Oxford: Oxford UP, 2000.

Lee, Hermione. *Virginia Woolf*. New York: Vintage, 1996.

Levenson, Michael, ed. *The Cambridge Companion to Modernism*. Cambridge: Cambridge UP, 1999.

Lewis, Jane. *The Politics of Motherhood: Child and Maternal Welfare in England, 1900–1939*. London: Croom Helm, 1980.
Light, Alison. *Forever England: Femininity, Literature and Conservatism Between the Wars*. London: Routledge, 1991.
Logenbach, James. "Modern Poetry." *The Cambridge Companion to Modernism*. Ed. Michael Levenson. Cambridge: Cambridge UP, 1999. 100–129.
Lorsch, Susan E. "Structure and Rhythm in *The Waves*: The Ebb and Flow of Meaning." *Essays in Literature* 6 (1979): 195–206.
Mackie, Erin, ed. *The Commerce of Everyday Life: Selections from* The Tatler *and* The Spectator. Boston: Bedford, 1998.
Magnus, Kathy Dow. "The Unaccountable Subject: Judith Butler and the Social Conditions of Intersubjective Agency." *Hypatia* 21.2 (2006): 81–103.
Mann, Alfred. *The Study of Fugue*. New York: Dover Publishing, 1986.
Mansfield, Katherine. *Stories*. New York: Vintage, 1991.
Marcus, Jane. "Britannia Rules The Waves." *Decolonizing Tradition: New Views of Twentieth-Century "British" Literary Canons*. Ed. Karen R. Lawrence. Urbana: U of Illinois P, 1992. 136–161.
———. *Virginia Woolf and the Languages of Patriarchy*. Bloomington: Indiana UP, 1987.
Marinetti, F. T. "The Founding and Manifesto of Futurism 1909." *Futurist Manifestos*. Ed. Umbro Apollonio. London: Thames and Hudson, 1973.
McClintock, Anne. *Imperial Leather: Race, Gender and Sexuality in the Colonial Contest*. New York: Routledge, 1995.
McDowell, Linda. *Gender, Identity & Place: Understanding Feminist Geographies*. Minneapolis: U of Minnesota P, 1999.
McGee, Patrick. "The Politics of Modernist Form; or, Who Rules The Waves?" *Modern Fiction Studies* 38.3 (1992): 631–50.
McHale, Brian. *Postmodernist Fiction*. New York: Methuen, 1987.
McVicker, Jeanette and Laura Davis, eds. *Virginia Woolf and Communities: Selected Papers from the Eighth Annual Conference on Virginia Woolf*. New York: Pace UP, 1999.
Minow-Pinkney, Makiko. *Virginia Woolf and the Problem of the Subject: Feminine Writing in the Major Novels*. New Brunswick: Rutgers UP, 1987.
Mitchell, W. J. T. *Landscape and Power*. Chicago: U of Chicago P, 1994.
Moore, Madeline. "Nature and Community: A Study of Cyclical Reality in *The Waves*." *Virginia Woolf: Revaluation and Continuity*. Ed. Ralph Freedman. Berkeley: U of California P, 1980. 219–40.
———. *The Short Season Between Two Silences: The Mystical and thePolitical in the Novels of Virginia Woolf*. Boston: Allen & Unwin, 1984.
Moore, Olive. *The Apple is Bitten Again. Collected Writings*. Elmwood Park: Dalkey Archive P, 1992.
———. *Celestial Seraglio. Collected Writings*. Elmwood Park: Dalkey Archive P, 1992.
———. *Fugue. Collected Writings*. Elmwood Park: Dalkey Archive P, 1992.
———. *Spleen. Collected Writings*. Elmwood Park: Dalkey Archive P, 1992.
Moran, Patricia. *Word of Mouth: Body Language in Katherine Mansfield and Virginia Woolf*. Charlottesville: UP of Virginia, 1996.
Morgan, Genevieve. "Elizabeth Dalloway Talks Back; Students and the Mrs. Dalloway Experience." *Virginia Woolf and Her Influences: Selected Papers from the Seventh Annual Conference on Virginia Woolf*. Ed. Laura Davis and Jeanette McVicker. Plymouth: Plymouth State College, 1997. 234–38.
Nadel, Ira B., ed. *The Cambridge Companion to Ezra Pound*. Cambridge: Cambridge UP, 1999.
Nicholls, Peter. *Modernisms: A Literary Guide*. Berkeley: U of California P, 1995.

O'Brien, Catherine. *Women's Fictional Responses to the First World War: A Comparative Study of Selected Texts by French and German Writers*. New York : Lang, 1997.

Osterhammel, Jürgen. *Colonialism: A Theoretical Overview*. Trans. Shelley Frisch. Princeton: Wiener, 1997.

Onions, C. T., ed. *The Oxford Dictionary of English Etymology*. New York: Oxford UP, 1966.

Paccaud-Huguet, Josiane. "The Crowded Dance of Words: Language and Jouissance in *The Waves*." *Q/W/E/R/T/Y* 5 (1995): 227–40.

Phillips, Kathy J. *Virginia Woolf Against Empire*. Knoxville: U of Tennessee P, 1994.

Potter, Jane. *Boys in Khaki, Girls in Print: Women's Literary Responses to the Great War, 1914–1918*. Oxford: Clarendon P, 2005.

Rainey, Lawrence. "The Cultural Economy of Modernism." *Cambridge Companion to Modernism*. Ed. Michael Levenson. Cambridge: Cambridge UP, 1999. 33–69.

Raitt, Suzanne, and Trudi Tate, ed. *Women's Fiction and the Great War*. Oxford: Clarendon P, 1997.

Richardson, Dorothy. *Pilgrimage 1: Pointed Roofs*. New York: Popular Library, 1976.

Riley, Denise. *War in the Nursery: Theories of the Child and Mother*. London: Virago, 1983.

Rivers, William H. R. "Instinct and the Unconscious: A Contribution to a Biological Theory of the Psycho-Neuroses. Chapter X: Dissociation" (1920). *Classics in the History of Psychology: An Internet Resource Developed by Christopher D. Green*. York University, Toronto, Ontario. Posted March 2000. <http://psychclassics.yorku.ca/Rivers/chap10.htm>.

Robb, George. *British Culture and the First World War*. Houndsmills: Palgrave, 2002.

Roe, Sue. "The Impact of Post-Impressionism." *The Cambridge Companion to Virginia Woolf*. Ed. Sue Roe and Susan Sellers. Cambridge: Cambridge UP, 2000. 164–190.

Roe, Sue, and Susan Sellers, ed. *The Cambridge Companion to Virginia Woolf*. Cambridge: Cambridge UP, 2000.

Ruotolo, Lucio P. *The Interrupted Moment: A View of Virginia Woolf's Novels*. Stanford: Stanford UP, 1986.

Said, Edward. *Culture and Imperialism*. New York: Vintage, 1994.

Saffire, William. "The Way We Live Now: 6–25–00: On Language; Never Said It." *New York Times Magazine*. 25 June 2000: 22.

Scott, Bonnie Kime. *The Gender of Modernism*. Bloomington: Indiana UP, 1990.

———. *Refiguring Modernism, Volume Two: Postmodern Feminist Readings of Woolf, West, and Barnes*. Bloomington: Indiana UP, 1995.

Schaffer, Talia. *Literature and Culture at the* Fin de Siècle. New York: Pearson, 2007.

Sharpe, Jenny. *Allegories of Empire: The Figure of Woman in the Colonial Text*. Minneapolis: U of Minnesota P, 1993.

———. "Figures of Colonial Resistance." *The Post-Colonial Studies Reader*. Ed. Bill Ashcroft, Gareth Griffiths, and Helen Tiffin. London: Routledge, 1995. 99–103.

Sherry, Vincent. *The Great War and the Language of Modernism*. New York: Oxford UP, 2003.

Shiach, Morag, ed. *The Cambridge Companion to the Modernist Novel*. Cambridge: Cambridge UP, 2007.

Showalter, Elaine. *Hystories: Hysterical Epidemics and Modern Media*. New York: Columbia UP, 1997.
Silver, Brenda. *Virginia Woolf Icon*. Chicago: U of Chicago P, 1999.
Simpson, Kathryn. "'Queer Fish': Woolf's Writing of Desire Between Women in *The Voyage Out* and *Mrs Dalloway*." *Woolf Studies Annual* 9 (2003): 55–82.
Smith, Angela K. *The Second Battlefield: Women, Modernism and the First World War*. Manchester: Manchester UP, 2000.
*The South Carolina Review* (Virginia Woolf International) 29.1 (1996). Clemson: Clemson Digital P.
*The Space Between: Literature and Culture 1914–1945*. Fort Hays: Fort Hays State U.
Spivak, Gayatri Chakravorty. "Three Women's Texts and a Critique of Imperialism." *The Post-Colonial Studies Reader*. Ed. Bill Ashcroft, Gareth Griffiths, and Helen Tiffin. London: Routledge, 1995. 269–272.
Squier, Susan Merrill. *Virginia Woolf and London: The Sexual Politics of the City*. Chapel Hill, U of North Carolina P, 1985.
Stalla, Heidi. "Empire and Elveden: New Light on *The Waves*." *Virginia Woolf Bulletin* 12 (2003): 20–29.
Strachey, Lytton. *Eminent Victorians*. New York: Penguin, 1984.
Sypher, Eileen B. "*The Waves*: A Utopoia of Androgyny?" *Virginia Woolf: Centennial Essays*. Ed. Elaine K. Ginsberg and Laura Moss Gottlieb. New York: Whitston Publishing, 1983. 187–213.
Tate, Trudi. *Modernism, History, and the First World War*. Manchester: Manchester UP, 1998.
Thane, Pat. *Borderlines: Genders and Identities in War and Peace 1870–1930*. Ed. Billie Melman. New York: Routledge, 1998.
Theweleit, Klaus. *Male Fantasies*. Minneapolis: U of Minnesota P, 1989.
Torgovnick, Mariana. *Primitive Passions: Men, Women and the Quest for Ecstasy*. New York: Knopf, 1997.
Trotter, David. "The Modernist Novel." *The Cambridge Companion to Modernism*. Ed. Michael Levenson. Cambridge: Cambridge UP, 1999. 70–99.
Tuchman, Barbara W. *Guns of August*. New York: Presidio, 2004.
Vlasopolos, Anca. "Staking No Claims for Territory: The Sea as Woman's Space." *Reconfigured Spheres: Feminist Explorations of Literary Space*. Ed. Margaret H. Higonnet and Joan Templeton. Amherst: University of Massachusetts Press, 1994. 72–88.
Wallace, Miriam L. "Theorizing Relational Subjects: Metonymic Narrative in *The Waves*." *Narrative* 8.3 (2000): 294–323.
Warner, Sylvia Townsend. *Lolly Willowes: or the Loving Huntsman*. London: Virago, 1995.
West, Rebecca. *The Judge*. New York: Dial P, 1980.
Williams, Mark. "Mansfield in Maoriland: Biculturalism, Agency and Misreading." *Modernism and Empire*. Ed. Howard J. Booth and Nigel Rigby. Manchester: Manchester UP, 2000. 249–74.
Wilson, John. *Noctes Ambrosianae*. Redfield: New York, 1854.
Winston, Janet. "Something Out of Harmony": *To the Lighthouse* and theSubject(s) of Empire," *Woolf Studies Annual* 5 (1996): 39–70.
Woolf, Virginia. *Between the Acts*. New York: Harvest, 1969.
———. *Mrs. Dalloway*. New York: Harvest, 1953.
———. *A Room of One's Own*. New York: Harvest, 1957.
———. *Three Guineas*. New York: Harbinger, 1963.
———. *To the Lighthouse*. Hertfordshire: Wordsworth Editions Limited, 1994.
———. *The Waves*. New York: Harvest, 1959.

———. *A Writer's Diary: Being Extracts from the Diary of Virginia Woolf.* Ed. Leonard Woolf. New York: Harvest, 1982.

Zwerdling, Alex. *Virginia Woolf and the Real World.* Berkeley: U of California P, 1986.

# Index

**A**
Abject: 5–9, 11, 16, 23, 28–31, 35, 37–38, 42, 46–47, 49–50, 105–107, 110–111, 113–129, 132, 134, 142 n7–9, 143 n15–16, 159 n52–55, 161 n9, n11, 162 n14–15
Alsace: 8, 22–23, 110, 111–112, 114–115, 117, 119, 121–126, 129, 133, 163 n24

**B**
Baucom, Ian: 10, 38
Beer, Gillian: 151 n 37
Bhabha, Homi: 11–12, 70, 150 n33, 151n1
Boone, Joseph Allen: 7, 167
Borders: 4, 6, 8–9, 12–13, 24, 27, 30–31, 34, 46, 70, 113, 122, 127, 131–132, 162n16
Bourton: 31, 33, 35, 40–41, 144n11
Bowlby, Rachel: 144n12
Butler, Judith: 14 n5

**C**
Cain, P.J. and A.G. Hopkins: 10, 147n8
City: 2, 11–12, 31, 36–38, 57, 78, 144n2, 144n11,
Civilization/civilized: 33–34, 37, 41, 47, 52, 56, 57, 78, 95, 96, 98, 99–102, 104, 116, 128, 147n8, 154n15, 157n45
Cixous, Hélène: 142 n11
Class: 17, 25, 26, 30, 37, 41, 44–45, 47, 96, 97, 98, 99, 100, 104, 142n10, 149n21, 156n35
Colonialism: 9, 10, 11, 12, 13, 18, 22, 32, 34, 36, 39, 41, 42, 52, 63, 98, 99, 127–128, 145n16, 156n36
Conclusions/endings: 18, 19, 22, 23, 24, 72, 73, 92, 102, 103, 104, 111–113, 129–134
Conrad, Joseph: 10, 156n37; *Heart of Darkness*, 93, 150n31
Corporeum: 1–2, 4–5, 12–13, 18–19, 22–24, 76, 134, 136–137
Countryside: 2, 12–13, 22, 25, 31, 33–34, 38, 41, 67, 90–91, 95, 122, 132, 144n11, 149n25

**D**
Domesticity: 27, 28, 31, 39, 41, 46, 54–55, 59–60, 62–63, 65, 70–71, 95, 109, 151n35
DuPlessis, Rachel Blau: 17, 45–46, 51, 144n10

**E**
Eliot, T.S.: 15, 49, 75, 77, 101, 104–105, 107–108, 130, 132, 153n10, 159n54, 160n56–57, 165n4
Embodiment: 1, 4–7, 11–13, 15, 19–24, 54, 56, 66, 161n7; female, 1, 3, 4, 5–7, 8, 11–13, 15, 19–24, 26, 27, 28, 29, 30, 31, 34, 36–37, 38, 54, 56, 66, 74–90, 91–105, 106, 107, 109, 110–111, 113, 115, 121, 129–130, 134, 136, 137, 141n6, 144n4; geographic, 1, 2, 4, 5, 7, 8, 12–13, 19, 23, 24, 25–26, 31, 33, 35, 36, 43, 74, 76, 90–91, 95, 110, 120–125, 126, 134, 137; national/imperial, 1, 2, 4–5, 6, 7, 11, 19–20, 23, 24, 25–26, 33, 35, 38–39, 43, 74, 77, 98, 100, 102, 110, 121–122, 126, 128, 134,

137; textual, 1, 4–5, 7, 12–13, 15, 19, 23, 24, 25, 30, 31, 43, 74, 76, 77, 103, 106, 107, 137, 141n6; empire, 2, 9–12, 20, 22, 24, 150; and the feminine, 2, 11, 12, 24, 33, 37–39, 41, 42–43, 46, 92, 97–104, 121, 126, 136; and patriarchy, 2, 22, 24, 28, 37, 38, 41, 42, 47, 96, 97, 98, 99, 121, 135, 136
Escape: 2, 7, 23, 31, 32–33, 36, 40, 75, 93, 96, 110, 112–113, 117, 119–120, 123, 125, 128–129, 134
Esty, Jed: 147n6
Experimentation: 1–5, 7, 13–24, 25, 26, 30, 31, 43, 45–46, 47–49, 50, 52, 54, 68, 72, 92, 103, 105, 106, 109, 111–113, 129–131, 133–134, 137, 147n29

## F

Felski, Rita: 17, 46, 48–50, 115–116, 134
Female embodiment/ physicality: 1, 2, 5, 7–8, 11–13, 18, 20 ,21, 23, 24, 26–28, 30–38, 40, 45, 50, 54, 56, 66, 74–91, 91–103, 104, 107, 109, 110–115, 121, 125, 129–130, 134, 136, 141n6, 144n4, 155n23, 161n7
Female subjectivity: 4, 5, 13, 15, 16, 18, 20–23, 24, 26, 27, 30, 32–33, 35, 40, 41, 44, 48, 49, 50, 56, 61–62, 72, 74, 75, 77–90, 91–103, 106, 108, 109, 110–113, 115–116, 117, 120, 123, 125, 129–130, 133–134, 136–137, 144n7, 159n55
Feminine, the: 1–2, 5–14, 15, 16, 18, 19–20, 21, 22–24, 26–27, 28, 31–32, 33, 35, 37–39, 40, 46, 49, 50, 72, 74–90, 91–94, 95, 96, 97, 107, 109, 110–111, 113–114, 115, 116, 118–121, 123–124, 126–134, 137, 141n6, 142n7, 142n8, 142n9, 143n13, 143n15, 145n19, 148n13, 149n21, 151n37, 152n39, 153n7, 155n23, 159n51, 159n52, 160n56, 164n29
Fin de siècle: 48, 146 n27
Flight: 113, 134, 143 n18, 160 n1
Foria: 75, 87–88, 91–95, 98–100, 102, 107–109, 123, 153n6, n13, 157 n44, 158 n47; Forio, 153n6, 154n16, 157n45
Form, literary: 71, 93, 143n14; conclusions, 2, 18–19, 22–24, 103, 129–130, 132, 133; experimentation, 2, 5, 13, 14, 15, 25, 26, 30, 31, 43–45, 47–49, 50, 51, 525, 60–61, 69, 71, 101, 111–113, 129–130, 131–133, 143n16; female, 13, 14, 15, 26, 31–33, 38, 44–45, 48–49, 50, 107, 112, 129, 130, 132; modernist, 7, 107, 130, 131, 133, 137; patriarchy, 7, 28, 312, 35, 38, 78, 80, 82, 85, 90–91, 116, 118, 120, 131, 133; traditional, 26, 31, 44, 48–49, 71, 102, 130–131, 133
Friedman, Ellen G. and Miriam Fuchs: 132, 144n10, 146n28
Friedman, Susan Stanford: 16, 41, 44
Froula, Christine: 141n3, 144n11
*Fugue*, 1, 14, 16, 18, 22–23, 110–134, 137; and dissociation, 16, 111–121, 123–126, 129, 134; and Harrion, 22–23, 110, 110–117, 121–122, 124, 127, 129–132, 160n3, 161n7, 161n11, 162n14; and Lavinia, 14, 16, 22–24, 110–134, 137; and maternity, 22, 110–111, 114, 118–119, 123–124, 127–128, 132, 134; and nationalism, 23, 111–113, 122, 125–129; and Sebastian, 22, 23, 111, 117, 119, 120, 128–129, 131, 132; and subjectivity, 18, 22, 110–115, 117–121, 125, 127–130, 132–134

## G

Garrity, Jane: 55, 146 n26, 147 n5, 148 n14
Gikandi, Simon: 69, 93, 150 n29
Grosz, Elizabeth: 6–7, 27, 29, 144 n2

## H

Harvey, David: 131
Haunting: 32, 36, 146 n21
Heywood, Leslie: 15, 48, 104
Homeland: 12; and England/Britain, 8–9, 12, 20, 33, 52–54, 59–60, 62–63, 65, 66–68, 70–71, 72,126, 128, 147n7, 149n21; and Germany, fatherland, 121,

163n20; Alsace as abject homeland, 125
Hybridity: 11, 110, 126, 150n33, 152n1; and the body, 12, 22, 28, 41, 74–90, 93, 95–99, 101–104, 105, 109, 110; and colonization, 11, 12, 74, 88–90, 99, 100, 126; and identity, 8, 11, 28, 34, 41, 48, 70, 72, 74–90, 91, 95, 99, 100, 108, 126, 151; textual, 12, 51, 69–70, 72, 74, 77, 101, 102, 109, 110, 126, 137
Hynes, Samuel: 1, 3, 35, 38, 43, 141n3
Hysteria: 16, 82, 105, 121–122, 143n15, 155n26, 159n52, 160n56, 163n21

I

Identity: 1, 13, 16–18, 21–22, 24, 112, 150n33, 151n34, 152n39; and the body, 1, 2, 12, 13, 20, 21, 26–27, 28, 29, 30, 31, 35, 36, 38, 39, 41, 43, 47, 48, 50, 51, 74, 75–90, 91, 94, 97, 101, 104, 105, 107, 112–115, 117–118, 136; female, 3, 4, 21, 22, 24, 25, 26, 28, 29, 31–35, 36–37, 38, 40–43, 44, 48, 51, 55, 59, 74–90, 91, 94, 95, 96, 97, 98, 104, 106, 109, 113–115, 117–119, 125, 135–6, 141n6, 144n13; formation, 3, 7, 8, 25, 27, 28, 35–36, 38, 41, 44, 46, 47, 48, 51, 59, 72, 74–76, 77–78, 83–85, 88–91, 95, 100, 101, 105, 108, 109, 112, 114, 152n39; and the nation, 1, 4, 9, 10, 12, 20, 24, 25, 26, 36–40, 43, 52, 71–72, 91, 102, 121–123, 129, 136, 141n6; and the land, 1, 8, 12, 13, 19, 20, 23, 24, 26, 32, 33, 34–35, 74–77, 91–95, 99, 103, 121–122, 136; and the text, 1, 13, 16, 17, 24, 31, 33, 36, 40, 43, 44, 46, 47, 49–51, 71–72, 74, 77, 102, 108, 115, 119, 136
Imagination: 53–55, 142n10; and the feminine, 37, 49, 55, 60–61, 71–72, 76, 81, 82–85, 88–90,105; and identity formation, 2, 3, 40, 43, 44, 48, 49, 51, 68, 70, 76, 81, 84–85, 89–90, 93, 94, 105, 107

Imagism: 153n10, 158n50
Imperialism: 1–4, 9–10, 11, 13, 18, 20, 52, 121, 125–127, 145n16, 149n23, 151n35, 155n23, 157n42; and complicity, 2, 4, 5, 8, 9, 10, 18, 19, 25, 37–38, 41, 42, 74, 77, 126–129; and violence. 8, 10, 12, 13, 21, 34, 42, 52, 58–60, 62–70, 72–73, 125–127
Interwar period: 2–3, 8, 14, 18–19, 34, 46, 55, 165n1
Irigaray, Luce: 76, 142n9, 159n53, 162n19
Ischia: 153n6, 154n16, 157n45

K

Katz, Tamar: 53–54
Kent, Susan Kingsley: 144n7, 148n11, 163n22, 165n1
Kime Scott, Bonnie: 147n29
Kirby, Kathleen: 34, 77, 82, 90, 95, 109
Kirby, Vicki: 16, 105
Kristeva, Julia: 7, 16; abjection, 5–9, 11, 16, 23, 28–31, 35, 37–38, 42, 46–47, 49, 105–106, 142 n7–8, 143n15–16, 159n54–55, 161n9, 162n15; *Powers of Horror*, 143n16, 159n54

L

Land: 1–16, 18–24, 110–111, 121–126, 132, 144n11; and feminization, 2, 7–8, 10, 11, 12, 16, 20, 21, 25, 26, 31–37, 38, 50, 62–63, 65–66, 74, 77, 90–91, 92, 93, 94–103, 109, 110–111, 121–126, 132; and identity, 3, 7, 8, 23, 25, 31, 32, 33–38, 41, 42, 43, 50, 66, 75–76, 91, 92–100, 102, 108, 109, 111, 112, 117, 121–122, 123, 125, 136; and nationalism, 3, 4, 8, 26, 33–35, 36, 38, 50, 66–67, 77, 91–93, 95, 110, 125–126; and patriarchy, 7, 19, 33–35, 36, 38, 42, 62, 90–91, 135
Landscape: 2, 3, 4, 6–8, 13, 16, 19–20, 22, 25–26, 28, 31, 33, 35–37, 50, 60, 62–63, 65–67, 91–96, 99, 109, 110–111,115, 121–126, 132, 145n13, 146n20, 150n28, 160n3, 163n23
Language: 2, 16, 113, 121–122, 124, 128–129, 131–132, 159n52,

159n55; and the feminine, 16, 24, 27, 29, 31, 32–33, 38, 40, 46–47, 48, 61, 92, 104, 106, 113, 121, 123, 128, 131, 159n52; and identity formation, 2, 13, 17, 18, 25, 26–27, 28, 29, 32–33, 37–38, 42, 43–44, 47, 48, 61, 103, 104, 106, 113, 121–122, 124, 128, 132; and patriarchy, 2, 15, 16, 27, 28, 30, 33, 37–38, 43, 46–47, 50–51, 86, 106, 129, 133, 135; and subjectivity, 5, 27, 30, 31, 32–33, 46–47, 48, 51, 61, 106, 110, 129; and tradition, 16, 27, 28, 32–33, 37–38, 41–42, 43, 44, 45, 47, 49, 77, 121

Light, Alison: 141n3, 142n10, 149n21, 164n29

London: 8, 12, 25–26, 33, 35, 39, 41, 45, 75, 88, 95, 110, 112, 154, 163n23

## M

Marcus, Jane: 20, 52, 56, 71, 147n7, 150n32

Marriage: 4, 5, 21, 27–31, 41–42, 75, 109, 154n14, 160n3

Maternal/maternity: 2, 4–6, 8, 12, 16, 21–23, 27–29, 31, 35, 41, 42, 48, 56, 74–83, 75–76, 86–87, 90–91, 96–98, 100, 102, 105–107, 109–111, 118–119, 123–124, 126–127, 129n20, 132, 134, 146, 152n5, 153n5, 154n14, 154n15, 155n21, 156n29, 156n30, 157n41, 161n9, 162n15

McClintock, Anne: 8, 34, 63, 90, 93, 97, 156n33

McDowell, Linda: 34, 79, 94

McGee, Patrick: 70, 147n7, 149n22

Minow Pinkney, Makiko: 7, 28

Mitchell, W.J.T.: 124–125, 150n28

Modernism, literary: 1, 3, 7, 13–14, 15, 19, 24, 25, 48–49, 77, 87–88, 104; and anorexia, 15, 48, 104–105, 108, 133, 137, 147n6, 153n7, 153n9, 153n10, 153n11, 154n15, 160n57; and modernist aesthetic, 15, 17, 45, 49, 131, 153n7, 153n10

Moore, Madeline: 165n2

Moore, Olive: 1–3, 6–7, 12, 13–16, 18–23, 74–90, 135, 136, 137, 139; *The Apple is Bitten Again*, 75, 135, 139, 155n27, 162n16, 164n32; *Celestial Seraglio*, 74, 152n5; *Fugue*, 1, 14, 16, 18, 22–23, 110–134, 137; *Spleen*, 1, 6, 21, 22, 74–90, 110, 111, 137

Moran, Patricia: 28–29, 50, 55, 63

*Mrs. Dalloway*: 1–4, 8–9, 18–20, 23, 90, 110, 111, 131, 137; Clarissa, 2–4, 7–8, 9, 12–13, 18–20, 24; Elizabeth, 29, 32–33, 36, 41–42, 144n12, 144n13, 145n19, 146n21; Hugh Whitbread, 35, 36, 40; Miss Isabel Pole, 38; Lady Bruton, 2, 18, 31, 36, 40, 42–43, 45, 47, 146n24; Miss Kilman, 2, 18, 40, 41–42, 45, 146; Peter, 25, 31–32, 33–38, 46, 50–51, 136; Sally, 2, 8, 19, 30, 31, 40–41, 45, 47, 137, 146n20, 146n27; Septimus, 18, 20, 31, 32, 38, 45, 51, 131, 136

## N

Narrative: 2, 7, 13–14, 16, 18, 20–24, 68, 110–112, 126, 129–133, 144n10, 146n26, 150n30; Construction, 17, 21–22, 31–32, 40–41, 44, 45–48, 51, 52, 70–71, 93, 95, 96, 104, 108, 111–112, 130–132; Experimentation, 2, 6, 13–14, 16, 18, 23–24, 32, 43–48, 50–51, 52, 70–72, 92, 110–111, 129–131, 133; and identity, 13, 16, 17, 21, 27, 30–31, 44, 46, 50, 51, 94, 112, 131, 133; and structure, 17, 20, 31, 43, 44–46, 70–71, 108, 110–112, 126, 129–131, 133, 160n56

Nation/nationalism: 1–5, 7, 11, 13, 52, 110–113, 121–123, 125–126, 129, 144n7, 145n18, 146n22, 147n10, 149n19, 152n39, 163n24; and figureheads, 13, 25, 34, 38–40, 42, 43, 54–58, 95, 122, 126; and ideals/ideology, 2, 5, 7, 10, 11, 12, 25, 34–36, 37–38, 40–41, 43, 47, 52, 60, 66, 77, 112, 121–123, 126; and patriarchy, 2, 25, 30, 34–36, 40, 42–43, 47, 129; and women, 8, 25, 26, 33–34, 36, 37, 38, 39–40, 40–43, 50, 55, 74–75,

91, 94, 110–111, 113, 121–123, 126, 129, 136
National identity: 1–3, 8–10, 12–13, 20–22, 24, 52, 54–55, 59, 70–71, 121, 123, 128–129; and female identity, 2–3, 4, 8, 10, 12, 13, 18, 20, 22, 25, 26, 33–35, 37, 38, 39–41, 43, 47, 50, 54, 55, 59, 75, 91, 93, 108, 121, 123, 128–129, 136; and icons, 25, 33, 35–39, 61, 121
New, the: 87, 89, 130
Nicholls, Peter: 105, 107–108, 131–133, 153n7, 153n11, 158n50, 159n54, 160n57

O

Otherness: 6, 12, 30, 36, 49, 53, 93, 98–100, 106, 109, 127, 142n7, 151n33, 152n39, 161n9

P

Pastoral: 3, 8, 12, 13, 19–20, 25
Patriarchy: 2–5, 7–9, 12–13, 15–16, 18–25, 28–30, 33–35, 37, 40–43, 46–47, 49, 53–55, 57–58, 62, 71–72, 74, 76–78, 80, 82, 85–86, 92, 94, 96, 101, 106, 116, 118, 120, 131, 136, 145, 160n2, 161n9
Phantoms: 22, 151 n33
Phillips, Kathy: 11, 28, 39, 53, 59, 144n6, 145n19, 145n20, 147n7, 149n19, 149n23, 163n22
Primitive, the: 11–12, 37, 57–60, 72, 78–80, 82, 92–93, 98–101, 108–109, 116, 149, 153n12, 153n13, 161n12

R

Richardson, Dorothy: 14, 49

S

Sea: 56, 58, 62–65, 67, 69, 94
Sharpe, Jenny: 52, 59–60
Showalter, Elaine: 163n21
*Spleen*: 1, 6, 21, 22, 74–90, 110, 111, 137; and the body, 6, 21, 22, 74–90, 91, 95, 99, 101, 103, 104; and civilization, 6, 78, 98, 99, 100, 101, 104–109; and conception, 21–22, 74–77, 78, 84–90, 96; and England, 6, 21–22, 75, 87–88, 90–91, 92; and Ruth's father, 75, 92, 96, 109, 156n36, 157n43; and the land, 6, 7, 21, 22, 74–77, 78, 90–91, 93; and Italy/Forio, 22, 75, 88, 91, 92, 93, 94, 97, 98, 102, 122, 153n6, 154n16, 156n28, 156n35,157n45, 158n45, 163n32, 163n25; and "make it new", 22, 77, 87, 101–102, 108, 143n17; and maternity, 6, 21, 22, 74–83, 85, 87, 90, 91–92, 97–109; and the modern woman, 74–76, 87–90, 97, 104; and monster/monstrosity, 6, 80, 87–89, 96, 98, 101, 102, 107; and nationalism, 6, 74, 76–78, 88–90, 91, 93, 94, 98, 108, and reproduction, 21, 22, 74, 75, 79, 92, 97, 101, 104, 105; and Richard, 6, 21–22, 75, 87–88, 91, 92, 95, 96, 101, 102, 103, 107, 108, 109, 156n29; and Ruth, 6, 21–22, 24, 74–75, 77–78, 80, 83–91, 92, 94–109, 137; and the soul, 82–88; and the Victory of Samothrace: 83–84, 90, 95, 101, 155n23
Stream-of-consciousness: 2, 7, 13–15, 18–20, 25–26, 30–31, 43–44, 47, 49–50, 83, 102, 136–137
Subjectivity: 3–4, 13–16, 20–23, 110–113, 115, 117–120, 123, 124, 127–130, 132, 134; female, 3–4, 13–16, 20–23, 26, 27, 30, 32–33, 36, 41, 44, 48, 49, 50, 56, 61–62, 72, 75, 77–90, 91, 93, 94, 97, 98, 101–109, 110–113, 115, 117, 120, 123, 125, 129–130, 132–134, 136–137; split subjectivity, 23, 27, 30, 36, 39, 51, 75, 78, 80, 83–90, 98, 102, 105, 111–115, 117–119, 125, 127–130, 134, 136

T

Textual experimentation: 1–5, 7, 13–24, 53–54, 68, 71–72, 74–90, 110–111, 113, 129, 131, 134, 137; and textual form/shape, 3–5, 7, 12, 13–24, 25–26, 30, 31, 43, 44, 45–47, 48–50, 51, 101, 103, 104, 108, 110, 111, 112, 113, 124, 129, 133–134, 136–137

Thane, Pat: 55, 150n29
Theweleit, Klaus: 141n6
Time: 3, 17, 31, 32, 35, 44, 72, 83, 150n28, 158n50, 163n27
Torgovnick, Mariana: 10–12, 37, 57, 58, 72, 78, 98, 153n12, 156n37, 161n12
Tradition: 22, 23, 48, 73, 77, 102, 104, 107–108, 122, 160n56, 160n57

**V**

Victory of Samothrace: 83–84, 90, 95, 101, 155n23

**W**

Warner, Sylvia Townsend: 154n17
West, Rebecca: 14
*The Waves*: 1–2, 13–14, 19–20, 74, 78, 90, 137; Bernard, 21, 69–70, 150n32, 152n39; Birds, 62, 65–66, 69; and empire/colonies, 13, 19, 52–53, 54, 55, 56, 58, 59, 61, 63, 64, 65, 66, 67, 70, 71, 72, 73; and the episodes, 13, 24, 59, 69–72; and female embodiment, 13, 53, 54, 56, 58, 60, 61, 62, 63, 66, 72; and female identity, 53, 54, 55–60, 61, 72, 73; and gender, 20, 55, 57, 59, 62, 63, 64; and home, 53, 59–60, 62–63, 65, 67, 70, 71; and homeland, 52, 53, 54–55, 59, 60, 62, 63, 65–66, 67, 68, 70, 71; and imperialism, 20, 52, 53, 55, 56, 58, 59, 60, 62, 63, 64, 65, 67, 68, 69, 70, 72, 73; and the interludes, 21, 52, 53, 54, 55, 56, 57, 58, 59–60, 61, 63–65, 67–72; and land: 20, 53, 60, 62, 63, 65, 66, 67; and Louis' beast, 64, 69, 149n26; and patriarchy, 53, 54, 57, 63; and the primitive, 57–60, 64, 72, 78; and shadow imagery, 21, 54, 60–61, 64, 72; and sun imagery, 20, 52, 53, 54, 55–62, 63, 67–68, 70–72; and textual experimentation, 53, 54, 55, 68, 69, 70, 71, 72, 73; and war, 58, 59, 63, 64, 66–68; and waves, 62–68, 71
Wild, the, wilderness, or the wild land: 8, 31, 41, 92, 93, 92–95, 100, 137
Winston, Janet: 145n17
Woolf, Virginia: 1–4, 7, 12, 13–15, 18–21, 75, 135–137; *Between the Acts*, 33, 145n14, 152n38; *Mrs. Dalloway*: 1–4, 8–9, 18–20, 23, 90, 110, 111, 131, 137; *A Room of One's Own*, 14, 57, 96, 135, 142n12, 144n8, 148n16, 157n41, 164n32; *Three Guineas*, 156n34, 163n24, 165n2; *To the Lighthouse*, 144n6, 145n15, 145n17; *The Waves*, 1–2, 13–14, 19–20, 74, 78, 90, 137

**Z**

Zwerdling, Alex: 165n2

For Product Safety Concerns and Information please contact our EU
representative GPSR@taylorandfrancis.com
Taylor & Francis Verlag GmbH, Kaufingerstraße 24, 80331 München, Germany

www.ingramcontent.com/pod-product-compliance
Lightning Source LLC
Chambersburg PA
CBHW070613300426
44113CB00010B/1510